CULTURAL ECONOMIES
PAST AND PRESENT

Texas Press Sourcebooks in Anthropology,
No. 18

Cultural Economies

PAST AND PRESENT

by Rhoda H. Halperin

UNIVERSITY OF TEXAS PRESS

AUSTIN

Requests for permission to reproduce material from this
work should be sent to Permissions, University of Texas
Press, Box 7819, Austin, TX 78713-7819.

⊗ The paper used in this publication meets the minimum
requirements of American National Standard for
Information Sciences—Permanence of Paper for Printed
Library Materials, ANSI Z39.48-1984.

Library of Congress Cataloging-in-Publication Data
Halperin, Rhoda H.
    Cultural economies past and present / by Rhoda H.
Halperin. — 1st ed.
        p.   cm. — (Texas Press sourcebooks in
anthropology ; no. 18)
    Includes bibliographical references and index.
    ISBN 0-292-73089-6 (c : alk. paper). —
ISBN 0-292-73090-X (p : alk. paper)
    1. Economic anthropology. I. Title. II. Series.
GN448.H34   1994
306.3—dc20   94-15762

CONTENTS

PREFACE AND
ACKNOWLEDGMENTS

I started out to write a book about Polanyi which would be in part a translation and interpretation of his powerful but often obtuse models and concepts of the economy. Many of my colleagues urged me to write my own book—volume 2 of *Economies Across Cultures*. I resisted another theoretical book for some time, still clinging to the idea that Polanyi needed to be translated into straightforward English and that what was really needed was a critical biography of Polanyi for economic anthropologists—not just for ethnologists, but for archaeologists and ethnohistorians as well.

Indeed, my colleagues were, to some degree, right; while my thinking has always used Polanyi as a reference point, it has gone beyond his formulations in both sympathetic and highly critical ways. What I have done in this book is to take off from Polanyi's models and concepts by giving Polanyi a Marxist and an anthropological reading. I have created and redefined concepts for the analysis of economies in their cultural and institutional contexts. In the process, I have embellished, changed, and interpreted Polanyi's cross-cultural concepts of the economy. My hope is that this book will speak to archaeologists and historians as well as to ethnographers of the economy in cultural systems, past and present.

Many people helped me with this book over several years. The book began while I was on leave at MIT in 1988–89. To the Anthropology Program there, especially to Jim Howe, Jean Jackson, and Martin Diskin, I owe a great deal. Also to Alison Salisbury and Abby Moser, who made my life so comfortable at "the institute." Patricia McAnany, Tom Killion, Bob Connolley, Vern Scarborough, Michael Smyth, Lin Poyer, Tom Håkansson, Joel Halpern, and Andy Hofling gave me many useful comments, as did my students in our seminars in economic anthropology. Sandy Daniels Solove and Lora Anderson helped with the typing. Margie Mendell, director of the Karl Polanyi Institute of Political Economy at Concordia University in Montreal, was a very generous guide through the Polanyi archives. I thank the Institute for allowing me to make use of some of Polanyi's unpublished work in this book. Andre Levesque of McGill University's history department also helped the process enormously. Kristin Quinn, a graduate student in our department, came to the rescue at the eleventh hour to usher this manuscript to press. My very special thanks to Barry Isaac who has listened many hours to some of my best and some of my worst ideas. His advice and editorial assistance cannot be measured.

The materials in chapters 3, 4, and 5 have appeared in *Research in Economic Anthropology*, edited by Barry L. Isaac. Another version of chapter 7 appeared in *Perspectives on the Informal Economy*, edited by M. Estellie Smith. Some of the case materials in chapters 5 and 8 have appeared in my book *The Livelihood of Kin*, published by the University of Texas Press. There I thank Theresa May for her many helpful and encouraging conversations.

My family has put up with the takeover of our house by papers and books for many years. This book and its artifacts and many versions have occupied several rooms. "Have you taken over this room now too?" one teenager asked incredulously, but without a negative tinge in his voice. I thank Michael and Bill for their patience with this project and Sam for his help with the title and the figures.

CULTURAL ECONOMIES
PAST AND PRESENT

INTRODUCTION

This book is about the cultural and institutional constructions of economies. It focuses on concepts and processes and creates models for understanding economic processes in cultural systems. The term "cultural economies" refers to an analytical perspective which examines economies as they are embedded in and constructed by cultural systems that are larger and more powerful than particular individuals or particular historical moments; it has a cross-cultural approach to economies that focuses on patterns and processes in the past and in the present. By emphasizing economic processes and patterns as they are culturally and institutionally constructed, *Cultural Economies Past and Present* deemphasizes individual behavior and economistic, utilitarian forms of economic rationality and deals instead with patterns of economic organization. As a book about cultural systems and economic processes it also emphasizes contexts—cultural, institutional, and temporal—and does not treat economic actors as units of analysis. In fact, this project is meant to serve as a critique of the ethnocentrism, methodological individualism, and psychological reductionism that are still so common in conventional economic anthropology.

Cultural Economies Past and Present is organized according to key concepts, and it explores much new and some old ground. As a "concept book," it is the first of its kind. I hope it will be useful to a range of scholars and practitioners who, in turn, will refine and embellish these concepts, adding along the way to the conceptual repertoire. This book follows in the historical and institutional traditions of Marx and Polanyi both by focusing on concepts, such as economy, ecology, equivalencies, householding, storage, and informal economy (to name a few), for understanding how economies are organized in cultural systems and by emphasizing concepts, models, and paradigms that move toward a general theory of economic organization.

As I said in the preface to *Economies Across Cultures* (1988), although I am a third-generation intellectual descendant of Karl Polanyi, my disagreements with the members of the original Polanyi group, especially with George Dalton, but also with Harry Pearson and Walter Neale, have been quite deep. Most in the Polanyi group have vehemently denied the positive associations between Marx and Polanyi (Dalton 1981; Neale personal communication)—a testimony, perhaps, to the long-term effects of a McCarthyite witch-hunting political climate upon a whole generation of scholars. I continue to admire Polanyi's efforts to create a general theory of the economy and I operate within the same institutional paradigm as Polanyi—a paradigm that originated with Marx. However, the anthropological vantage point of a broad-based, cross-cultural perspective has enabled me to maintain a critical sense of disbelief about certain aspects of Polanyi's theoretical framework, especially those that romanticize pre-capitalist economies and that argue for separate paradigms for analyzing capitalist and pre-capitalist economic systems. Despite these disagreements, I have tried to build upon and elaborate Polanyi's ideas. Since Polanyi died before I became an undergraduate student, I never had the benefits of his charismatic personality or powerful teaching. On the other hand, I have had the advantage of distance from Polanyi, the man.

In recent years Polanyi's economist daughter, Kari Polanyi-Levitt, and her colleagues at the Karl Polanyi Institute of Political Economy in Montreal, including Margie Mendell, Daniel Salee, Andre Levesque, and many others, have supported cultural and institutional approaches to economies that embrace Marxism. The formation of the Polanyi Institute is itself a cultural and institutional feat, for not only does it provide an archive of Polanyi's work, but its conferences and lecture series bring scholars from all over the world to elaborate Polanyi's ideas. I was delighted when Kari, upon reading *Economies Across Cultures*, remarked to me: "I can't believe that an American got it right!" I interpret her statement to be a strong critique of the economism and the methodological individualism that continues to dominate economic anthropology in the United States.

The concepts in this book make up an analytical tool kit for studying economic processes across cultures and over time. They may be used for the two main purposes of description and comparison. The concepts are intended to facilitate the writing of what Geertz called "thick descriptions" of economic processes—production, distribution, and consumption—in all economies, past and present. They will also make possible comparisons for the purpose of understanding similarities, differences, and changes between and among contemporary and past economies. For unless our concepts are clear, comparable data cannot be collected. Comparable data are difficult to come by precisely because we use concepts inconsistently and because we examine similarly named economic processes through different theoretical lenses. It is not surprising that we come up with noncomparable data. What one anthropologist means by production is usually not the same as what another means. Similarly, the analytical tools for understanding the organization of land, labor, trade, gift exchange, commodity, and barter are all left almost to serendipity, or at least to the idiosyncrasies and presuppositions of individual anthropologists. Without clear concepts that guide the collection of comparable data, we have no systematic way of understanding similarities and differences among economic processes in cultural systems; attempts to understand how and why economies change are almost impossible without comparable data sets. I offer the concepts in this book as examples; they are only some of those that can be created and used for the comparative study of economic processes across cultures and over time; there are many more yet to be formulated and refined.

In this book I have started with Polanyi's models and concepts, and have given him both a Marxist and an anthropological reading. My thinking represents a synthesis of substantivism and Marxism, but it diverges considerably from the "pure" (if there is such a thing) and, especially, the doctrinaire versions of both. I have created some new concepts, resurrected some old ones, and refined others; in the process, I have expanded upon, changed, and criticized Polanyi's attempts at a general theory of the economy. I have done so in ways that should be useful to contemporary anthropology in the broadest sense of the discipline—that is, by including archaeologists and ethnohistorians as well as cultural anthropologists (see Lamberg-Karlovsky 1989; Dunnell 1989; and Binford 1989). The audience for this book, then, is not confined to ethnologists alone, but includes economic historians, archaeologists, and ethnohistorians as well as other scholars in social, cultural, and economic studies, particularly institutional economists. Archaeologists have also contributed to this book's case materials and thereby to the refinement of concepts.

The concepts treated here are both basic and sophisticated; I have tried to present them so that their relationship to the institutional paradigm is clear. This paradigm originated with Marx and was elaborated by Polanyi in the form of a rudimentary generic model of the economy. Before talking about either the institutional paradigm or the generic model of the economy, it is important to understand the historical and theoretical trends and themes that precipitated the various formulations of the institutional paradigm—those writings through which the institutional paradigm was originally formulated and is still being elaborated. These themes run very deep in the social sciences, and they play off against one another in complicated and positively reinforcing ways. The themes are dominated by methodological individualism in various forms—first classical political economy, then marginal-utility economics, and just recently, more sophisticated models from ecology and evolutionary biology.

Chapter 1 uses Anthony Giddens' discussion of "structure and agency" (1979) as a backdrop against which the institutional paradigm and a generic model of the economy can be understood and elaborated. The chapter is a discussion and critique of forms of methodological individualism in economic anthropology, including the formalist school and optimal foraging theory. Here I take the opportunity to link to theory in economic anthropology some of the issues that have been raised about relationships of individual behavior, institutions, and culture in social theory generally and in the history of anthropological thought particularly. The chapter stresses the limitations of methodological individualism for understanding pattern, variation, and change in economic processes. It concludes with two ethnographic examples that illustrate contrasts between institutional/cultural and individualistic/behavioral analyses. Hidden structures mold economic processes; these structures and cultures are not always apparent in surface behaviors.

The second chapter first summarizes the key features of the institutional paradigm, because it contains the theoretical foundations for a generic model of the economy and for the development of comparative concepts in economic anthropology. The second part of chapter 2 outlines the main features of a generic model of the economy as it is grounded in the institutional paradigm. This model has scarcely been recognized by any of the schools in economic anthropology, whether formalist, substantivist, or Marxist (see Gledhill and Larsen 1982; and Gilman 1989). As a result, there have been serious misuses of Polanyi's basic concepts and, even more importantly, the basic, cross-cultural approach to the analysis of economic processes that is contained in the generic model has not been elaborated theoretically or applied practically. The subsequent chapters (3–8) focus on concepts that can be related to different parts of the generic model and the institutional paradigm. Presenting the concepts in this way requires some repetition of the basic features of the generic model from chapter to chapter.

In chapter 3, "Economy and Ecology: Basic Concepts, Their History, and Applications," there is an historical review and critique of classic works in economic and ecological anthropology. The framework for this critique is provided by the core concepts of the generic model of the economy, especially the primary concepts of locational and appropriational movements, which Polanyi referred to as "changes of place" and "changes of hands." Binford's (1980) concepts of "foragers" and "collectors" are scrutinized in light of these concepts, and the implications for economic organization are discussed.

A lengthy discussion of "The Concept of Equivalencies in Economic Anthropology" appears in chapter 4. Equivalencies pervade all economies; they indicate how much of what to transact and in what form, in what order, and in what rhythms. I have provided a broad spectrum of applications of the concept by using a variety of ethnographic and archaeological examples covering problems of production, distribution, exchange, trade, and consumption. Equivalencies are a clearer and more useful way of getting at the patterns of exchange and value than is barter (Chapman 1980; Humphrey and Hugh-Jones 1992). The concept of equivalencies is not restricted to processes of exchange. If what I am calling "equivalency-formation processes" can be understood in relation to the institutional paradigm, the contexts for exchange can be taken into account in ways that are not possible using the concept of exchange or barter.

The concept of equivalencies overrides all kinds of exchanges, including those of gifts and of commodities. My approach to equivalencies also avoids the problem of psychologically reductionistic explanations so easily used when individuals are the focus of analysis. Focusing on equivalencies gives cultural and institutional factors primacy and allows for an understanding of how systems of exchange—gift, barter, etc.— are organized (institutionalized) in different cultural and temporal contexts. This approach also avoids the ethnocentrism inherent in marginal-utility economics (Humphrey and Hugh-Jones 1992:17). The last part of the chapter traces the concept of equivalencies in Polanyi's thought and includes a transcribed segment of the interdisciplinary seminars on "Economic Aspects of Institutional Growth," held at Columbia University in the early 1950s. Among other things, these transcripts show how comparative cross-cultural concepts were created through the interactions of economists, anthropologists, and historians.

Chapter 5, "Householding: Resistance and Livelihood in Rural Economies," uses my data from a region of northeastern Kentucky to treat householding as a form of economic integration. Householding operates in contexts where complex economic processes (organized by different institutional arrangements) and combinations of economic processes organize units of production and distribution in stratified, state-level societies. Like the other forms of integration, reciprocity, redistribution, and exchange, householding is a model, not a label or a category for pigeon-holing economies or economic processes. In this chapter I argue that the concept of householding is designed to handle complexity, change, and especially resistance to dependency on capitalism in cultural systems where there are constant tensions between the demands of elites and the material and cultural requirements of people who stand on the lower rungs of state stratification systems. The concept of householding is not designed for small-scale economies in stateless societies. It was created by Polanyi to understand the rural and disempowered segments of states.

Householding per se has received relatively little attention in economic anthropology—perhaps because householding is not confined to households (Maclachlan 1987; Netting et al. 1984; Wilk and Ashmore 1987); neither does it, as a form of economic integration, require households. I treat householding as a concept that has the same status as the other forms of economic integration in the generic (institutional) model of the economy. Householding, in its various forms and folk expressions, is a common form of peasant resistance. While the particular example of householding comes from northeastern Kentucky, the concept has applicability in many peasant economies in nation-states. An additional case of householding from Guatemala is presented for comparative purposes in chapter 8, "Time and the Economy."

In chapter 6 I deal with "Storage as an Economic Process." The title of the chapter is important because it indicates a focus on storage per se, not on storage as an indicator of something else, such as sedentism, stratification, or complexity. I treat the relationships between storing processes and those of production and distribution in an evolutionary context.

Chapters 7 and 8, on the concepts of informal economy, and time and the economy, respectively, are exploratory and experimental in that they present models and develop concepts in nontraditional ways—these ideas either have not been presented in the literature of economic anthropology or have been presented in narrow, somewhat ethnocentric ways. "A Cross-Cultural Treatment of the Informal Economy" is an effort to use the institutional paradigm to create a truly cross-cultural model of the informal economy and to use it to explore variability in economic processes within cultural systems. The model of informal economy here is nontraditional in that it is not limited to negative concepts—for example, so-called black-market, underground, or hidden economies in modern nation-states.

Using Johannes Fabian's book *Time and the Other* as its starting point, chapter 8, "Time and the Economy," explores the temporal dimensions of economic processes through a series of cases, each of which involves a different model of time. The chapter begins with a discussion of the timing of householding in Guatemala and continues with Evans-Pritchard's analysis of ecological and structural time, concluding with additional ethnographic and archaeological case materials that focus on time as it reveals features of economic organization. The last case is an archaeological study of water management in the Maya lowlands that focuses on a slow, accretionary model of state formation as proposed by Vernon Scarborough (1993).

The final chapter, "Looking Backward and Forward on Concepts of the Economy," reviews some of the discourse of economic anthropology in an historical framework. It draws heavily from a piece on primitive economies written by Ruth Bunzel for Boas' 1938 reader, *General Anthropology*. Bunzel provides a discussion of concepts that is consistent with the institutional paradigm. Her framework was very sophisticated for its time, and her discussion allows us to focus on the issue of comparison in a broadly historical and theoretical context. It also allows for a discussion of concepts that have not been treated anywhere else in the book and it contains some implicit, but sorely needed, models of property. It becomes clear in this chapter that developments in economic anthropology parallel closely developments in the history of anthropological theory as a whole.

Materialist and Humanistic Approaches to the Study of Economic Processes

"The economy" refers to all processes of material-means provisioning in every cultural system, past and present. The approach, however, is not strictly materialistic; nor is it strictly scientific in the positivist sense of that term. Rather, I have combined scientific and humanistic methods for understanding the economy in its many forms throughout time. Concepts must be created and explored for understanding the relationships between material and symbolic processes of culture as they work to construct economic formations and strategies. Chapter 5, on householding and resistance, for example, deals with the ideological and symbolic systems that rural people in Kentucky call "the Kentucky way." The context for householding is a material provisioning strategy that requires participation in a variety of capitalist and non-capitalist institutional arrangements in different combinations.

The reasons for emphasizing the formation, clarification, and elaboration of concepts and their relationships to the collection and analysis of data are relatively simple and straightforward. In economic anthropology we have had an incredible proliferation of concepts and terms: modes of production, reciprocity and redistribution, prices, markets, forces and relations of production, exploitation, optimization, commoditization, etc. Many of the same concepts and terms have been used metaphorically, descriptively, and analytically in different institutional and historical contexts. Some have been used to describe behaviors in specific kinds of cultural and social contexts; others have been used with little attention to or understanding of context. Still more concepts have been employed in ways indicating that their users do not understand the differences between the organizational principles of economic processes that are configured differently in different kinds of cultural systems, and individual behavior pure and simple (Plattner 1989).

Current students of the economy, especially those who came of age after the formalist-substantivist debate of the 1960s and the 1970s, and during a period when Marxism was no longer a social science taboo, have not been able to develop a common vocabulary. By a common vocabulary I mean clearly defined concepts with definite uses. Such a vocabulary has been difficult to develop because many basic concepts have been either assumed or dismissed. Also, students have lacked a powerful and consistent paradigm—a theoretical framework on which to "hang" their concepts and their data. There is a great need, then, to construct a clear theoretical framework. This framework requires that we resurrect some old, but nonetheless basic, concepts and set down and elaborate new concepts, questions, and models that can be used by students and practitioners of economic anthropology—archaeologists, ethnohistorians, and ethnographers alike. We need a revitalized economic anthropology that incorporates archaeology.

The emphasis on concepts for understanding economic organization takes as its first priority the analysis of pattern, variation, and change in economies across cultures. In this sense, it is an extension of my previous book by that title (Halperin 1988). But whereas *Economies Across Cultures* focused on paradigms and schools in economic anthropology, and elaborated different forms of the comparative method, I deal in this book with individual concepts and problems that are illustrated by using specific archaeological as well as ethnographic case materials.

My hope is that once anthropologists are equipped with useful conceptual tools for the field and the library, they will be able to collect and analyze data directed toward understanding principles of economic organization. While this is certainly not only a "how to" book or a handbook, it can be used as such. The basic components of production and distribution processes, for example, should be understood by all anthropologists before they go to the field. By basic components I mean that fieldworkers must understand how to think about production processes in terms of the general questions that are possible to ask about production. The same can be said for other economic processes such as distribution. So also should questions about spatial and temporal units of description and analysis be made explicit.

That ethnocentrism and romanticism should be avoided at all costs goes without saying, but without concepts that deal with non-market economies and non-capitalist forms of resistance to capitalism, as well as with the basic elements of capitalism, economic anthropologists risk imposing assumptions upon their analyses that may distort what they are trying to say. It is no better to impose a market-driven supply and demand system on egalitarian horticulturalists in the Amazon Basin than it is to assume that working-class people in the United States, many of whom live on the margins of urban industrial capitalism in state systems and rely on a combination of extended family ties and the informal economy for their livelihoods, can be understood with the same non-market concepts that are appropriate for understanding stateless kin-based economies in tribes and chiefdoms. At the same time, it is impossible to understand the complex relationships between subsistence and cash economies in the absence of concepts that allow us to cross and criss-cross between differently organized economic processes: capitalist, pre-capitalist, and non-capitalist. By differently organized economic processes I mean processes that are organized by combinations of qualitatively different institutional arrangements.

There are several additional reasons to emphasize concepts for understanding principles of economic organization. One has to do with the strong tendencies, especially in archaeology, toward mistaking subsistence typologies or behaviors associated with subsistence activities for principles of economic organization. For example, hunting-and-gathering, horticulture, and agriculture take many organizational forms and occur on very different scales depending on their context. Tribal peoples practice horticulture with and without domesticated animals in the Amazon Basin as well as in the highlands of New Guinea; the Maya built pyramids and a complex state system while eating as their staple food maize produced by combining swidden agriculture (horticulture) with a variety of intensification techniques (e.g., raised fields). Humans remained the major source of energy. To assume that similar subsistence technologies occur in the same kinds of cultures and that they are all homogeneously organized is to gloss over the issue of explaining the organizational features of economic processes and, therefore, to ignore the problem of variability within subsistence types. Hunter-gatherers, for example, cover a range of organizational types from simple, small, nomadic groups, to complex, chiefdomlike cultural systems (Cassell 1988; Ellanna 1988).[1]

Another reason to emphasize economic organization is the confusion between the physical movements of goods and resources (including people) in space and the organization of economic processes. For example, just because an obsidian blade moves from point "a" to point "b" does not say anything about how or why the blade moves. I elaborate this point in chapter 3 specifically in connection with a critique of Binford's (1980) distinction between "foragers" and "collectors."

Thirdly, the idea that a description of a task, especially a work task, can be accepted as an analysis of the underlying institutional arrangements that shape and attach meaning and importance to that task has given us the illusion that we understand more about the nature of work, the division of labor, and the organization of production processes than we actually do. The discussion of time and the economy in chapter 8, especially Jane Guyer's material on gender and the organization of production, treats these issues in some detail.

To summarize, in order to get at economic organization, we must take a critical approach to past work that glosses over organizational issues by omission or simply by naiveté. This critical approach must be constructive, however, because it does not suffice merely to point out the flaws in a model or in an argument; one must come up with alternatives. Ethnographic and archaeological examples must be used to illustrate specific questions, problems, and concepts. Ironically, perhaps, it is the archaeologists who have the richest data on movements of material things through time and space. With a few exceptions, what they do not have is the analytical tool kit to understand the institutional arrangements that drive these movements.[2] Such a tool kit must be fashioned by creating a dialogue between archaeologists and cultural anthropologists interested in problems of economic organization (see Hirth 1984).

One   METHODOLOGICAL
INDIVIDUALISM:
STRUCTURE
AND AGENCY
IN ECONOMIC
ANTHROPOLOGY

*Parsons' actors are cultural dopes, but Althusser's
agents are structural dopes of even more stunning
mediocrity.*
(ANTHONY GIDDENS 1979:52)

The basis for the institutional paradigm, which
provides the overarching framework for this book, and which originated
with Marx and was elaborated by Polanyi, can be found in a critique of
methodological individualism. Recently, there has been a great deal of
discussion about the relationships between individuals' actions and decisions and the larger historical, institutional, and cultural contexts in
which they live. Anthony Giddens has coined the terms "agency" and
"structure" to refer to actors and institutions respectively (1979). Some
scholars have even argued that the critical debates in economic anthropology have all centered around controversies over whether economic
anthropologists study the behaviors of individual actors or the workings
of institutions and processes (Cancian 1966; Isaac 1993).

In light of these considerations, it seems important to provide a place
in this book for a discussion of some of the forms of methodological
individualism and the analytical costs and benefits of adopting such a
theoretical perspective. By methodological individualism I refer simply
to the use of individuals and their behaviors (or actions) as the units of
description and analysis. "Behavior" here refers to individual behavior,
not to the behavior of groups or systems. This critique of methodological individualism provides an opportunity to link to economic anthro-

pology some classic issues in the history of anthropological thought: Is the anthropological enterprise the study of culture or the study of behavior? What are the relationships between individuals, behaviors, institutions, and culture? These relationships have not been brought out in economic anthropology. As will be seen below, some people practice methodological individualism without knowing it, even when it is the very system that they are challenging.[1]

The limitations of methodological individualism are numerous. Patterned responses (or processes) in cultural systems cannot be accounted for by methodological individualism. This means that it cannot explain why cross-cultural differences or similarities occur. As we will see in chapter 8, it also has a very difficult time dealing with changes in patterns and processes. We are interested in patterns manifested by economic processes: production, distribution and consumption, storage, equivalency formation, those of resistance, and other more informal ones. If we posit the same rational, utilitarian motives to individuals in all cultures, and if we assume that all humans allocate scarce means towards alternative uses, all economic processes in all cultures would appear to be identical.

It is also true that economic anthropology has developed very few concepts or useful terminologies for treating economic matters in anything other than individualistic (person-oriented) terms. I will use Anthony Giddens' analysis of structure and agency as a basis for framing my discussion, and will end this chapter with some brief examples that illustrate some of the ways in which an institutional approach contrasts with one of methodological individualism.

Methodological individualism has had many—often hidden—forms in economic anthropology, all of which have involved focusing attention on the behavior of individual actors, rather than on the operations of the larger processes of which individuals are a part. Usually the behavior of people is described in terms of their actions or decisions, in isolation from, or subordinate to, the larger historical, cultural, and institutional structures of which they are a part (Barlett 1980). In its most extreme form, methodological individualism is highly ethnocentric, especially when it has imposed a utilitarian, "choice-making under conditions of scarcity" form of rationality upon actors. To assume that all humans make rational choices is problematic, but to assume that this approach tells us anything about patterns of similarity and difference in economic processes is even worse. Believing that all humans operate under the same kinds of rationality with the same kinds of priorities, systems of logic, and ways of operating is certainly a form of ethnocentrism. A focus on economic behavior per se is conducive to such interpretations (Plattner 1989).[2]

I will begin with Giddens' contemporary treatment because it parallels almost exactly the key issues, as I see them, in the history of economic anthropology, and because it has received such widespread attention in anthropology as a whole. Throughout the discussion, I will interweave theoretical issues in social theory and anthropology with those in economic anthropology.

Giddens begins by pointing out that agency and structure are usually seen as polar opposites: "'action' and 'structure' normally appear in both the sociological and philosophical literature as antinomies" (1979:49). Indeed the focus on agency (methodological individualism) at the expense of structure (institutions) in economic anthropology has not only failed to relate action theory to problems of institutional structure and transformation, but it has ignored or at best merely paid lip service to historical, cultural, and institutional contexts altogether. One has only to take a quick look at the table of contents of the most recent textbook in economic anthropology edited by Plattner (1989) to see that most of the focal chapters have the words "economic behavior" in their titles. Phrases such as "economic behavior in bands" (Cashdan 1989), "economic behavior in tribes" (Johnson 1989), "economic behavior in peasant communities" (Cancian 1989), and "economic behavior in markets" (Plattner 1989) immediately leap out. What do these phrases mean? What are their implications for understanding pattern and variation in economic processes across cultures and over time? I should note at the outset that this focus on economic behavior is understandable on two grounds. First, it is easier to observe and analyze individual behavior than it is to understand the institutional arrangements that drive it; after all, we can see agents, but we cannot see structures. And aside from the often cryptic and largely unelaborated concepts put forth by Polanyi, economic anthropology has lacked the concepts for analyzing anything other than economic action. Even Marx's concepts of the forces and relations of production—although useful and designed to get at institutional and historical features of societies—are so abstract that they are often difficult to operationalize. In fact most of the concepts Marx created (alienation, surplus, exploitation, class) were specific to the analysis of capitalism, and do not take us very far in pre-capitalist and non-capitalist contexts.

Leslie White

In twentieth century anthropology Leslie White is the theorist who most persistently and clearly argued against methodological individualism, although he did not use that term. His arguments were aimed at several different areas. One had to do with White's objections to biological and psychological reductionism in the social sciences. Another, and more positive, point had to do with his insistence that culture is not only the subject matter of anthropology, but the system that explains patterns and variations in the variety of cultures found in the world. White said, for example, in an essay entitled "The Individual and Cultural Process":

> *Thus, we do not account for differences between Chinese and Swedish culture by appeal to the physical, somatological, and innate psychological differences between the Chinese and Swedish people. We know of no differences between cultural traditions, no specific feature of the cultural process, that can be explained in terms of innate biological properties, physical or mental. On the other hand, we can explain the human behavior of Chinese and Swedish peoples as biological organisms in terms of their respective cultures.* (1987:285, ORIGINAL 1950)

For White, individuals are a vital part of cultural processes, but these processes cannot be explained in terms of individual psychological characteristics.

> *The individual himself is not irrelevant to the culture process. On the contrary, he is an integral and in one sense a fundamental part of it. Individuals do indeed enamel their fingernails, vote, . . . But the individual is irrelevant to* an explanation *of the culture process. We cannot explain the culture trait or process of enameling nails in terms of innate desire, will, or caprice. We can, however, explain the behavior of the individual in terms of the culture that embraces him.* (1987:286)

In short, what anthropologists study is not individual behavior, but culture, understood as a set of integrated and multitiered systems. White was very definitely influenced by Karl Marx and by Emile Durkheim (1949:330). The latter argued that the whole is greater than the sum of its parts and that social facts exist apart from the behaviors of individuals; he thereby provided the conceptual grounding for White's work.

White developed his own set of concepts and methods for countering methodological individualism. These took the form of the science of "culturology." For White, the study of culture with a capital "C" was the method for analyzing institutions and processes that are ongoing and that change and evolve over time, regardless of the particular individuals who are involved. By focusing on energy as the key factor in culture change—more precisely on the amount of energy a given culture can harness per capita per year—White could begin to develop some quantitative measures for dividing the "apples" and "oranges" of human cultures.

White saw culture as a system that could be divided into three subcategories:

> *Culture is an organized, integrated system. But we may distinguish three subdivisions within, or aspects of, this system. For our purpose, we shall distinguish three subsystems of culture, namely, technological, sociological, and ideological systems. The technological system is composed of the material, mechanical, physical, and chemical instruments, together with the techniques of their use, by means of which man, as an animal species, is articulated with his natural habitat . . . here we find the tools of production, the means of subsistence, the materials of shelter, the instruments of offense and defense. The sociological system is made up of interpersonal relations expressed in patterns of behavior, collective as well as individual. In this category we find social, kinship, economic, ethical, political, military, ecclesiastical, occupational, professional, recreational, etc., systems. The ideological system is composed of ideas, beliefs, knowledge, expressed in articulate speech or other symbolic form. Mythologies and theologies, legend, literature, philosophy, science, folk wisdom, and common sense knowledge make up this category.*
> (1949:364)

Here we have, in economic anthropological terms, the essence of Marx's theory of culture—what Marx would have called "the social." Note White's emphasis on systems and patterns of behavior and the care with which he attends to all the dimensions (layers) of culture. But cultures change, and it was the concept of evolution—specifically cultural evolution—that gave power to White's theory. As Peace has recently put it in his discussion of the political context of White's cultural evolutionism, "White believed society had evolved and was continuing to evolve and that socialism was the next, and higher, stage of development after capitalism" (1993:141). White's concept of evolution subordinated the individual to the larger cultural system. The larger technological, sociological, and ideological processes mold individual action. Cultures, then, are the units of change: cultures evolve, individuals do not.

Giddens on Problems of Agency and Structure

Giddens points to Marx as the most important thinker on relationships between agency and structure:

> Marx's writings still represent the most significant single fund of ideas that can be drawn upon in seeking to illuminate problems of agency and structure. (1979:53)

He proceeds to draw upon Marx to elaborate a dialectical relationship between agency and structure. Giddens states that (1979:53) "notions of action and structure *presuppose one another* dialectically" (emphasis his), and that two factors are necessary for a theory of institutions: (1) "the incorporation of temporality into the understanding of human agency," and (2) the inclusion of "power as integral to the constitution of social practices." I deal with the issue of temporality in chapter 8, "Time and the Economy," and with the issue of power in chapter 5 on householding, which is seen as a form of resistance in state systems. In chapter 8, time and temporality are not focused on human agency. Rather, "Time and the Economy" deals with the temporal dimensions of economic processes in different historical, cultural, and institutional contexts. There I draw on the work of Johannes Fabian as well as that of Nancy Munn, Jane Guyer, and Vernon Scarborough.

One of the most interesting and important aspects of Giddens' concept of agency is that it has institutional and cultural components built into it.

For example, to Giddens, action is "a continuous flow of conduct" (1979:55). Action is thus repetitive and patterned. He treats regularized action as "situated practices" (1979:56). Giddens' concept of structure also includes agency. For Giddens, structuring properties consist of "rules and resources recursively implicated in the reproduction of social systems" (1979:64). On the next page he adds historical dimensions to rules by saying: "Rules can only be grasped in the context of the histori- cal development of social totalities as recursively implicated in practices." Notice that this feature of recursivity (repetition, as well as cycles that feed back upon themselves) is important for both concepts, structure and agency. Rules and practices only exist in conjunction with one another. Giddens defines institutions as being embedded in social systems just as agents are embedded in structures:

> Structures do not exist in time-space except in mo-
> ments of the constitution of social systems. But we can
> analyze how "deeply layered" structures are in terms
> of the historical duration of the practices they recur-
> sively organize, and the spatial "breadth" of those
> practices: how widespread they are across a range of
> interactions. The most deeply layered practices consti-
> tutive of social systems in each of these senses are
> institutions.
> (1979:64–65)

If we take this notion of "deeply layered practices" as a working defi- nition of institutions, we have not only a good beginning for a critique of methodological individualism, but a useful way of understanding in- stitutions, their longevity, and their trajectories in cultural systems. It should also be mentioned here, however, that this notion of "deeply lay- ered practices" sounds very much like Kroeber's superorganic concept of culture (1952); this concept was resurrected and relabeled in Bourdieu's concept of "habitus" (1979). Culture in this sense may be understood, perhaps, as one of the layers, and a thick one at that.

Giddens' theory of structuration posits a concept of "duality of struc- ture" that asserts the "mutual dependence of structure and agency." I would argue, however, that Giddens has built concepts of structure and institution into his concept of agents. In contrast to Parsons' actors and Althusser's agents, those of Giddens are neither cultural nor structural dopes. Rather, Giddens' agents are, at least theoretically, institutional and cultural geniuses. This makes Giddens' agents very different from the actors of methodological individualism.

Forms of Methodological Individualism in Economic Anthropology

Methodological individualism has had a long history in economic anthropology. In fact, one school of economic anthropology (the formalist school [LeClaire and Schneider 1967]) began as an offshoot of methodological individualism's archetype, conventional economics (Robbins 1962; Samuelson 1967). Central to the formalist position is the assumption that individuals (the key units of description and analysis) in both capitalist and pre-capitalist economies behave in similar rational and utilitarian ways. Operating on assumptions of scarcity, maximization, and the primacy of individual self-interested choices, conventional economic concepts designed for market capitalism have become the main menu of concepts for formalist economic anthropology. The classic historical examples can be found in the work of Melville Herskovits and, later, Raymond Firth.

Herskovits' *Economic Anthropology*, the first comprehensive textbook in the field, began with a discussion of "economizing and rational behavior."[3] His emphasis on universals is testimony to the powerful influence of the mature discipline of economics upon the fledgling science of economic anthropology. What is perhaps most striking, however, is the hard-core, utilitarian methodological individualism that is the basis of all of Herskovits' work and that has carried over into the work of present-day economic anthropologists. Herskovits' statement below could be found just as commonly in a textbook on conventional economics:

> It can also be taken as cross-culturally acceptable that,
> on the whole, the individual tends to maximize his
> satisfactions in terms of the choices he makes. Where
> the gap between utility and disutility is appreciable,
> and the producer or consumer of a good or service is
> free to make his choice, then, other things being
> equal, he will make his choice in terms of utility
> rather than disutility.
> (1952:18)

Firth, too, in a manner similar to that of Herskovits, emphasizes economizing by individuals (1967:4).

Both Herskovits and Firth were ambivalent towards conventional economics, however. Clearly, any theory that postulated the universal applicability of concepts based on a capitalist example had to be ethnocentric. As anthropologists, Herskovits and Firth realized the significant qualitative differences between primitive, peasant, and capitalist economies. They must have seen that by postulating universals based on assumptions about the behavior of individuals, they were avoiding the issue of explaining variation in economic forms. Yet neither Herskovits nor Firth made significant progress toward institutional or comparative analysis. Herskovits resorted to an encyclopedic approach that described economic behavior in primitive societies in endless detail. Firth also wrote huge volumes on a variety of different economies but he never provided concepts for understanding even the essentials of his descriptions in comparative terms.

Following Herskovits and Firth came a plethora of ethnographic cases written by anthropologists who tried to use the terminology of conventional economics in essentially non-capitalist contexts (Tax 1953; Pospisil 1963; Epstein 1968; Schneider 1974). Theoretical accompaniments included work by Burling (1962), Cook (1966a, 1966b, 1969), and others. Perhaps the most often quoted of the ethnographic cases is Pospisil's account of the Kapauku Papuans who, as Isaac (1993) points out, were anthologized by LeClaire and Schneider (1968:381–394) under the heading "The Kapauku Individualistic Money Economy." If Pospisil had set out to write the textbook on methodological individualism, he could not have done a better job, for he writes of them as extreme individualists (1963:3). But as Isaac points out, by quoting a passage that LeClaire and Schneider did not include in their anthology, what we really have in capitalistic clothing is a pre-capitalist economy in which hoarding of wealth is taboo and individuals who fail to comply with the Kapauku requirement of generosity are frequently put to death (Pospisil 1963:49, quoted in Isaac 1993:223). One wonders whether, in fact, Pospisil's theoretical ax was indeed that of extreme methodological individualism rather than that of conventional economics. The title of Harold Schneider's *Economic Man* (1974) certainly reinforces any individualistic notions that may have gone unnoticed by readers of Pospisil's work.

The New Formalism

Recent work in economic anthropology still exhibits methodological individualism. With a few exceptions it pervades the recently edited Plattner volume on economic anthropology (see especially chapters by Plattner, Barlett, Gladwin). Decision-making models are prime examples of methodological individualism (Barlett 1980; Gladwin 1982). To take another example, the notion that individual productivity must be measured, regardless of the context, is only one rather blatant instance of methodological individualism. After noting that there is widespread sharing of food within hunter-gatherer bands, one author says that the effects of food sharing on individual productivity have not yet been adequately explored (Cashdan 1989:26). From descriptions of individual behavior, formalists and methodological individualists assume the universality of nineteenth-century market capitalism. They do this by ignoring context and attaching the same assumptions to the behavior of all individuals. The difficulty of course is that variability is difficult to discern; at best economies vary in degree, not in kind. Quantitative distinctions can be made, not qualitative ones. According to this methodology, pre-capitalist economies become miniatures of capitalist economies.

The idea that pre-capitalist economies operate according to qualitatively different organizational principles (institutional arrangements) cannot be accommodated if all individual economic actors are created and analyzed equally. Among other things, one corollary is that economies of highly variable levels of complexity can be assumed to be comparable.

While formal models and their application have changed greatly since the heyday of the formalist-substantivist debate, certain strains of methodological individualism remain remarkably intact. Optimal foraging models are prime examples of utilitarian methodological individualism. I have written about these elsewhere (Halperin 1988) as one of several examples of formal atomistic models to indicate the use of methodological individualism, but I did not discuss methodological individualism per se.

FORMAL ATOMISTIC MODELS

Formal atomistic models are models of agents, and they developed from conventional microeconomic theory. Their key units of analysis are still rational, self-seeking individuals, but they perform slightly different (and more complex) functions in these models than they did in the old formal economic anthropology. Whereas the individuals of the old formalist economic anthropology functioned as universal actors, the individuals of formal atomistic models function *both* as universal actors and as ideal ones.

Formal atomistic models were established solidly for the subfield of economic anthropology with the publication in 1975 of Stuart Plattner's edited collection *Formal Methods in Economic Anthropology*. Plattner's work was a turning point because it added a new and powerfully scientific dimension to the concept of the formal. Plattner employed individual decision-making units as both universals and ideals against which reality could be measured. Prediction and simulation are two of the main functions of formal atomistic models (see Plattner 1975*b*). It is interesting to note that Platter has, in his recent edited volume (1989), gone back to a position that is closer to the old version of formalism, namely that it is universal; he does not emphasize modeling nearly as much in his 1989 volume as he did in the 1975 work. He himself argues that the book has an empirical emphasis. Nonetheless Plattner's work provided the groundwork for even more sophisticated formal models.

FORMAL PROCESSUAL MODELS

As I have argued elsewhere (1988) formal processual models contrast with formal atomistic models. The former are models of processes—the units of analysis are institutions and processes. Reciprocal sharing processes vary from one culture to another; those of band-level hunter-gatherers are different, for example, from the ones practiced by so-called complex, tribal-level hunter-gatherers whose populations are larger and more sedentary. In order to create such models, however, kinship groups, bands, and camps would be the relevant units of analysis (see also Cowgill 1989 and Yellen 1989). It should also be possible to construct models that facilitate analysis of peasant economies so that we can predict and explain the success or failure of agrarian reform at the village level. This could be done in terms of such subjects as the distribution of political offices among families over time, the quality and number of political and economic ties between local, regional, and national elites, and the size and quality of the local land base. A sufficient number of descriptions of agrarian reform attempts exist in the literature to allow models of this sort to be constructed.

Formal processual models are much less elegant than formal atomistic models. Their units are complicated processes or sets of social relations occurring in cultural systems at different times and in different places.

Also, many different assumptions can be attached to the units. While optimization is still a prominent assumption in existing processual models, the models are not formulated in terms of maximizing individuals, but rather in terms of an overall adaptive strategy for the group (Keene 1979). Chayanov (1966) used the peasant family farm as the unit of analysis. Thus, it is not formal modeling per se that is problematic for economic anthropology, it is the choice of units and attached assumptions. Formal processual models are models of structures.

OPTIMAL FORAGERS AND OPTIMAL DIETERS: INSTITUTIONAL GENIUSES OR CULTURAL DOPES?

Optimal foraging analyses of hunter-gatherer subsistence patterns are perhaps some of the best-known examples of formal atomistic models. In some respects, they represent methodological individualism at its extreme. These models postulate rational, choice-making individuals as their units of analysis and they assume scarcity of time as well as of other resources. Winterhalder and Smith's (1981) version of optimal foraging strategy assumes that foragers maximize their net rates of energy while foraging, a postulate that has been subject to question (Martin 1983). Yesner's (1981) patch-use model not only assumes that movements between patches are random, but that the seasonal factors that shape the composition of resources in a "patch" can be ignored.

One of the best descriptions of yet another version of optimal foraging models is Elizabeth Cashdan's of the model of optimal diet choice:

> The optimal diet model assumes a homogeneous environment, where resources are encountered randomly. Each food type has a cost (the time taken to procure and process it, often called "handling time") and a benefit (the net caloric value of the food). The profitability of a food type, then, can be measured by the ratio of benefit to cost, and an optimal forager should prefer the most profitable food items. . . . This decision depends on the trade-off between "handling" time, the time it takes to get the item once it is encountered, and "search" time. If a forager chooses only the most profitable items, he will have a high

> rate of return for each item once he encounters it, but
> he will have to spend a lot of time "searching" for the
> food item. If he is willing to be less selective, he will
> spend less time searching, but he will have a lower
> rate of return when actually procuring and processing
> the prey. . . . The optimal diet breadth occurs . . .
> when the decrease in search time gained by adding
> food types just equals the increased handling time of
> procuring them.
> (1989:29–31)

Cashdan (1989:31) goes on to mention that in later formulations of this model, the optimal number of food types is determined by comparing the profitability of each food type, once encountered, with the average return rate for all food types of higher rank (see Hawkes, Hill, and O'Connell 1982).

With a sarcastic tone, Martin criticizes the assumptions contained in optimal foraging models of all varieties because they are predicated on a utilitarian brand of methodological individualism:

> Travel between patches and the search for patches is
> thus like a random walk in an environment in which
> patches are distributed randomly and uniformly rela-
> tive to the movements of the forager. The forager has
> no foreknowledge of patch distribution or other ways
> of moving directly to the more productive patches and
> therefore "loses" nothing in the way of travel time by
> moving about randomly and utilizing patches as
> encountered.
> (1983:621)

Martin's point, of course, is that these assumptions are not warranted in the case of hunter-gatherers. The ethnographic record shows that the movements of hunter-gatherers in the environment are flexible but highly structured and purposeful. These movements are based on an intimate and extensive knowledge of the environment, including not only the location and sources of key resources, but also the patterns and origins of resource variation on an annual and seasonal basis (see Cohen 1989).

Following up on some of the points above, Cashdan herself presents some useful alternatives to the methodological individualism of optimal foraging models in a discussion of seasonal variation among hunter-gatherers. She mentions three factors that provide hunter-gatherers with flexibility and stability: mobility, group size, and storage: "At the simplest level, storage evens out temporal variation in resource abundance, and trade does the same for spatial variation" (1989:33). She goes on to point out that hunter-gatherers "track" environmental variation by adjusting to it through changes in location and local group size; they live in relatively large "macroband" camps during part of the year and disperse into smaller "microband" family-sized groups during the remaining months (1989:33).

Cashdan does not, however, detail the specific principles that organize production units, large and small, during these different seasonal phases in group size. Larger groupings can be responses either to resource abundance or to scarcity, depending upon the exigencies of production processes. Nor does she analyze storage in relationship to production and distribution processes in any systematic way. A quick reading still leaves one with the impression that individuals are making the decisions about group size and location as well as whether or not to share resources. While she writes (1989:37) of "a strong ethic of sharing and 'generalized reciprocity,'" she refuses to acknowledge that sharing is deeply institutionalized through kinship and marriage in virtually all hunter-gatherer cultures, both simple and complex. Her methodological individualism, combined with a certain degree of ecological reductionism, gets in the way of her analysis. Her facts are right, but she lacks the concepts to avoid methodological individualism. I deal with these issues in the chapters on storage (chapter 6) and on ecological and economic anthropology (chapter 3). One cannot assume that either individuals or ecological processes drive economic organization.[4]

Finding Structures and Agents in Fieldwork in Economic Anthropology

The critical question seems to be: What kinds of structures are defining and driving what kinds of agents? Once these are defined, we can begin to collect comparable data and begin to create models for understanding pattern and variation. I offer two examples from my own fieldwork. The first comes from Grenada, West Indies; the second from the United States.

I. GRENADA 1969

The following example is based on fieldwork on the Caribbean island of Grenada in a coastal village (population 400) whose livelihood processes include: seine fishing, wage labor on locally owned and run banana plantations, kitchen gardening with small livestock (chickens and pigs), and a few local shopkeepers (these were primarily rum shops). Two elite families dominate the village and own a large banana plantation; bananas are exported to the Netherlands on a weekly basis. Most non–elite people are related through ties of blood, marriage, or godparenthood. A strong ideology of equality prevails. The phrase "We is all one people here" can be heard in many village settings.

In the late 1960s I witnessed repeated shouting matches between groups of women fish-vendors clustered on one side of the seining beach, and their common-law fishermen-husbands gathered around baskets of fish at the other. The arguments often lasted for an hour or more. The men and women were arguing over the price the vendors would pay the fishermen for specific quantities of fish; they were buying the fish to sell in the large urban marketplace in the capitol city of St. Georges. Upon their return from the marketplace to the village the vendors shared the profits of the fish sales among themselves. On many days it appeared as though the men and women, who were couples residing in the same household, were competing economically.

What was going on here? Men and women operate, for the most part, in separate, although related, social, cultural, and economic domains. Women are responsible, along with the members of their female kin networks, for the maintenance of households and for reproduction. Men, while they certainly contribute resources to their current households, have obligations in several other households as well as in the domain of politics, both at the village level, and, in some cases, beyond the village. These male obligations require resources, whether in the form of cash or credit. To look simply at the face value of the arguments over the price of fish does not tell us anything about the structures within which men and women live and work.

Seine fishing requires substantial numbers of people from the village to help "haul in" the nets from the shore. Each person who helps is entitled to a share of the catch. This is one of the major sources of protein in the village. In addition, virtually every household in the village has its own "kitchen garden" which is equivalent to the Mesoamerican *milpa* in

METHODOLOGICAL INDIVIDUALISM

PHOTO I. *Fishermen and fish vendors, Grenada, West Indies.*
Photo by the author.

PHOTO 2.   *Fishermen and fish vendors surveying the catch, Grenada,
                            West Indies. Photo by the author.*

PHOTO 3.   *Fish vendor surveying the catch, Grenada, West Indies.
                            Photo by the author.*

the sense that it contains a variety of fruit trees and vegetable plants, including bananas, breadfruit and cassava (manioc), which are major staples of the diet. In addition each household has a few chickens, often one or two pigs, and perhaps a cow or two for milk. Fish sales, then, provide cash, but they are by no means the major source of subsistence. Many village residents, both men and women, work for cash on the local banana plantation.

If we view the shouting matches between fish vendors and their common-law husbands in this context, we can begin to see that the operative structures (institutions) here are not households and the operative agencies (actors, and the roles they play) are not husbands and wives. Rather, the operative agencies are fishermen and women fish-vendors, who happen to be common-law spouses, but who operate primarily as members of male and female peer groups. As noted above, women control and maintain reproduction, which is based in households and female kin networks in the village and the region; men are responsible for maintaining their peer groups (which are usually associated with one of the two political factions in the village). Men must also maintain the fishing operation itself—boats, nets, etc. Agricultural activities work differently. Milk from cows that are usually tethered some distance away in the mountain, and the products of kitchen gardens, are produced by the labor of men and women, respectively, and used jointly for household maintenance.

There are several points to be made here with regard to the organization of economic processes. First, the relevant structures and the definition of agents depend, not only on context, but on specific kinds of productive processes. Secondly, we see different structures—the household, the peer group (male and female), the village itself—operating simultaneously, but for different purposes. Fish production is organized by the male peer group. Fish distribution and the sharing of the catch among people who help to haul the nets is a village function. Outsiders are not permitted to help. On most days, seine fishing is a cooperative (village) effort in which all who help receive their rightful share of the catch from the captain of the fishing crew. No fish are taken to the marketplace. It is only after this village distribution has occurred that the remaining portion of the catch is taken to the capitol city to be sold. Distribution of profits from fish sales is under the aegis of the female peer group, while households organize the basic subsistence activities involving livestock and kitchen gardens. Both men and women work as agricultural wage laborers on the local banana plantation and contribute their wages to household maintenance. Often such wage labor is performed on a sporadic basis, although sometimes work is more regular.

We can see that the contexts within which people work are both complex and fluid. People move in and out of different structures in simultaneous and, often, overlapping patterns. The structures are critical however; without understanding these structures, a great deal of behavior can easily be misinterpreted.

2. AN URBAN EXTENDED-FAMILY ECONOMY IN THE U.S.

This example is taken from an ongoing research project in an urban Appalachian area that is currently experiencing rapid economic development. This working-class community is culturally diverse and racially integrated. While it has experienced dramatic changes over the past twenty years (demographic decline, infrastructural disintegration, and a city-generated economic development plan) and appears on the surface to be deteriorating, its core families have resided in the neighborhood for at least four generations; in many cases they have been here as long as long as seven to eight generations. Strong family and home-place orientations are common, as are high levels of participation in informal economic sectors (odd jobs and work obtained through kin networks). Mutual support through kin and neighborhood networks is the primary mark of community membership.

Tricia McDonald takes out life insurance on her informally adopted mother (Ruby Kale), a lifelong resident of the community, and on her adoptive grandmother, Beatrice Kale. Tricia works as an administrative secretary in a major corporation in a midwestern city. Her husband is a construction worker.

Tricia's adoptive mother, Ruby, held a variety of wage-earning jobs (factory worker, convenience-store manager, barmaid) but now spends her days watching her grandbabies. Her major work, however, is for her community. She is a fifth-generation resident, and she is committed to the preservation of this Appalachian community's culture and heritage. As former chairperson of the housing subcommittee and as former president of the community council, she is a well-known and respected figure at City Hall. Every day, Ruby transports her "daughter," Tricia, and Tricia's biological mother, Nadine, to and from work in the central part of the city. She often stops at City Hall to drop in on the mayor or his staff-people. Ruby uses Tricia's American Express card and has, as her primary cash income, her own mother's pension check. She makes a home for virtually all neighborhood children in her small apartment; this includes feeding them and lending them money.

Sharing of resources among extended family and community members is not uncommon in the inner city U.S. (Stack 1972; Susser 1986). Two features make this case interesting for economic anthropology. The first is that kinship here is not biologically but culturally constructed; livelihood and reproductive patterns are deeply embedded in kinship and community. The second is that Tricia appears in the census data as employed; the assumption on the part of the mainstream hegemonic culture is that her income supports her biologic nuclear family. The unit of distribution (the structure, in Giddens' terms) is assumed to be the nuclear family. Ruby, on the other hand, is at best an unpaid baby-sitter or an unemployed barmaid, according to the census. Such would be the interpretation of a methodological individualist.

Life-course is a hidden but important structure in this case. Different kinds of work tasks and different expectations regarding their share of the extended family's resources are appropriate for people at distinct points in their life-course. Traditionally in this community, grandmothers exit from the mainstream labor force or they take night jobs so that they can "watch" their grandbabies during the day. Women of reproductive age are expected to work outside the home, just as Ruby did when she was raising her adopted daughter. In large part, however, the needs of the extended family network demand that an intergenerational division of labor be created among women. The priority here is not profit, or even upward mobility, but rather the maintenance of the extended family, preferably in its community of origin. People sacrifice their own self-interest in favor of the benefit of the family and the community; this is why community work is so important, even though it is not economically beneficial for individuals.

SUMMARY

This discussion of methodological individualism began on a rather abstract level, using Anthony Giddens' concepts of structure and agency as the framework. It has reviewed critically the various forms of methodological individualism in economic anthropology, including the formalist school and optimal foraging theory. It has concluded with two examples from my own fieldwork that are designed to show the hidden structures and the hidden cultures that operate to shape economic processes. These hidden structures and cultures are not mysterious to the anthropological fieldworker; but they are not apparent to the casual observer or to the person who assumes individual utilitarian rationality.

| Two | MARX'S INSTITUTIONAL PARADIGM AND POLANYI'S GENERIC MODEL OF THE ECONOMY |

I n this chapter, I want to set out some of the theoretical foundations for what is to follow in the rest of the book. First I will summarize the key features of what I have called the institutional paradigm (Halperin 1988) because it contains the theoretical foundations for a generic model of the economy and for the development of models based on comparative concepts in economic anthropology. The institutional paradigm originated with Marx[1] and was elaborated by Polanyi and others (Kahn and Llobera 1981) through the use of historical, archaeological, and ethnographic data.

In the second part of this chapter I will outline the main features of a generic model of the economy as an outgrowth of the institutional paradigm. In fact, I will argue that the beginnings of the generic model of the economy are to be found in Polanyi's attempt to elaborate and render operational in a cross-cultural context Marx's general categories: the forces and relations of production. I will argue further, and throughout the course of this book, that a generic (institutional) model of the economy that derives from and elaborates on the institutional paradigm provides the basis for the development of comparative, cross-cultural concepts of the economy. The concepts from the generic model are thoroughly grounded in the institutional paradigm, however, and that fact must never be lost.

Polanyi provided the beginnings of such a generic model and did so by building on the preliminary institutional and historically based models of Marx; this is heartening in that it establishes guideposts for attaching some data to abstract concepts and thereby for refining those concepts in the context of the institutional paradigm. Polanyi added two key ingredients to Marx's institutional paradigm: (1) ethnographic data, mostly from the early American cultural anthropologists and from the early British structural-functionalists, primarily Bronislaw Malinowski and Raymond Firth; and (2) models that identified, in a very formal and abstract way, patterns of economic processes. The best known of Polanyi's models are his forms of economic integration: reciprocity, redistribution, exchange, and householding. These have not been recognized as models. Most often, in fact, the various forms of economic integration have been taken to be types of economies or types of exchanges (Codere 1968; Fried 1967; Sahlins 1972; Stanish 1992).

The theoretical framework into which Polanyi placed these data was dynamic, historical, evolutionary, and, some might argue, dialectical. He accepted neither the method nor the theory of British or American functionalism. In the process Polanyi went beyond Marx in formulating concepts for the analysis of economies across cultures. He did this by developing models for different kinds of economic processes which were institutionalized differently in distinct historical and cultural contexts. This chapter is also intended to provide the theoretical foundations for a "concept" book on economies past and present that builds upon both Marx and Polanyi in both critical and sympathetic ways.

I should emphasize at the outset that what I am calling Polanyi's generic model of the economy—really a model of material livelihood in cultural systems—has gone virtually unrecognized. While there certainly has been the general recognition that Polanyi was working toward a general theory of the economy (Schroyer 1991; Polanyi-Levitt 1990) there has been no discussion of Polanyi's concepts of locational and appropriational movements; these concepts provide the basis for his generic model. Neither has there been any discussion of the relationships between the concepts of locational and appropriational movements and Polanyi's forms of economic integration.

PART I. MARX, THE INSTITUTIONAL PARADIGM, AND THE CRITIQUE OF ECONOMISM

The basis for the institutional paradigm can be found in a critique of methodological individualism calling for a shift in the unit of economic analysis from the individual to society and its institutions (see Kahn 1990). Whereas Adam Smith and the classical political economists focused on individuals and their "natural propensities" to "truck, barter and exchange one thing for another," Marx argued for the embeddedness (contextualization) of economic activities in larger social and historical contexts—in essence, culturally and institutionally constructed economies. The political economists claimed that a system of order would automatically and naturally result from the sum total of individual exchange activities, and their argument was that the whole is indeed equal to the sum of its parts. Marx, on the other hand, maintained that social, cultural, and historical contexts operate separately from any particular individual activities. Identical activities or behaviors are, in fact, different in different social and historical (institutional) contexts (White 1949, 1959; Sahlins 1960).[2] To say this more simply, economies differ not just in degree, but in kind.[3]

The movement from a focus on individuals to one on institutions indeed constituted a paradigm shift for the social sciences (Kuhn 1962). But, as I have indicated in the previous chapter, this change is contested regularly in anthropological studies of economies as well as in the social sciences generally (Giddens 1979, 1982).[4] Methodological individualism has taken many forms in economic anthropology, from the conventional economic stances of the formalists of the formalist-substantivist debate (LeClaire and Schneider 1968; Schneider 1974), to the assumptions of optimal foraging models in more recent discussions.[5] Marxism, too, has its many types, from French structural Marxism (Terray 1972, 1975) to more recent British versions (Ingold 1979, 1980, 1983). Not all Marxists subscribe to the institutional paradigm; even among those who do, some use the institutional paradigm in ethnocentric ways such that the categories of capitalist economies are imposed in non-capitalist and pre-capitalist economic formations (Clammer 1978a).

The important point for economic anthropologists is that the paradigm used determines the ways' in which one defines and analyzes all economic processes. Often, the paradigm is hidden or implicit or, in some cases, mixed. Logically we can understand that, for example, production processes appear to be different if one begins with the individual instead of with societies or cultures at particular points in time. There is a timelessness to methodological individualism, which assumes that if individuals are behaving in certain ways, they will do so forever. I will discuss some of these issues in chapter 8, "Time and the Economy." Building an alternative paradigm to methodological individualism in-

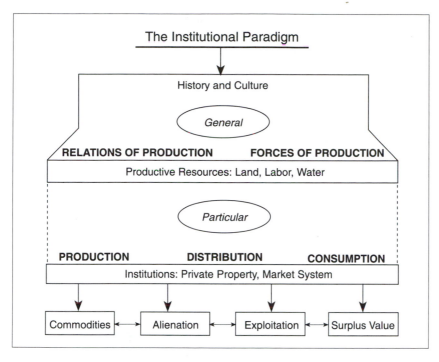

FIGURE I.   *The Institutional Paradigm*

volves the close examination in their historical contexts of economic processes and the institutions organizing them.

The Institutional Paradigm and its Concepts: Marx, the Institutional Paradigm, and the General Problem of Production

Marx approached production processes on two levels, general and particular: the first level consisted of those elements in production processes shared by all economies at all times and places; the other consisted of particular features of production in specific institutional contexts—more clearly, the production processes organized by specific institutions in particular cultural contexts or societies, as Marx would have it. He framed his general discussion of production in comparative (what Harris [1979] came to call "etic") terms. These comparative terms are considerations for analyzing all systems of production in all societies during all historic (and, we should add, prehistoric) periods. Marx was aware of the abstract nature of general categories and, therefore, of the need to keep particular systems of production in mind when formulating them. The following is a quote from Marx's *The Grundrisse* (1973:85); it is a short but complicated passage with both historical and evolutionary overtones. It contains an explicit critique of "modern economists" as well as some general guidelines for fashioning analytic tools for understanding similarities, differences, patterns, and variations in ancient and modern economies:

> *[A]ll epochs of production have certain common traits, common characteristics.* Production in general *is an abstraction, but a rational abstraction in so far as it really brings out and fixes the common element and thus saves us repetition. Still, this* general *category, this common element sifted out by comparison, is itself segmented many times over and splits into different determinations. Some determinations belong to all epochs, others only to a few.* [Some] *determinations will be shared by the most modern epoch and the most ancient. No production will be thinkable without them; however, even though the most developed languages have laws and characteristics in common with the least developed, nevertheless, just those things which determine their development, i.e., the elements which are not general and common, must be separated out from the determinations valid for production as such, so that their unity—which arises already from the identity of the subject, humanity, and of the object, nature—their essential difference is not forgotten. The whole profundity of those modern economists who demonstrate the eternity and harmoniousness of the existing social relations lies in this forgetting.*

To translate this a bit, Marx is arguing that general and common features of production must be separated and distinguished from the particularities of specific production systems. Marx is referring here to both general—forces and relations of production that are valid for all systems of production—and specific categories—the variations among systems of production as they evolve in cultural systems. The general categories can be seen as models for understanding the key elements and common denominators of all production processes. The important point here is that the common denominators of production—for example, productive resources such as labor, land, tools, and water—must be understood to vary according to historical, cultural, and institutional setting. Under capitalism, the surplus value siphoned off by capitalists by virtue of the fact that they own the means of production and can essentially put less into the product than they get out of it (wages, etc.) is an outgrowth of the institutions of private property and the market system. Profit is possible under capitalism because of the particular way property and exchange are organized. Theoretically, and actually, the same technical production processes—for example, factories that produce identical things—can operate under completely different institutional arrangements. Notice that Marx's critique operates on at least two levels here. He is criticizing capitalism as a system and he is criticizing our concepts for understanding it. Marx's concepts of alienation, exploitation, surplus value, etc., are only a few of his particular concepts involved in this double critique. As we will see below, Polanyi sympathized with Marx's double critique.

In a further critique of economism, Marx takes on those who gloss over critical differences in historical and institutional arrangements:

> The bourgeois economy thus supplies the key to the ancient, etc. But not at all in the manner of those economists who smudge over all historical differences and see bourgeois relations in all forms of society. One can understand tribute, tithe, etc., if one is acquainted with ground rent. But one must not identify them. Further, relations derived from earlier forms will often be found within it only in an entirely stunted form. For example, communal property. Although it is true, therefore, that the categories of bourgeois economies possess a truth for all other forms of society, this is to be taken only with a grain of salt. They contain them in a developed, or stunted, or caricatured form etc., but always with an essential difference.
> (1973:105–106)

Here Marx has taken on one of the most important corollaries of economism and methodological individualism. That is, he is saying, in his phrase "always with an essential difference," that economies—in this case forms of property or forms of the organization of productive resources—vary in kind (qualitatively), not just in degree (quantitatively). Land for example is very different if it is a commodity for sale than if it is a resource to be used only to yield a staple crop for a group of subsistence producers. In the case of such subsistence producers neither the land nor the crops grown on it are commodities. The land is a productive resource and the crops are simply subsistence goods. All producers are also consumers of needed amounts of products. These are some of the essential differences to which Marx refers.

Marx: Relationships between Production, Distribution, and Consumption Processes

For Marx it appears that production is primary and that the organization of distribution and consumption processes follows from the organization of production. But if one examines his terminology carefully, it is clear that Marx is using terms such as distribution in a broad sense to mean allocation. Distribution processes are also involved in production because distribution must occur in order to allocate productive resources such as land and labor, which must be distributed among people in order for them to work and engage in production processes.

> In the shallowest conception, distribution appears as the distribution of products, and hence as further removed from and quasi-independent of production. But before distribution can be the distribution of products, it is: (1) the distribution of the instruments of production, and (2) which is a further specification of the same relation, the distribution of the members of the society among the different kinds of production. (Subsumption of the individuals under specific relations of production.)
> (MARX 1973:96)

We must understand these statements on both the general and particular levels—the particular involving specific kinds of institutional arrangements, or what Marx called particular relations of production. In general terms, Marx is talking about such basic elements of production as the linking of people and resources: people need tools in order to work, they must have access to land, etc. But Marx is aware that, under capitalism, those who have greatest access to the means of production, namely the capitalists who own factories, tools, machinery, etc., also have the greatest access to the products of labor. Thus he writes of the relationships between the distribution of products and the "distribution" of "instruments of production," or "the distribution of the members of society among the different kinds of production." One can read this as a simple description of the division of labor, a "who does what" kind of statement; or one can read this as a description of a class-stratification system. Under capitalism, people who work are not just laborers, pure and simple, but labor that can be bought and sold for a price in a system of market capitalism—in short, people are commodities or commodified labor.

Marx is asking the following questions about the organization of production and of productive resources. How are cultural systems organized for the purposes of allocating productive resources such as labor, land, and water to groups and individuals so that production can begin? How do these allocations affect the distribution of products? All production processes require assembling and allocating resources. The question is, how might this be done in cultural systems at different times and places and under different ecological constraints?

Polanyi asked the same questions. He gave production a prominent place in his analysis of the economy by asserting that the dominant form of economic integration (reciprocity, redistribution, market [capitalistic] exchange, and householding) is the one that organizes productive resources. Here he provides us with a brief description of some of the kinds of non-market institutional arrangements that organize land and labor:

> Dominance of a form of integration is here identified
> with the degree to which it comprises land and labor
> in society. So-called savage society is characterized by
> the integration of land and labor into the economy by
> way of the ties of kinship. In feudal society the ties of
> fealty determine the fate of the land and labor that
> goes with it. In the floodwater empires land was
> largely distributed and sometimes redistributed by
> temple or palace, and so was labor, at least in its de-

*pendent form. The rise of the market to a ruling force
in the economy can be traced by noting the extent to
which land and food were mobilized through exchange, and labor was turned into a commodity free
to be purchased in the market.*
(1957:255)

In *The Great Transformation*, Polanyi clearly stated his concern for discov-
ering "order in production and distribution processes in pre-industrial
societies" (1944:47). This was the dual focus of his institutional critique
of economism.

The institutional paradigm, then, emphasizes social and historical
context and downplays the importance of individuals in favor of the
larger (superorganic) forces and structures that shape what Durkheim
would call social facts. Examples of such structures include kinship
groups, forms of political organization, and institutions such as the *kula*
as described by Malinowski (1921, 1922).

The institutional paradigm (see fig. 1), at its highest and most abstract
level of generality, emphasizes Marx's concepts: "relations of production" and "forces of production." The concept "relations of production"
refers to the relationships among individuals in institutional settings, the
essence being that in different institutional settings, relations of production will be different:

*In production, men not only act on nature but also on
one another. They produce only by cooperating in a
certain way and mutually exchanging their activities.
In order to produce, they enter into definite connections and relations with one another and only within
these social connections and relations does their action
on nature, does production, take place.*
(MARX AND ENGELS, CITED IN GIDDENS,
1971:35)

We can begin to see that the institutional nature of the concept of
relations of production is quite clear. Social connections and relations
refer to the kinds of ties that operate to organize the unit. These ties may
be based on kinship, political relations, connections to a particular place,
etc. The concept of relations of production, however, in itself does not
impose any particular organization or set of institutional arrangements
on a given economy or, more particularly, on the organization of any

given resource. In this respect it is a truly comparative, cross-culturally applicable concept. The important point here, though, is that social relations of production do shape the organization of all resources, albeit in different ways. The concept "forces of production" refers to technical arrangements. We will return to this below.

PART II. POLANYI'S GENERIC MODEL OF THE ECONOMY: AN OUTGROWTH OF THE INSTITUTIONAL PARADIGM

Beginning with the *Great Transformation* (1944) and continuing with the coedited *Trade and Market in the Early Empires* (1957), and the posthumously published *The Livelihood of Man* (1977), Karl Polanyi's work had a revolutionary impact on the subfield of economic anthropology; he built on and, to some degree, paralleled the work of Marx for the social sciences.

Unfortunately, much of Polanyi's very sophisticated, abstract, and truly cross-cultural conceptual tool kit was not recognized; it has been misunderstood and often ignored. As a result, Polanyi's concepts have become atrophied for lack of use and they have not been elaborated or critiqued properly.

Some Preliminaries: Polanyi's Codes

Polanyi is very difficult to read; his essays in *Trade and Market*, the book that most anthropologists read, are written in a sort of code, so as to avoid association with Marx during the 1950s. So too do many of the other essays in *Trade and Market* walk on political eggshells. Given the cross-cultural and comparative nature of his concepts, and their links to Marx and the institutional paradigm, there is a great need to decipher the codes. Here Polanyi's unpublished manuscripts are very helpful. Many of these were written in the 1930s and 1940s in Europe.

One very subtle aspect of the code was Polanyi's humanistic approach that focused on pre-capitalist economies and the development of concepts for understanding non-market economies. Often, Polanyi's humanism was equated with socialism, an important aspect of his thought. What most people did not understand was that his humanism was an essential aspect of his critique of capitalism as a system and that it was a preliminary attempt to create a generic model of the economy. It was indeed subtle and indirect. His humanism was interpreted as romanticism and his concepts dismissed as applicable only to primitive economies. His critique of capitalism and his attempts to develop a generic set of concepts for understanding economic processes were muddled by a combination of McCarthyism and a brand of development economics that was interested in transforming economies in precisely the ways most abhorrent to Polanyi.

Polanyi's Use of Models: Formal Institutional Models of the Generic Economy

Polanyi's primary aim was to formulate and use models in order to analyze economic processes. His main contribution to the analysis of economic organization took the form of a still unrecognized and even less understood formal (in the sense of ideal) model of the generic economy, in part derived from Marx (see fig. 2). This model specifies the general elements found in all economies. Polanyi's generic model consists of a series of hierarchically related models that are driven by his insistence that all economies consist of "instituted" (socially organized) processes geared towards material-means provisioning. It is true that his model has been very difficult to identify, much less understand. Polanyi stated it in the sketchiest of terms and used an abundance of encoded language. Nevertheless, Polanyi insisted that models were essential for the understanding of economies across cultures:

> *Descriptions shall provide details of social situations and processes, spelling out who does what, to whom, under what circumstances, how frequently, and to what effect. Quantitative determination of phenomena is sought wherever possible. Locational patterns, processes, mechanisms, operations and their functioning may be illustrated to advantage through the use of models.*
> KARL POLANYI. NOTES ON ECONOMIES.
> MEMO 25. MARCH 1956. COLUMBIA
> UNIVERSITY INTERDISCIPLINARY PROJECT.
> ECONOMIC ASPECTS OF INSTITUTIONAL
> GROWTH, P. 14.

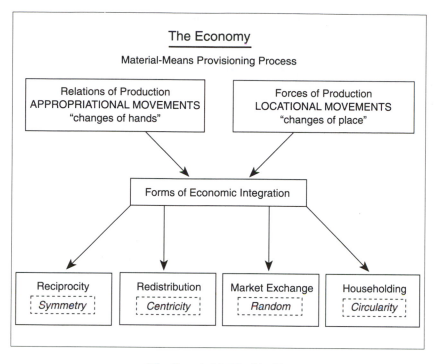

FIGURE 2.   *The Generic Model of the Economy*

Polanyi's formalism provides the key to his scientific analysis of economies across cultures. By formal I mean the specification, development, and use of ideal models (at several different levels of abstraction) for understanding pattern and variation in economic processes across cultures and over time. Polanyi's was a formal institutional model of the generic economy.

The generic model has formal features of the following sort. It begins with a set of concepts and terms that can be used with equal appropriateness in all economies at all times and places. In this respect, in Polanyi's generic model, the most general concepts, which are at the highest levels of abstraction, resemble those of Marx—specifically his concepts, forces, and relations of production. But whereas Marx went on to develop concepts for the analysis of capitalism, in particular ideas such as alienation and surplus value, Polanyi's concepts kept the entire range of economies in the human cultural experience in mind; they remained general, albeit with certain limitations and restrictions. These restrictions can be understood as domains of applicability.

The structure of Polanyi's generic model is hierarchical. It can be used appropriately for a range of economies: capitalist, pre-capitalist, and non-capitalist; pre-industrial, industrial, and post-industrial; even mixed economies manifesting combinations of capitalist and non-capitalist institutional arrangements. This model sets out a framework for understanding pattern and variability in economic processes across cultures and over time. Polanyi's formal model began with general concepts for the purpose of developing a generic model for analyzing economies across cultures. Marx's institutional paradigm started with general concepts and developed particular concepts for understanding capitalism. It will be seen below that the power of Polanyi's model for cross-cultural analysis derives, in part, from its formal features.

Because Polanyi's formalism has not been recognized, the full scientific potential of his models has not been realized; interpretations and applications of his concepts have been narrower than Polanyi intended. Understanding the models and their potential requires a contemporary anthropological vantage point oriented toward comparative studies of material processes. Knowledge of both theory and ethnography is essential for distilling the features of the models and their usefulness in different cultural and historical contexts.

To emphasize the formal elements of Polanyi's writing, however, might be interpreted by some as a form of blasphemy. How could anyone suggest that a man who took such a strong antiformalist stance might, in fact, have used a kind of formalism himself? It is the specific kind of formalism that is of importance here.

Polanyi's Sources: Marx and Anthropology

Polanyi's formalism and hence his science of the economy derive from two sources: Marx and anthropology. In an unpublished manuscript of Polanyi's dated 1938, the following passage points not only to Polanyi's Marxism, but to his early interest in anthropology as a scientific enterprise. Polanyi realized the cross-cultural potentials of Marx's several concepts:

> *Marxism is not a system of knowledge, but an interpretation of social and historical facts. It is prophetic teaching—the most important since Jesus—a revelation of truth become active in history. It is also a scientific method . . .*

> *The starting point for Marx is anthropology in its fullest sense, i.e., a science of the nature of man. This science is the basis of Marx's method. It deals not with man as an individual, but with mankind, the genus man. Man's nature is the result of the history of human society. Since history is the progressive realization of freedom, it should be added that it is man as a member of the community, not man as an individual, who becomes free. . . .*
>
> *Man is not merely a thinking being, but a part of the material world, who cannot be abstracted from it. Man, though he may not be able to live by bread alone, cannot exist without bread. The economic system is the basis of society . . .*
>
> *The form of society depends on the nature of the means of production and on the conditions under which production is carried on—the property system being the legal aspect of the latter. A society, according to Marx, consists only if the relationships are human.*[6]

Here in plain and simple prose is a statement containing all of the major elements of Polanyi's thought: his science, his humanism, his concern with freedom, his focus on society and its institutions, his critique of capitalism. Since my main purpose here is to discuss the nature of Polanyi's formal model of the economy, I will not dwell on the origins of the model (see Halperin 1988).

The Substantive Economy: A Formal Construct

Polanyi saw the substantive economy in formal scientific terms. His concept of the substantive economy involves models of economic processes; these models are arranged hierarchically and operate at different levels of abstraction. Locational and appropriational movements provide the framework for his formal, cross-cultural model of the economy. They are patterned after Marx's forces (locational) and relations (appropriational) of production. Reciprocity, redistribution, market exchange, and householding are subsidiary models. Polanyi's formalism came relatively late in his career and is most prominent in *Trade and Market in the Early Empires* (1957). The concept of the substantive economy—so essential to Polanyi's formal treatment of the generic economy—was not present as such in *The Great Transformation*; neither were his concepts of locational and appropriational movements. These did not appear in print until 1957 when *Trade and Market* was published. Polanyi's formal models represent refinements of concepts presented earlier in descriptive terms; reciprocity and redistribution are two examples.

The fact that he used the same concepts first in descriptive terms (1944) and then as models (1957, 1977) has not been recognized, and has led to misinterpretation. Also, the fact that in *The Great Transformation* Polanyi organized and presented the historical and ethnographic data that were to provide the basic assumptions for his formal models has, likewise, been overlooked.

At this point, it should be apparent that I am using a very different definition of formalism—and indeed of anthropology—than the one commonly used by the so-called Polanyi group. Formal models are heuristic devices designed to get at certain problems. Model-building involves establishing a series of expectations under known or assumed conditions and then comparing these expectations with empirical data. In other words, formal models compare an artificial or ideal order with a real order. Polanyi's formal models were by no means devoid of content, however. On the contrary, he was careful to demonstrate his sensitivities to qualitative and, to some degree, quantitative differences in economic systems of many types. The models are tailored to different types of cultural systems with different technologies, ways of dividing labor and allocating land, etc. The models are also designed to deal with different kinds of analytic problems. In Polanyi's case, the overall problem is that of understanding the place (read origin, structure, and function) of economies (processes of material provisioning) in cultural systems.

Ecological and Institutional Aspects of All Economies

Polanyi's concepts of locational (ecological and technological) and appropriational (institutional) movements provide the framework for his formal, cross-cultural model of the economy. That is, the combinations of locational and appropriational movements, which he defined as "changes of place" vs. "changes of hands," constitute all of the logical possibilities for understanding the relationships among the material elements in cultural systems. Polanyi said: "Between them, these two kinds of movements may be said to exhaust the possibilities comprised in the economic process as a natural and social phenomenon" (1957:248). The concepts of locational and appropriational movements are elaborated in the next chapter. His forms of economic integration are lower-level models of appropriational movements, although they contain locational elements as well. We can begin then to see the outlines of a hierarchically structured model of material-means provisioning processes.

Polanyi's model of the generic economy derives from his definition of the substantive economy. Since all societies have economies, the substantive economy covers the cross-cultural record (it is not restricted to non-market economies). The question then becomes one of identifying the components of economic processes. For Polanyi the economy can be understood on two levels, which correspond to his concepts of locational and appropriational movements:

> The substantive economy must be understood as being constituted on two levels: one is the interaction between man and his surroundings (locational movements of people and/or goods in space for example); the other is the institutionalization of that process (appropriational movements as in principles of labor recruitment). In actuality, the two are inseparable; we will, however, treat of them separately.
> (1977:31 PARENTHESES MINE)

It should be realized that there are many versions of the concepts of locational and appropriational movements. The important point for now is that they together provide the basis of Polanyi's model of the generic economy: "Together the two kinds of movement complete the economy as a process" (1977:32). Economies are understood abstractly and formally as instituted processes involving certain kinds of interaction. Instituted means organized in the sense of something that is not idiosyncratic or random. In Anthony Giddens' terms, "instituted" refers to the structure. The principles of organization and the relevant units vary enormously, and this is precisely the point, to get at the variation. "Process" for Polanyi involves "analysis in terms of motion. The movements refer either to changes in location, or in appropriation, or both" (1957:248). That this is a dynamic, not a static or "equilibrium," model of the economy is apparent from the outset.

Summary of the Generic Model of the Economy

Polanyi's formal model of the economy is hierarchically organized, with the dual ecological and institutional concepts at the top of the hierarchy. The concepts of locational and appropriational movements cover both the ecological (locational) and the institutional (appropriational) dimensions of the economy. These points are further elaborated in chapter 3. If we go back to figure 2 for a moment, we can see that the generic model of the economy begins with a basic definition of the economy as the material-means provisioning process for all cultural systems. This process, in turn, can be conceptualized in terms of two analytically distinct kinds of processes, which Polanyi called "movements" in order to indicate their dynamic nature and the fact that they are constantly changing and transforming themselves. Here Polanyi comes very close to Marx's concept of the dialectic, but notice the terminology he uses—the word "movements" is not only a very subtle replacement for the dialectic, it is colorless as well. From here Polanyi goes to lower levels of abstraction in his forms of economic integration. These forms of integration are patterns of locational and appropriational movements. The forms represent different possible structures that are, again, formal models taking on different content in different cultural and historical contexts. Thus, reciprocity takes many forms, different in small-scale pre-capitalist societies from in post-industrial working-class communities (see chapter 2). The same principle applies to redistribution, market exchange, and householding, for they take on different forms in different contexts.

If we look at figure 3, we can see that the basic economic processes of production, distribution, exchange, and storage can be understood generically as well. All of these processes are comprehensible in terms of locational and appropriational movements, which in turn can be further specified in terms of the forms of economic integration in different contexts. These forms can be understood, in part, as logical possibilities; one, all, or some combination of two or more forms of economic integration can organize processes of production, distribution, exchange, and storage, even trade.

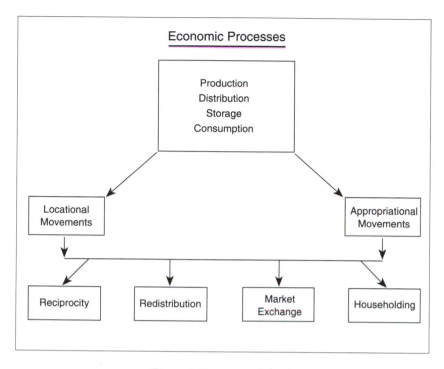

FIGURE 3.   *Economic Processes and the Generic Model of the Economy*

The generic model of the economy is considered formal because it allows the analyst to establish a series of expectations under assumed conditions. These assumptions are arbitrary and must be devised by the analyst. All economies consist of locational and appropriational movements, whose specific forms vary from one kind of economy to another. There are patterns in these movements which Polanyi formalized as forms of economic integration (reciprocity, redistribution, market exchange, and householding). "Forms of economic integration" is an analytical, not a descriptive, concept that requires locational and appropriational movements. Used analytically, these concepts are not mere classifiers; they are parts of a formal model of the economy. To delineate this as succinctly as possible:

> *1. Reciprocity, redistribution, market exchange,*
> *and householding are, first and foremost, comprised of*
> *movements. These movements are not just of goods in*
> *the process of distribution, but of the whole range of*

things that can move in the material-means provision-
ing process, from production to consumption.

2. The character of the movements is determined
by the structure(s) within which they occur. For ex-
ample, many different kinds of structures can bring
about reciprocity as a form of economic integration as
long as the "movements are between correlative points
of symmetrical groupings" (1957:250). Movements
between correlative points of symmetrical groupings
are the most succinct formal statement of reciprocity as
a form of integration.

Many different structures can employ redistribution as a form of economic integration. Chiefly feasting in tribes and chiefdoms and Aztec
tribute are two different examples. All redistributive systems must involve "centripetal movements of many upon one central figure followed
by an initiative of that central figure upon the same many" (1957:viii).
Polanyi and Arensberg present redistribution by actually using the term
formal: "Formally, BA/CA/DA/EA/FA are followed by an event A/
BCDEF in unison or repartition" (1957:viii). Market exchange was
also presented formally by Polanyi and Arensberg: "Now, formally A/
BCDEF took place no oftener than B/ACDEF or F/ABCDE . . ." They
described this as "fluid randomizing" (1957:ix). There are different kinds
of reciprocal, redistributive, and market systems. Householding was not
described by Polanyi in formal terms, but it does have formal features of
circularity, as we will see in chapter 5. The four forms of economic integration must be understood as formal models that (1) are designed to
get at the variability and (2) operate within the overall generic model as
an elaboration and specification of the concepts of locational and appropriational movements. Polanyi said: "We might think of the forms of
integration as diagrams representing the patterns made by the movements of goods and persons in the economy, whether these movements
consist of changes in their location, in their appropriation, or both"
(1977:36). If we think of the forms of integration as diagrams or models
their formal features become even clearer.

For Polanyi, a diagrammatic presentation would appear as follows:

Arrows connecting points that are symmetrically
arranged in regard to one or more axes might stand for

> *reciprocity; redistribution would require a star-shaped*
> *diagram, some arrows pointing towards the center,*
> *others away from it; and exchange could be pictured*
> *as arrows connecting random points, each directed*
> *both ways.*
> (1977:36)

Notice that he has dropped householding here, perhaps for political reasons that associate householding with socialism. The important point is that the kinds of symmetrical organizations, central points, and randomly directed arrows (market systems) are variable in this formal framework (Dilley 1992). Without understanding locational and appropriational movements and their importance in Polanyi's formal model of economies past and present, all of Polanyi's concepts, including the forms of economic integration, are difficult to understand. At best they can be so abstract and vague that they are used generally with too little attention to pattern and variability.

If we agree that all sciences use models, and that economic anthropology is, at least potentially, a cross-cultural science, then the issue is not whether or not to use models, but what kinds of models to use. Interpreting Polanyi's concepts as models or as components of models is new in economics and in economic anthropology.

Polanyi's models are what I have elsewhere called formal processual models, not formal atomistic models (Halperin 1988). They are not based upon individuals as the units of analysis, but rather upon institutions—organizational principles, social and political structures. The real advantage of formal processual models is to be found in their potential for comparative analysis and in their avoidance of methodological individualism.

In sum, the formalism in Polanyi's thought is not to be confused with the formalism of the formalist-substantivist debate. His own brand of formalism, with its emphasis on logical possibilities that could be exhausted by the concepts of locational and appropriational movements, was, ironically enough, closer to Frank Knight's. Knight, a very traditional economist, recognized that conventional economic theory was not to be applied literally because it was but a model of logical possibilities that never occurred in the real world. Methodologically, Polanyi's thinking was much closer to Knight's than to the ideas of those who tried to romanticize and humanize his ideas. Knight and Polanyi were proposing two very different kinds of formal models, with different assumptions, different units of analysis, and different domains of potential applicability. While Knight's was a formal model of capitalist market economies, Polanyi's formal model pertained to economies across cultures. The limits, as well as the potentials, of Polanyi's formal models remain to be explored in the context of the institutional paradigm.

Three　　ECONOMY AND
ECOLOGY: BASIC
CONCEPTS, THEIR
HISTORY, AND
APPLICATIONS

Th
his chapter uses Polanyi's generic model
of the economy, specifically his concepts of locational ("changing place")
and appropriational movements ("changing hands"), to examine the
concepts of ecology (locational movements) and economy (appropriational movements). The confusion between, and often the equating of,
economy and ecology is still common in anthropological studies of
material-means provisioning processes in cultural systems. Hatch (1973)
used all three words, economic, subsistence, and ecological, in the title
of his review article, thereby erring on the side of redundancy and avoiding entirely the issue of choosing one or another of them. Today, even
though the mud-slinging debates of the 1960s and early 1970s are behind
us, and reductionism and the crudeness of cultural materialism's calorie
counting have been recognized, the conceptual tools for organizing our
knowledge of economic processes are still not well developed.

While many (thick and thin) descriptions relevant to material processes can be found in virtually every ethnographic account, no matter
how general or tightly focused, the presence and quality of any particular description usually are a matter of happenstance: a reflection of what
the anthropologist noticed or considered to be "economic"—subsistence
patterns, items of material culture, trade patterns, food distribution, and
the like. At best, such a situation makes comparative work extremely
difficult. We may know a lot about sweet-potato gardening in one culture
and command large amounts of information about salt trade patterns in
another, but a pair of equally "thick" descriptions of two such entirely
different aspects of the economy will not provide the data necessary for
making comparisons, even if the two cultural systems are very similar

and even if the same aspects, locational or appropriational, of these processes are used consistently. In addition, what constitutes subsistence gardening or trade may vary from one ethnography to the next. In short, we find variation in empirical practices, in the kinds of observations made, and in what is actually described.

Many classic ethnographies focused on material processes, both economic and ecological. Within the British school, for example, we can think immediately of Malinowski's treatment of the *kula* trade in *Argonauts of the Western Pacific* (1922), Firth's exhaustive ethnographic treatment of the economy in *Primitive Polynesian Economy* (1929), and Evans-Pritchard's *The Nuer* (1944), with its focus on ecology and shifting settlement patterns. Both *Argonauts* and *Primitive Polynesian Economy* are classics in economic anthropology; in contrast, *The Nuer* contains considerable amounts of economic and ecological data but has been ignored, for the most part, by ecologists and economic anthropologists alike. As we will see in chapter 8, Evans-Pritchard also raised the issue of time and the economy in some useful as well as in some highly problematic ways. In the United States, anthropologists such as Herskovits (1952), Belshaw (1965), Dalton (1961), Bohannan (1955), Pospisil (1963), and others paid almost no attention to ecological matters, whereas Netting's (1968) work on the Kofyar, Gross's (1975) work on the Amazon Basin, and Harris's (1979) *Cultural Materialism* focus on ecological variables while slighting critical aspects of economic organization. More generally speaking, ecological anthropology certainly treats matters of material livelihood, but most of its practitioners pay little if any attention to the concepts of economic anthropology.

The economy/ecology separation is curious in light of the fact that economic and ecological anthropology treat many of the same problems: subsistence patterns, production and distribution processes, storage, and trade and exchange, to name a few. The words "economy" and "ecology" derive from the Greek root "oikos." "Economics" originates in the Greek *oikonomikos*, which combines *oikos* (household) with the root *nem*, meaning to regulate, administer, and organize (Finley 1973; Polanyi 1957*a*). "Ecology" also comes from the Greek *oikos*, in its meaning of habitation. Netting quotes the biologist Ernst Haeckel, who coined the word ecology in 1870 and understood it to mean:

> *the study of the economy, of the household, of animal organisms. This includes the relationships of animals*

*with both the inorganic and organic environments,
above all the beneficial and inimical relations that
Darwin referred to as the conditions of the struggle for
existence.*
(1977:1)

We should not be surprised that there has been some overlap and confusion in the use of the concepts of economy and ecology (cf. Bates
1961). Clear analytic distinctions between ecology ("changes of place")
and economy ("changes of hands") are difficult to draw. Nevertheless, if
the subfields of economic and ecological anthropology are to remain the
primary arenas for the analysis of livelihood processes in the cross-
cultural record, then we must understand exactly what kinds of economic processes they examine and we must use concepts that are
appropriate.

This chapter deals with the problematical relationships between economic and ecological anthropology from the point of view of understanding processes of material livelihood. These relationships have been
assumed rather than analyzed. Both economy and ecology have been
used—sometimes separately and at cross-purposes, and sometimes interchangeably—to denote material processes (Netting 1977). In some instances, ecology subsumes economy; in others, the reverse is true. Re-
arrangements of people and resources in the landscape (changes in spatial
arrangements; here, *locational movements*) are mistaken for changes in
rights of access to resources or for alteration in the organization of labor
(changes in institutional arrangements; here, *appropriational movements*)
(cf. Binford 1980). Relationships between these two kinds of spatial and
institutional changes certainly exist, but they are not identical. The
distinctions between "changes of place" (locational movements) and
"changes of hands" (appropriational movements) are the focus of this
essay.

The differences between economic and ecological anthropology can
best be understood in terms of a series of variations upon these two fundamental but largely unrecognized concepts, locational and appropriational movements. These concepts, originally put forth by Karl Polanyi
(1957a) but elaborated and extended here, are important for three reasons. First, they are the central concepts underlying the two subfields of
economic and ecological anthropology. Second, as noted earlier, taken
together, the two concepts provide the framework for a formal, cross-

cultural model of the economy. Third, the two concepts can be used to clarify some conceptual as well as some terminological confusions in the archaeological and ethnographic literature on processes of material livelihood. If we understand the basic conceptual distinctions between "changing place" (locational movements) and "changing hands" (appropriational movements), then we will be able to sort out the terminology and the data that signal the spatial (locational) and the organizational (appropriational and institutional) components of economic processes. In this chapter, I will demonstrate the utility of thinking about economic and ecological anthropology in terms of these underlying and hitherto unspecified concepts.

More specifically, this chapter suggests ways of relating economic and ecological anthropology by analyzing the transformations that have occurred over time in the relationships between the two underlying concepts of locational and appropriational movements. Taking 1930 as the starting date for economic anthropology—shortly after Malinowski published *Argonauts*—I use the two concepts to trace the relationships between economic and ecological anthropology until about 1985. I wish to emphasize at the outset that the concepts themselves did not change. Indeed, they were not explicitly stated or analyzed. What changed were the relationships between the two implicit concepts (locational and appropriational movements) and the schools (formalist, substantivist, and Marxist) and paradigms (formal, ecological, and institutional) in economic anthropology (see Halperin 1988). The transformations themselves have been complex. They often have involved several stages and more than one paradigm. Elsewhere, I have elaborated the relationships between the schools and the paradigms in economic anthropology (Halperin 1988). The important point to understand here is that the transformations signal some new approaches to the analysis of pattern and variation in economic processes. Most significantly, perhaps, the transformations are positive, integrate economic and ecological anthropology, and provide an alternative to methodological individualism.

Locational and Appropriational Movements: "Changes of Place" and "Changes of Hands"

As concepts, locational and appropriational movements originated with Karl Polanyi (1957a), who gave them powerful but not easily understandable or applicable definitions. The concepts must be clarified by using an anthropological vantage point to modify and elaborate Polanyi's definitions.

"Changes of place" or locational movements consist of one or more of the following: (1) *transfers from one physical space to another*, involving (a) physical transfers of goods or of people from one place to another, as in movements of work crews, or (b) physical transfers of productive resources, such as tools; (2) *physical changes* in the material stuff of livelihood, for example, changes in the physical condition of a foodstuff (raw to cooked, whole to divided, seeds to plants); (3) *energy transfers*, such as the relocation of resources and storage facilities from one place to another or the relocation of a village vis-à-vis ecological zones.

"Changes of hands" or appropriational movements, in contrast, consist of (1) *organizational changes*, or (2) *transfers of rights*. Organizational changes involve changes in the principles allocating resources or goods, e.g., a shift from communal land tenure to private property. Butchering game is a locational movement, but sharing the meat is an appropriational movement. Even if butchering and sharing occur at nearly the same time, the two kinds of movements, locational and appropriational, can and must be separated analytically. Transfers of rights change people's access to and control over goods and resources. The ability to control goods and resources used in the production of surpluses to maintain large populations and the ability to acquire goods for simple and direct consumption by producers are both examples of appropriational movements.

Polanyi's metaphor, "changes of hands," implies changes in control over resources (for production) and over production (for distribution). One of the best examples of appropriational movements is transfers of rights to land, clearly a stationary resource. These land transfers can occur under a variety of institutional arrangements—kinship-driven inheritance such as was found all over tribal Africa, politically driven redistribution such as we find in pre-industrial states, or market-driven sale of land, to name a few examples. Labor organization, on the other hand, usually involves both locational and appropriational movements, i.e., moving people to the site of production as well as assigning them tasks. To take another example, appropriational movements include people making decisions about whether to engage in one kind of productive task or another, say, hunting vs. gathering or working in a factory vs. working on a farm or in a kitchen garden. Recruiting people to work—whether by a big-man or a chief in a pre-capitalist society, or by a larger, more impersonal labor market under capitalism—involves both locational and appropriational movements.

As I have noted earlier, Polanyi's discussion of locational and appropriational movements is contained in his famous chapter in *Trade and Market in the Early Empires*, "The Economy as Instituted Process," where it follows his presentation of the substantive concepts of the empirical economy defined "as an instituted process of interaction between man and his environment, which results in a continuous supply of want-satisfying material means" (1957a:248). Process, for Polanyi, involves "analysis in terms of motion. The movements refer either to changes in location, or in appropriation, or both" (1957a:248). In Polanyi's view, the economy is a set of dynamic processes undergoing constant transformations. It is not a static entity, as in a structural-functionalist view of a system in a steady state. I should emphasize again that while Polanyi used ethnographic data on the economy collected by people in the British structural-functionalist school (Malinowski and Firth, especially), he did so simply because these were the primary ethnographic data available. As the title of his famous book, *The Great Transformation*, suggested, he placed the data in a dynamic framework, the characteristics of which are often missed by people who want to associate Polanyi with the rich but rather stagnant data sources. In point of fact, Polanyi took ethnographic facts, somewhat cavalierly at times, from whatever resources he had at hand. He used data from American cultural anthropologists as well—Boas, Benedict, Lowie, Herskovits, and Mead, to name a few.

Polanyi's definition of the economy is powerful because these two kinds of movements, locational and appropriational, together make up the components of his general, formal model of the economy that can be used for comparative, cross-cultural analysis. The combinations of locational and appropriational movements constitute all of the logical possibilities for understanding the relationships among the material elements in cultural systems. As Polanyi (1957a:248) put it: "Between them, these two kinds of movements may be said to exhaust the possibilities comprised in the economic process as a natural and social phenomenon." The words "natural" and "social" reveal Polanyi's awareness of the ecological and institutional components of economic processes. His use of the word "movement" is somewhat unusual, but Polanyi commonly used words in unusual and often confusing ways. Taken in the context of his definition of the substantive economy as a series of ongoing and changing processes, however, the word makes sense.

Polanyi put forth, then, a formal model of the economy that is widely applicable. Such formalism in Polanyi's thought is not to be confused with the formalism that entered into the so-called formalist-substantivist debate. In that debate, the formalists attempted to apply to all economic systems, pre-capitalist and capitalist, the concepts and categories of one group of formal models, those of conventional microeconomic theory. Polanyi was certainly opposed to that line of formalist thinking. His own brand of formalism, with its emphasis on logical possibilities that could be exhausted by the concepts of locational and appropriational movements, was very different.

Polanyi's model of the economy may be considered formal because it allows the analyst to establish a series of expectations (usually, ideal expectations) under presumed conditions (see Halperin 1985, 1988). According to the model, all economies consist of locational and appropriational movements; the specific forms taken by these movements vary from one economy (culture) to the next. Such a model provides guidelines for identifying the relevant variables for analyzing particular kinds of movements in specific kinds of cultural contexts.

To say that the concepts of locational and appropriational movements provide the basis for a general formal model of economies that can be used cross-culturally does not mean that only one (in the sense of universal) model will suffice. Rather, out of the primary, general model, we can generate subsidiary models for analyzing particular kinds of problems in different kinds of cultural systems. Locational and appropriational movements provide the basic conceptual framework for both the general and the subsidiary models. For example, in band-level societies, locational and appropriational movements will have different components with different assumptions attached to them than will be the case in state-level societies. In other words, small-scale systems will have qualitatively different kinds of locational and appropriational movements from those of large systems.

The concepts of locational and appropriational movements do not correspond to the material and the ideological realms of culture, respectively. Used properly, however, the models can aid in making the link between the two. This will become clearer in the chapter on the concept of householding, in which locational and appropriational movements play an important part. While the discourses vary, the movements, in different cultural contexts, remain very similar and retain their householding pattern (see chapter 5). This is true whether we are talking about rural Kentucky, rural France (Weinberg 1975), or rural Guatemala (Annis 1987).

Patterns of Thinking in Economic and Ecological Anthropology: Problematics and Potentials

Polanyi's elaboration of the concepts of locational and appropriational movements established patterns of thinking in both economic and ecological anthropology. First, for Polanyi, production falls under the category of locational movements:

> *Locational movements include production, alongside of transportation, to which the spatial shifting of objects is equally essential. . . . This type of movement of the elements represents an essential of the economy in the substantive sense of the term, namely, production.*
> (1957A:248)

Unfortunately, he placed distribution under the rubric of appropriational movements:

> *The appropriative movement governs both what is usually referred to as the circulation of goods and their administration. In the first case, the appropriative movement results from transactions, in the second case, from dispositions.*
> (1957A:248)

This dichotomy (appropriational movements associated with distribution and locational movements with production) is unfortunate. By associating production with locational movements, and distribution with appropriational movements, the appropriational (read: institutional or relational) aspects of production and locational (read: spatial, ecological, or technological) aspects of distribution are eliminated from the framework. Clearly, both systems of distribution and systems of exchange involve locational and appropriational movements, but Polanyi eliminated these possibilities from his scheme.

Systems of production also involve appropriational as well as locational movements of productive resources such as land and labor. Since Polanyi's scheme dealt with production and distribution in completely different terms, though, the study of economies as systems of both production and distribution was impeded. Why did Polanyi create such a seemingly unreasonable dichotomy? If we put the preceding aspects of Polanyi's thought together with the fact that he focused almost exclusively upon distribution processes (trade, markets, and exchange) in his written work, barely mentioning production processes, we can consider his dichotomies—locational/appropriational, production/distribution—as part of his masked Marxism (Halperin 1984). That is, by defining production sheerly in locational terms, he eliminated from consideration the appropriative (i.e., the exploitative) aspects of production under capitalist conditions.

This is not at all how Marx would have had it, for production and distribution are clearly intertwined and interrelated processes, as are the forces (locational movements) and relations (appropriational movements) of production. As I will show below, we need to unmask the Marxism and put locational and appropriational movements back together for an understanding of the workings of economic processes across cultures.

The Hidden Economics in Cultural Ecology: Ecology and Economics, the Early Period (1930–1980)

The separation of locational and appropriational movements and their respective association with production and distribution processes became the template for divorcing ecological from economic anthropology. Without anthropologists realizing it, locational and appropriational movements became solidified as two poles of an underlying dichotomy. Ecological anthropology focused on locational movements and production processes; economic anthropology examined appropriational movements and distribution processes (trade and exchange).

Before proceeding, I should mention that both early and late ecological studies have also dealt with problems that are much broader than the economy, namely, relationships between cultural and environmental behavior. In this regard, James Anderson (1973) has written at length about "an ecology of man," referring to the work of Geertz (1963), Harris (1968), Helm (1962), Sahlins (1964), Steward (1955), Vayda (1969), and Vayda and Rappaport (1968). Ecological variables have been used to explain a wide range of cultural practices—from ceremonies and rituals (Piddock 1965; Rappaport 1968a, 1968b) to camel raiding (Sweet 1965) and India's sacred cattle (Harris 1966). These studies do not concern me here. Rather, I shall focus on those ecological studies that deal with the aspects of production, distribution, and consumption processes—the hidden economics in ecological anthropology. Flannery's (1969) work on the ecology of food production in Mesopotamia is a classic example of this hidden economics. In that article, Flannery deals almost exclusively with locational movements. His summary is indicative of the article as a whole:

> The food-producing revolution in southwestern Asia is here viewed not as the brilliant invention of one group or the product of a single environmental zone, but as the result of a long process of changing ecological relationships between groups of men (living at varying altitudes and in different environmental settings) and the locally available plants and animals which they had been exploiting on a shifting, seasonal basis.
> (1969:303)

Likewise, Netting's (1965, 1968) work on the Nigerian Kofyar is a fascinating example of a focus on the locational aspects of production as an ecologically driven process. For Netting, both the organization of labor and the organization of land reflect ecological necessities, or at least make ecological sense. In that framework, institutional arrangements (appropriational movements) are dependent variables.

With a few exceptions (e.g., Carneiro 1961, 1981b), cultural ecology, particularly its earliest versions, gave social and institutional factors (appropriational movements) a low profile. Most such studies totally excluded institutional factors from discussions of production or shrouded institutional factors in some other terminology, often in a narrow or reductionist framework. Steward's (1955) concept of the "culture core" is important to consider in this context. As Robert Murphy (1981:175) points out, "Steward's anthropology had an earthy and common-sense orientation that regarded the exigencies of work and livelihood as among the most important of these determinants. . . . He saw the key to human culture in food-getting activities." Although Steward's work certainly had this economic orientation, he never made clear the relationship between economic and noneconomic activities in cultural systems, nor did he indicate the specific kinds of economic processes he had in mind. On the one hand, economic processes were at the center of the culture core; on the other, religion was also included, albeit as a subordinate element. More importantly for our purposes, because the economy is the independent variable in Steward's framework, its characteristics are assumed rather than detailed. Lumped into the culture core were both noneconomic relationships to the physical environment and subsistence practices, which consisted only of food procurement. Emphasis on food procurement has, in fact, persisted in cultural-ecological studies (Lee 1965, 1969, 1979, 1984; Lee and DeVore 1968). As a result, the systematic analysis of the economy qua economy has not been carried out by cultural ecologists. The concept of the culture core was, in fact, a clever way of masking the forces and relations of production. Indeed, the concepts of the culture core (Steward 1955) and energy (White 1949, 1959) were both part of the hidden Marxism in American anthropology in the 1950s (Murphy 1981; Carneiro 1981a). In a similar manner, primitive social organization (Service 1962) and the evolution of political society (Fried 1967) were conceptualized in such a way that the economy was taken as a given and therefore not examined. Social organization and political evolution could then be used as concepts behind which economic issues could be concealed.

The hidden Marxism, at least as far as the cross-cultural analysis of the economy was concerned, was both subtle and complex. While the economy clearly was at the foundation of all of these ecological/evolutionary analyses, the economy remained in the background, never becoming the object of direct study. For example, in *The Evolution of Political Society* (1967), Fried assumed that egalitarian societies had economies based upon reciprocity and that ranked societies had economies based upon redistribution (see also Codere 1950, 1968). Certain kinds of appropriational movements were assumed, but not analyzed or presented systematically. Fried focused on sorting political systems in qualitative terms, and he used very general economic processes and demographic scales as the basis for his typology.

In sum, while there was definitely a hidden economics in cultural ecology, the subtleties were difficult to untangle. For the most part, studies were tied to general, noneconomic problems such as ethnicity (Barth 1956), adaptation (Alland 1967; Bennett 1969; Cohen 1968; Damas 1969a, 1969b; Leeds and Vayda 1965; Meggers 1954, 1957; Sanders 1962, 1965; Sanders and Price 1968), and the like. Those analyses that appeared to deal with economic processes—such as Steward's, White's, and Fried's—have been difficult to decipher because they constructed a series of code words for economic processes. Some of the earliest works, while distinctly descriptive, had a clearer linkage of economy and ecology than did the work of the 1960s (Evans-Pritchard 1944; Forde 1934).

The focus on energy on the part of the early cultural ecologists enabled them to establish a series of categories for organizing the great variety of cultures in the world. Theirs was definitely a scientific enterprise. Cultural ecology also shifted attention from the ideological level of culture to the material level (Netting 1977:1). This was a shift from the exotic to the mundane, and it provided the beginning for a scientific approach in cultural anthropology.

The Early Economic Anthropology

The economic anthropology of the pre-1980 period, whether formalist or substantivist, focused on appropriational movements. This is a revealing point, for there seemed to be no common ground established between the two camps while the formalist-substantivist debate was going on. Even though formalists and substantivists used different units of analysis—the former dealing with individuals, the latter with institutions—and applied different assumptions to these units, neither camp paid a great deal of attention to locational movements. Sol Tax (1953) wrote of "penny capitalists" in Guatemala; Leopold Pospisil (1963) described rational, individualistic big-men in New Guinea; and Harold Schneider (1964) analyzed East African cattle as real capital, money, and consumption goods. In fact, whether market or non-market institutions or combinations of institutions were at issue, economic anthropology as a subfield was concerned almost exclusively with the organizational (appropriational) mechanisms structuring economic processes. That they viewed economic organization in individualistic terms and therefore restricted themselves to one particular kind of institutional arrangement, namely the market system, only speaks to the narrowness of the formalist school of economic anthropology.

The pre-1980 period also saw attention given to forms of non-market rationality and non-market economic organization (Polanyi et al. 1957; Godelier 1966). Polanyi's concepts of reciprocity, redistribution, market exchange, and householding were put forth as modes of economic integration. The range of institutions involved in the organization of economic activities expanded analytically to include kinship groups (in the case of reciprocity), centralized polities (in the case of redistribution), and capitalist market (in the case of supply-demand market exchange). Sahlins (1965, 1972) elaborated the concept of reciprocity by his rather formal typology: negative, balanced, and generalized reciprocity. Bohannan and Dalton (1962) pointed out the important organizational differences between *marketplaces*, which are physical locations in which goods could be bought, sold, traded, bartered, etc., and *market systems*, which have no essential geographical or spatial referents. Thus, the basic issue was: What kinds of institutional arrangements organize economic activities? While there were clearly locational aspects to the concepts under discussion, especially concepts such as reciprocity and redistribution, no attention was given to differences in distances traveled, overall ecological context, or levels of energy expended over space or time. Had attention been focused on these matters, some of the variability in redistributive systems, for example, might have been discovered (Brumfiel and Earle 1987). Also, some of the relationships between production and distribution processes might have been analyzed.

During this period, however, distribution processes took precedence over processes of production. Economic anthropology slighted production in its discussions of economies and focused instead on such exotic and colorful phenomena as marketplaces and ancient trading systems. Titles such as *Trade and Market in the Early Empires* (Polanyi et al. 1957), *Markets in Africa* (Bohannan and Dalton 1962), and *Traditional Exchange and Modern Markets* (Belshaw 1965) reflect the emphasis on distribution processes (see also Sahlins 1965). Prestige systems and systems of ceremonial exchange also received a great deal of attention—again, in the context of mechanisms of distribution. The literature on the potlatch (Piddock 1969; Suttles 1960; Codere 1950) and the cargo systems of Mesoamerica (Cancian 1965; DeWalt 1975; Greenberg 1981; Smith 1977) immediately comes to mind. In sum, the early economic anthropology was explicitly nonecological, focusing almost entirely upon appropriational movements, primarily distribution processes. "Changes of hands" took precedence over "changes of place."

The New Ecological Anthropology and the New Marxist Economic Anthropology

After 1980, the new ecological anthropology and the new Marxist economic anthropology employed the same basic dichotomy between locational and appropriational movements, but with some very different emphases. The new ecological anthropology continued to deal with locational movements, albeit in a much more focused and formalized manner. By formalized, I mean (as above) that ecological anthropologists developed ideal models as heuristic devices (analytic tools) that could be used to measure actual situations against expected or ideal conditions (Plattner 1975a, 1975b).

Using animal ecology, evolutionary biology, and Darwinian theory, ecological anthropologists selected individuals as the units of analysis. Various assumptions were attached to the behavior of these individuals. Remarkably, these assumptions were not unlike those associated with conventional economic theory. Optimal foraging models are cases in point (Cashdan 1983; Lee 1979; Winterhalder and Smith 1981; Bettinger 1980; Perlman 1980; Martin 1983; Yesner 1981; Keene 1979). As I indicated in chapter 1, these models follow in the tradition of methodological individualism by assuming both scarce resources and random movements by individuals in resource patches. The analyses do not attend to the organization of labor, to knowledge about how resources are arranged in space, to the seasonality of resource availability, etc. The aim of optimal foraging is for individuals to maximize their gains (benefits) while minimizing risks or losses. Using the individual as the unit of analysis eliminates the problem of examining organizational features, especially if the individuals are assumed to be moving about randomly.

While grand-scale problems of the relations between humans and environments (Moran 1979; Orlove 1980), adaptive strategies, and the like are still of central concern, ecological anthropology is now beginning to deal with economic topics and problems, often in a comparative framework. Subsistence patterns receive a great deal of attention, as do related problems of trade and exchange, storage, etc. In most instances, small-scale systems receive the most attention. Food procurement, energy use, and production processes are emphasized.

I have chosen the work of Roy Ellen (1982) and Michael Jochim (1981) to represent the new trends in ecological anthropology. While their approaches are different in many respects, both focus upon small-scale systems, are systematically formal, and are critical of the older cultural ecology, but in a way that is consistent with the early focus upon locational movements.

ROY ELLEN: *ENVIRONMENT, SUBSISTENCE, AND SYSTEM*

If the early cultural ecologists paid attention to livelihood processes in general (Netting 1977:5), the new ecologists deal purely and simply with food procurement in their treatment of economic processes. In Ellen's framework, cultures can be grouped according to their dominant subsistence technique. He recognized some difficulties— for example, that labels such as hunter-gatherer or swidden cultivator can be misleading and can "conceal critical variation" (1982:170). But while Ellen laments the narrow focus upon subsistence (defined as food procurement), he restricts his analysis to the examination of energy produced through procurement, even though he recognizes that this procedure presents some problems for dealing with such related subsistence activities as the processing of food. He says:

> *Perhaps the most notorious weakness has been the failure to provide data on the energy and the time cost of food-processing (to a large extent the work of females) together with the neglect or under-estimation of other activities technically and socially necessary for subsistence but not "food-getting" in the strict sense.* (1982:144–145)

Ellen proceeds, nevertheless, with a detailed analysis of the ecology of subsistence activities which, as he points out, "have been regarded as simple, undifferentiated, and tediously repetitive wherever they are found" (1982:123). Ellen's aim is comparative; he establishes a set of variables and categories for analyzing and comparing different subsistence patterns. What is most characteristic of his framework is his constant effort to separate the ecological from the economic. This effort involves the separation of locational from appropriational movements, with exclusive focus upon the locational, and the separation of spatial considerations from ideological concerns. Ellen (1982:130), summarizing Ingold (1979:274–277), defines ecological production as reproduction:

> *Ecological production may be defined as the creation of organic materials resulting in species and population reproduction. It is not to be confused with economic production, which is the creation of value in order to reproduce social and economic formations.*

Notice that economics is here conveniently taken out of the material realm and couched in ideological terms—"the creation of value." By "creation of organic materials," Ellen is referring, of course, to the production of energy—a topic, he notes, that has been of interest to anthropologists since Leslie White first speculated on the relationship between energy levels and cultural types. Cultures can be compared in terms of the calories produced, consumed, and expended per person per day (Ellen 1982:131–139). Measures of ecological efficiency can be calculated in terms of energy production divided by total human energy expenditure. Thus, one aspect of locational movements, namely, energy transfers, is evident in Ellen's framework.

Ellen's emphasis on locational movements becomes even more evident in his discussion of yield, effort, and efficiency though time. His use of certain words is worth noting here, because the language is deceiving. It falsely conveys an attention to organizational considerations (appropriational movements), whereas, in fact, extraction from the environment (locational movements) is the only concern. For example, Ellen uses phrases such as "the use and allocation" of effort through time and "patterns for the appropriation of non-domesticated resources" (1982: 154). He cites the classic essay by Mauss and Beuchat (1979:55), who were able to show how the seasonal availability of different animal species is directly linked to Eskimo patterns of nomadic movement and settlement.

What Ellen really means by appropriation in this context is extracting or gleaning resources. He is not concerned with the organizational features of ecological production here, but merely with its physical properties as determined by season. One other example will solidify this point. Ellen cites Nietschmann's (1973) study of the Miskito, with its careful calculation of variation in the numbers of species hunted each month, "to illustrate seasonal variation in resource appropriation and meat yields" (Ellen 1982:155). Below, I quote Ellen's summary of the Miskito data at some length in order to provide the reader with a sense of the variables considered. What is particularly evident is the emphasis on spatial arrangements of resources and movements of people (including distances traveled) on the landscape—in short, locational movements or "changes of place." Ellen writes:

> Seasonality is generally linked to the changing foci of resource appropriation. During the dry season much of Miskito food-getting is focussed on marine resources while in the wet season it shifts to terrestrial resources. The actual loci of hunting, fishing, agricultural and gathering activities radically shift during seasonal extremes. In the dry season food resources are generally more diverse, and this is related to depletion of agricultural foodstuffs. In the rainy season resources are more limited in quantity and kind, but the distances travelled to obtain them are reduced due to weather, hunting conditions and animal migration. Fishing activities increase to offset the loss of meat supplied through hunting. Neitschmann [1973: 119, 121–122, 160, 236] argues that the range and density of biotopes, the changes in their fauna and flora, and varying fruiting and crop maturity periods (many with overlapping phases) give rise to seasonal changes in the appropriation patterns of villagers, which permit a qualitatively and quantitatively balanced diet under subsistence conditions. By focussing on different means of food procurement at different times of the year, an average calorie consumption could be maintained between 2,000 and 2,800 per day for an adult despite major changes in the Miskito environment. (1982:157–158)

I should note that, for Ellen, one activity merely replaces another (e.g., fishing replaces hunting) in order to compensate for an actual or potential scarcity. There is no question that the collection of quantitative data on specific resources is critical to comparative studies of subsistence systems. The difficulties arise when Ellen's terminology (e.g., "appropriation") conveys a false sense of attention to the organizational features of these systems. In fact, only the spatial (i.e., locational) components of the system are being considered. Ellen's (1982:160–161) maps of ecological zoning should not be mistaken for economic organizational charts. Neither should they be interpreted as providing a total picture of subsistence.

Maps of ecological zoning can be used, however, to indicate the potentials of the system under specified ecological conditions. Such maps represent formal models based on locational features. They indicate the spatial components of subsistence systems formally specified by Ellen (1982:164) in the following: "The spatially patterned distribution of production and effort relates directly to the ecological structure of the exploitative area." In this formal sense, analyses are reductionistic, reducing subsistence processes to locational (spatial and physical, environmental and biological) characteristics.

MICHAEL JOCHIM: *STRATEGIES FOR SURVIVAL*

Perhaps the best example of an ecological analysis that is elegantly formal and reductionistically locational is Michael Jochim's (1981) *Strategies for Survival*. Jochim's assumptions of scarcity and system equilibrium underlie his model—which, like Ellen's, is concerned primarily with energy flows and procurement strategies. For Jochim, resources move back and forth to prevent shortages and to keep the needs of populations in balance with the available resources. Jochim's maintenance strategies, for example, are all geared towards system equilibrium, as are his concepts of storage and delayed exchange. Storage is a short-term strategy geared towards securing resources against actual or potential times of scarcity. Storage may also represent a strategy of time efficiency, designed to take advantage of the short-term availability of particular resources (1981:176). For Jochim, storage is predicated on seasonality and is much more likely to exist in northern and temperate latitudes. In the tropics, in contrast, alternatives to food storage, such as delayed exchange, operate as a means of anticipating resource shortages. Jochim writes:

> *By exchanging a current excess for a future return,*
> *people store credit and can expand the time utility of*

> *their production into lean periods. Delayed exchange
> is essentially a strategy that expanded the productive
> base of the practitioner. . . . As an anticipatory
> strategy, delayed exchange represents a two-way
> transfer of goods, separated by some timelag, and so
> must be distinguished from immediate trade, which
> involves the simultaneous transfer of materials. As a
> means of dealing with resource scarcity, delayed ex-
> change must represent transactions in goods that are
> utilized to compensate for their absence of scarcity,
> and so must be distinguished from ceremonial ex-
> change, which may involve the continuous circula-
> tion, without consumption or utilization, of goods
> that are not necessarily scarce at any point along their
> flow path . . . Like storage, delayed exchange repre-
> sents an insurance policy with certain costs.
> (1981:177–178)*

Jochim goes on to delineate the conditions for delayed exchange, cit-
ing the Pomo trade feasts (Vayda 1967) as one example. He emphasizes
that some differential in the timing of risk or production is essential to
the practice of delayed exchange as a strategy of anticipating resource
shortages (1981:178). From this point, Jochim proceeds to deal with the
relationships between the organization of exchange and the severity of
shortages. He writes:

> *The level of organization responsible for the transac-
> tions should show a direct relationship with the scope
> of risk and scarcity . . . The organization of ex-
> change would also reflect the severity of shortages.
> The more severe the shortage, the more important be-
> comes the income from delayed exchange. As depen-
> dence upon the exchange increases, the more necessary
> it may be to insure the reliable and timely flow of
> goods . . . As shortages become more severe, the ex-
> change should become more structured and more
> highly sanctioned.
> (1981:179)*

Here is where the analysis runs into problems, for Jochim tries to
make a logical leap from the locational (spatial) to the appropriational

(organizational) dimensions of the economy without considering the alternative possibilities. In other words, what begins as a physical description of the location of resources on the landscape, e.g., resource "A" in location "a" exchanged for resource "B" in location "b," becomes a matter of organization, a factor shaping the structure of exchange. Jochim fails to consider the other logically possible responses to such a situation of scarcity. For example, as the shortage of a resource becomes more severe, the population could: (1) relocate, (2) produce a substitute item, or (3) consume products lower on the food preference scale. One could think of many other possibilities.

In sum, as the new ecological analyses have become more formal and more quantitatively oriented, they increasingly derive organizational (appropriational) features from physical/spatial/ecological (locational) features. Elegant and parsimonious models have come to rule out complexity and reduce organizational considerations to locational movements.

The New Marxist Economic Anthropology

Theoretically, the revitalization of Marxist thought in economic anthropology should have brought locational movements (forces of production) and appropriational movements (relations of production) together under a single paradigm. In fact, however, after the mid-1970s, relations of production received much more attention than did forces of production. If the new ecology reduced institutions to ecology (locational movements), the new economic anthropology (Clammer 1978a; Seddon 1978; Bourdieu 1977) has gone to the opposite extreme. Ecological variables receive almost no attention.

The new economic anthropology, represented by several, often competing brands of Marxism, uses institutions as the analytic units, but in problematical ways. Concepts such as "class" are applied across cultures (Terray 1972; Clammer 1978a), even in cultural systems where the state was absent. Using the concept of class so broadly amounts to imposing the institution of private property upon lineage systems.

The new Marxism has also enlarged institutional arrangements to encompass entire social formations, called "social totalities" by some (Friedman 1974; Bourdieu 1977; Chevalier 1982). The concept of the social totality comes from Marx, but in the hands of structural Marxists it results in what Sherry Ortner (1984) has called a "seamless whole," in which economy and society overlap as intrinsic and inseparable parts of social formations, and the boundary between economic and noneco-nomic processes becomes virtually nonexistent. Thus, in order to study an economic problem, one must study the entire society or culture. Bourdieu's (1977) notion of "symbolic capital" is another example of Ortner's "seamless whole" problem, because it mixes the ideological and the material elements of cultural systems in a confusing fashion (see also Giddens 1979, 1981, 1982). In sum, for the new Marxist economic an-thropology, appropriational movements (institutional arrangements) are rendered unusable as units of analysis.

It should be noted here that there are other interpretations of Marx that I find more productive for the analysis of economies across cultures. The institutional Marxists, for example, consider economy and society to be analytically separate (Tuden 1979; Halperin 1988). The institutional paradigm, as I have called it, presumes a separation between economy and society by conceptualizing cultural systems in political terms, group-ing cultures with like political structures, and then examining pattern and variation in economic processes by analyzing organizational principles.

As I have outlined in chapter 2, the institutional paradigm consists of models that take institutions as the primary mechanisms for organizing production, distribution, and consumption processes (Cohen 1968). The concept of institution is an analytic construct that refers to an organiza-tional principle, mechanism, or device. Marx used "society" to refer to the organizational mechanisms as well as to the organizational contexts within which individuals or groups carry out production, distribution, and consumption processes. Polanyi (1944, 1957a) used "institution" and the phrase "institutional arrangements" to refer to organizational prin-ciples. As should now be clear, he also used "appropriational move-ments" to refer to institutions. Private property is an example of an institution that operates in the political context of the stratified nation-state. Age and kinship are two classic institutions that operate in all cul-tures, albeit in varying ways in different types of societies. Institutions must be understood abstractly as the principles (in Giddens' words, "structures") that organize the relationships within and between units of production, distribution, and consumption. Again in Giddens' terms, these relationships can be understood as "deeply layered practices" that make up and organize relationships (interactions). Tribute systems, long-distance trade systems, and the like involve multiple and complex prin-ciples, i.e., institutions.

The institutional paradigm (focusing on appropriational movements)

ECONOMY AND ECOLOGY

thus contrasts with the ecological paradigm (focusing on locational movements), which consists primarily of models that examine physical and biological variables in ecologically defined populations. The ecosystem, consisting of a set of interacting species of organisms and their physical environment, is the primary unit of analysis in the ecological paradigm (Rappaport 1968a, 1968b; Vayda and McCay 1975; Hardesty 1977; Orlove 1980; Ellen 1982; Gross 1983; Jochim 1981; Moran 1979). Among the central concepts are energy, population pressure, and carrying capacity. As Jochim (1981) demonstrates, ecological anthropology is strongly materialistic in the sense that it emphasizes food procurement, resource base, and, especially, protein sources, but also total caloric input and output.

The concepts of locational and appropriational movements underlie the new ecology and the new (Marxist) economic anthropology, even in the latter's competing forms and even when these movements are not yet explicitly recognized. The reason the terms locational and appropriational movements are so important is that they clearly distinguish the spatial components of systems from the organizational components. In the new ecological anthropology, locational movements are exaggerated; in the new economic anthropology, especially in its structural Marxist form, appropriational movements (institutions and organizational principles) take on a life of their own. We need to devise ways of putting these two essential aspects (locational and appropriational movements) back together, while keeping them analytically separate. Problems requiring the analysis of both locational and appropriational movements, such as the organization of labor, can be dealt with in a clear and precise manner once the concepts are clear. Precise formulation of research problems will aid this task.

I suggest the following steps: (1) break down the material-means provisioning process into its component parts of production, distribution (trade and exchange), and consumption; (2) decide which component or components are of primary interest; (3) decide which movements are primary—locational or appropriational. This procedure amounts to an examination of the institutional (appropriational) and the ecological (locational) components of livelihood. These distinctions between locational and appropriational movements are the critical ones, for they tell us what problems we are addressing. These are analytical separations, but they determine the kinds of empirical data we collect and the kinds of units we study.

Applications

The dichotomy between what I have referred to as the ecological and the institutional paradigms—manifested by a focus on either "changing place" (locational movements) or "changing hands" (appropriational movements)—has provided the underlying but unrecognized structure for a recent discussion between Louis Binford (1980) and Polly Weissner (1982). The concepts of locational and appropriational movements enable us to discover some of the confusions in their terminology and to sort out some of their basic points of agreement and disagreement.

Binford's article can be understood as a nearly perfect elaboration of the features of locational movements in hunter-gatherer systems. As such, it can be understood as an illustration of the use of the ecological paradigm for understanding one kind of system adaptation. Weissner's article, on the other hand, provides not only a critique of Binford, but also the beginnings of an analysis of appropriational movements for hunter-gatherer systems. She gets at some of the distinctive features of the institutional paradigm for hunter-gatherers.

Before examining some of the details of Binford's analysis, I must point out that his use of the term "organizational" is confusing and problematical. It does not deal at all with "changing hands." For Binford, organizational refers to spatial arrangements ("changing place"), not to institutional arrangements. He is interested in patterns of human mobility and in the arrangements of particular kinds of sites. In this respect, Binford's use of the term is deceiving in the same sense that Ellen's use of terms such as "appropriation" is deceiving. Binford uses terms that convey institutional meaning, but in actuality, as will be seen below, his subject matter is spatial arrangements, not institutional arrangements. In fact, the word "location" figures prominently in his discussion.

Binford begins his analysis of variability in hunter-gatherer systems with a set of assumptions:

> Human systems of adaptation are assumed to be internally differentiated and organized arrangements of formally differentiated elements. Such internal differentiation is expected to characterize the actions performed and the locations of different behaviors. (1980:4)

He then proceeds to specify the elements of hunter-gatherer systems in terms of different kinds of locational movements, namely, the movements of "foragers" versus the movements of "collectors." In essence, foragers move through space and therefore arrange their activities on the landscape differently than do the more sedentary collectors. A close examination of these two kinds of hunter-gatherer systems reveals specific characteristics of locational movements.

FORAGERS

According to Binford, who bases his model system of foragers upon the Gwi San as reported by Silberbauer (1981), foragers are characterized by seasonal residential movements among a series of resource patches: water, melon patches, etc. Foragers do not store foods, but instead gather their food daily. Thus, they move out from residential sites each day and return each afternoon or evening (Binford 1980: 5). Binford points out that there may be considerable variability among foragers in the size of the mobile group as well as in the number of residential moves made during an annual cycle. Some of the variables Binford examines for the more typical equatorial groups of hunter-gatherers include: number of residential moves, average distances between moves, and total distances covered during an annual cycle. Whether or not camps are located relative to locations of previous use is another consideration.

Binford's use of terminology reflects his attention to motion in space, i.e., points between which people move. For example, his summary of expectations regarding the archaeological remains of foraging strategies deals mainly with types of space and movement:

> There are apt to be basically two types of spatial context for the discard or abandonment of artificial remains. One is the residential base, which is, as we have seen, the hub of subsistence activities, the locus out of which foraging parties originate and where most processing, manufacturing, and maintenance activities take place. I have indicated that among foragers residential mobility may vary considerably in both duration and the spacing between sites . . . I have suggested that foragers may be found in environmental settings with very different incidences and distributions

*of critical resources. In settings with limited loci of
availability for critical resources, patterns of residential mobility may be tethered around a series of very
restricted locations such as water holes, increasing
the year to year redundancy in the use of particular
locations as residential camps. The greater the redundancy, the greater the potential buildup of archaeological remains, and hence, the greater the archaeological visibility.*
(1980:9)

Binford distinguishes "locations" from "sites." A location is a place
where extractive tasks only are carried out. These locations for foragers
are generally "low bulk" procurement sites. Binford (1980:9) points out
that the archaeological remains of locations may be scattered over the
landscape.

COLLECTORS

Contrasted to foragers, collectors are seen to
be characterized by different kinds of locational movements. Binford
writes:

*Logistically organized collectors supply themselves
with specific resources through specially organized
task groups . . . Collectors are characterized by
(1) the storage of food for at least part of the year and
(2) logistically organized food-procurement parties.
The latter situation has direct "site" implications in
that special task groups may leave a residential location and establish a field camp or a station from which
food-procurement operations may be planned and exe-
cuted. If such procurement activities are successful, the
obtained food may be field processed to facilitate transport and then moved to the consumers in the residential camp.*
(1980:10)

Binford's emphasis on different kinds of locational movements is impressive. Some movements occur before food processing, some after.

According to Binford, logistical strategies are labor accommodations to incongruent distributions of critical resources, that is, to circumstances where consumers are close to one critical resource but far from another, equally critical resource. Thus, sets of people rather than the whole group must leave the residential location, perform a procurement task at another place, and then return. Examples of such tasks include hunting sheep at a salt lick and procuring fish at fish weirs. For collectors, Binford designates three kinds of sites or locations: the field camp, the stations, and the cache. In his words:

> A field camp is a temporary operational center where a task group sleeps, eats, and otherwise maintains itself while away from the residential base. . . . Stations are sites where special-purpose task groups are localized when engaged in information gathering, for instance, the observation of game movement. Caches are common components of a logistical strategy and represent a temporary storage phase.
> (1980:11–12)

Binford's discussion is a detailed modeling of the elements of variability in the way hunter-gatherers are organized in space for subsistence purposes. Binford's (1980:15) summary is indicative of his focus on locational movements and upon ecological factors to explain variability:

> Foragers move consumers to goods with frequent residential moves, while collectors move goods to consumers with generally fewer residential moves. The first strategy, that of "mapping on," would work only if all the critical resources were within foraging range of a residential base. Logistical strategies (by collectors) solve the problem of an incongruous distribution among critical resources (i.e., the lack of a reliable supply of a critical resource within the foraging radius of a residential base camp presumably located with regard to an equally critical resource). Under conditions of spatial incongruity it must be appreciated that a residential move will not solve the problem. A move toward one location reduces that access to the other. It is under this condition that a logistical strategy is

> *favored. Hunter-gatherers move near one resource*
> *(generally the one with the greatest bulk demand) and*
> *procure the other resource(s) by means of special work*
> *groups who move the resources to consumers.*

While Binford refers to mapping on and to logistical strategies as organizational principles, these are locational, not appropriational movements—that is, they are movements from place to place, not (cultural or institutional) organizational principles.

Weissner's Critique

While Binford's analysis certainly is suggestive of ways of understanding how people are organized socially and how people gain access to resources, these are assumed rather than analyzed. Polly Weissner (1982) raises some of these issues in her comments on Binford's article. She delineates some of the elements of a model of appropriational movements for hunter-gatherers. Weissner emphasizes not locational strategies but what she calls social strategies for reducing risk. In the course of her discussion, she questions whether strategies of organization can be predicted from environmental variables alone. Stating this matter in slightly different terms, we can say that whereas Binford has emphasized what Marx referred to as the forces of production, Weissner emphasizes the social relations of production for hunter-gatherers. She outlines the following risk-reduction (reducing the probability of loss) strategies, all of which involve some aspects of the social relations of production: (1) prevention of loss, (2) transfer of risk or loss from one party to another, (3) storage (losses covered by previous accumulation), (4) pooling of risk or risk sharing.

The last is one of the more interesting from the point of view of appropriational movements. Weissner (1982:173) describes risk sharing as

> *a social method of "insurance" which combines principles of risk transfer with principles of storage, and storage of obligations. In pooling, risk is distributed over a broad segment of the population, so that loss is made more predictable and shared by those in the pool. Small everyday losses—gifts of food, assistance, etc.—are thereby substituted for larger, more indefinite ones, such as weeks without hunting success, pro-*

longed periods of sickness, etc . . . Many hunter-
gatherer societies use a form of risk pooling described
by Sahlins (1972) as generalized reciprocity, which
operates under the terms that he who has gives to him
who is in need, donors and recipients alternating as
the conditions of have or have not may be reversed.

Weissner notes that all of the risk-reduction strategies can be linked to Binford's strategies for organization around resources. Individually organized pooling of risk is largely associated with a "foraging" strategy, and centralized pooling, transfer, and storage are most frequently associated with a "collector" approach (Weissner 1982:173). Weissner deals with certain kinds of locational movements that are prohibited by Binford's framework, namely, exchange relationships between groups. The importance of Weissner's article, from an analytical and comparative perspective, is that she points to some of the critical social organizational dimensions of hunter-gatherer societies. These dimensions cannot be understood solely on the basis of spatial analysis (locational movements). Their understanding requires analysis in terms of principles of cultural systems that determine rights and obligations between and among people (appropriational movements). She deals not only with "changes of place" but with "changes of hands."

SUMMARY

Ecology itself cannot answer all the questions we
might wish to ask, it cannot even pose them. The as-
sistance it can render in the formulation of problems is
limited, and this is even more true when it comes to
problem solving . . . Ecological approaches and data
can only ever constitute part of a substantive analysis
of a particular social formation, which must also be
grounded in methodology and theory drawn from
other than ecological precedent.
(ELLEN 1982:275–276)

Perhaps the most important point to be derived from the foregoing discussion is that, while it is useful from an analytical perspective to differentiate the ecological from the institutional paradigm, and locational from appropriational movements, a combination of these components is needed for the analysis of economic processes. The challenge is one of meshing the ecological and the institutional. The concepts of locational and appropriational movements allow us to think our way out of this dichotomy of the ecological versus the institutional, and to relate these two critical components of economic processes. First, however, the necessary analytical distinctions between locational and appropriational aspects of economic organization must be made.

I propose a synthesis based on the following assumptions, which involve some redefinitions of the economy. First we must assume, as Ellen and others readily admit, that livelihood processes cannot be reduced to ecological variables. Secondly, we must assume that economy and ecology are not synonymous. Thirdly, we can assume a relationship between ecological and livelihood processes as well as a relationship between ecological and economic processes.

We may now define the economy broadly as the material-means provisioning process in cultural systems. Following Polanyi, the material-means provisioning process can be said to consist of locational plus appropriational movements.

We can now begin to solve some of the problems raised by Ellen (1982) and others regarding the limitations of the new ecological analyses. Ecological (locational) and institutional (appropriational) movements contribute differently to economies in different cultures at different times and places. While all economies contain both locational and appropriational movements, the movements differ in both degree and kind among economies. This line of thinking brings us back full circle to Polanyi's generic model of the economy as consisting of locational and appropriational movements. A synthesis of institutional and ecological components of the economy was something Polanyi hinted at but did not attempt. The advantages of this model are several: (1) it eliminates the problem of ecological reductionism by incorporating institutional components into the analysis of economic processes; (2) it avoids the problems presented by some of the Marxist analyses that attempt to deal with entire social formations as totalities; and (3) it eliminates problems of psychological reductionism that are so common in methodologically individualistic models because it emphasizes qualitative over quantitative differences. All economies cannot be said to be alike (more or less) because of the universal assumptions and characteristics attached to individuals and their behavior. The generic model of the economy, with its emphasis on structure over agency, does not allow agents to be institutional or cultural dopes.

By focusing on the economy as the material-means provisioning process—composed of processes of production, distribution, and consumption—and by incorporating both ecological (locational) and institutional (appropriational) components, we can keep the analysis focused and, at the same time, delineate specific problems for analysis. The model I have proposed has the advantage of bringing social systems back into the analysis without requiring analysis of whole social formations.

Four # EQUIVALENCIES IN ECONOMIC ANTHROPOLOGY

> *The main principle underlying the regulations of actual exchange is that the Kula consists in the bestowing of a ceremonial gift, which has to be repaid by an equivalent counter-gift after a lapse of time, be it a few hours or even minutes, though sometimes as much as a year or more may elapse between payments. But it can never be exchanged from hand to hand, with the equivalence between the two objects discussed, bargained about and computed. The decorum of the Kula transaction is strictly kept, and highly valued. The natives sharply distinguish it from barter, which they practise extensively . . .*
>
> *The second very important principle is that the equivalence of the counter-gift is left to the giver, and it cannot be enforced by any kind of coercion. A partner who has received a Kula gift is expected to give back fair and full value, that is, to give as good an arm-shell as the necklace he receives or vice versa. . . . If the article given as counter-gift is not equivalent, the recipient will be disappointed and angry, but he has no direct means of redress, no means of coercing his partner, or of putting an end to the whole transaction. What then are the forces at work which keep the partners to the terms of the bargain?*
> (MALINOWSKI 1922:95–96)

The purpose of this chapter is to explore the dimensions and implications of the concept of equivalencies for analyzing problems in economic history and anthropology, including ethnohistory and archaeology. Equivalencies, which indicate how much of what to transact and in what form, in what order, and in what rhythms, operate in all economies and for all facets of production, distribution, and consumption. Because equivalencies are so pervasive, the processes by which they are formed (hereafter, "equivalency-formation processes") can be said to be fundamental to all economies, regardless of how simple or complex. Yet, while we have many examples of equivalency-formation processes in economic ethnographies, there has been little explicit attention to this concept in the literature of economic anthropology. As a result, economic anthropologists, novices and experts alike, may or may not attend to the problem.

The concept of equivalencies was originally formulated by Karl Polanyi in the course of his analyses of the evolution of the market economy in *The Great Transformation* (1944) and as he was framing models of economic organization that would be usable cross-culturally and over time (Polanyi et al. 1957; Polanyi 1977). Since Polanyi, the concept of equivalencies has been used implicitly in our descriptions and analyses of economic processes, but it has not received the explicit discussion that is necessary to place it centrally in the analysis of economic processes.

Since the order in which I present the materials in this essay is somewhat unusual, I want to provide a description and rationale for it. This chapter has four parts. Part I places Polanyi's concept of equivalencies in the context of his generic model of the economy. This is not something that Polanyi himself ever did; also Polanyi's generic model has not been well understood by the field of economic anthropology. The aim here is to link the concept of equivalencies to Polanyi's generic model. Part II introduces a set of ethnographic and archaeological examples. I wish to explore how analysts have implicitly used the concept, so that some of its dimensions will become explicit in different evolutionary and historical contexts. Part III turns to a discussion and critique of the use of the concept of equivalencies in *The Social Life of Things*, especially the arguments of its editor, Arjun Appadurai, and his colleague, Igor Kopytoff.

The final part of the chapter, Part IV, returns to Polanyi and traces the concept of equivalencies in his published and unpublished work, including some excerpts and commentaries from the unpublished transcripts of the seminars Polanyi held at Columbia University in the early 1950s.

Polanyi was actually ahead of his time in the 1950s, in that he was asking questions and raising issues that are only now beginning to be addressed. Because Polanyi did not have the ethnographic and archaeological data that we have today, he was limited in his abilities to try out and develop his concepts. Examining Polanyi's concepts throws modern examples into sharp relief and, in turn, provides the opportunity to rebuild and elaborate them.

The Problem of Equivalencies

The Greeks of the ancient world were concerned with the problem of equivalencies long before economic theory of any sort was invented. Listen to what Hesiod, of the eighth century B.C., had to say about equivalencies:

> O Perses, store this in your heart; do not
> Let Wicked Strife persuade you, skipping work,
> To gape at politicians and give ear
> To all the quarrels of the marketplace.
> He has no time for courts and public life
> Who has not stored up one full year's supply
> Of corn, Demeter's gift, got from the earth.
> When you have grain piled high, you may dispute
> and fight about the goods of other men.
> But you will never get this chance again:
> Come, let us settle our dispute at once,
> And let our judge be Zeus, whose laws are just.
> We split our property in half, but you
> Grabbed at the larger part and praised to heaven
> The lords who love to try a case like that,
> Eaters of bribes. They do not know
> That half may be worth more by far than whole,
> Nor how much profit lies in poor man's bread.
> (HESIOD 1973:60)

In a similar vein, economic historian and classicist Moses Finley talks about different kinds of measuring rods and standards:

> A conventional measuring stick is no more than an
> artificial language, a symbol like the X, Y, and Z of
> algebra. By itself it cannot decide how much iron is

the equivalent of one cow, or how much wine. In Adam Smith's world that determination was made through the supply and demand market, a mechanism utterly unknown in Troy or Ithaca. Behind the market lies the profit motive, and if there was one thing that was taboo in Homeric exchanges it was gain in the exchange. Whether in trade or in any other mutual relationship, the abiding principle was equality and mutual benefit. Gain at the expense of others belonged to a different realm, to warfare and raiding, where it was achieved by acts, or threats, of prowess, not by manipulation and bargaining.
(FINLEY 1954:65–66)

The quarrels of marketplaces, the arguments about quantities of corn stored and gifts given and received, the divisions of land between brothers—in short, who gets what and for how much and in what form—all address the problem of equivalencies. Karl Polanyi (1944, 1957, 1977) first identified equivalencies as a generic alternative to price, which he saw as only one form of equivalency—a form set by forces of supply and demand in a price-making market system. Polanyi recognized that prices set in such a market system were also different from prices set and used in localized marketplaces. This is true precisely because the two kinds of prices (market system and marketplace) are determined by different equivalency-formation processes. In the former (market system), prices are set by impersonal and not at all localized supply and demand crowds, such as all the possible demanders for and suppliers of automobiles. In the latter (localized marketplaces), however, all sorts of complex factors enter equivalency-formation processes, from the personal relationships between the vendors to the time of day one happens to find buyers and sellers in the marketplace. The later it is, the less willing the vendors will be to take the goods back home, and so the lower the prices.

The important point here is that equivalencies are essential ingredients in all economic processes, whether we are considering different kinds of prices that are set by different institutional arrangements (market systems and marketplaces) or whether we are considering allocations of land and labor for production or the distribution of goods by means of long-distance trade or exchange. Polanyi mined sources on archaic and primitive economies to understand the problem of equivalencies in all of its variations. The economy and polity of Homer's Greece, for which poetry remains the only written source of information, was of both practical and theoretical interest to Polanyi.

Hesiod wrote the poem "Works and Days" to his brother as seasoned advice and counsel, but his view of equivalencies is at least as comprehensive and almost as sophisticated as that of any contemporary analyst. The sheer number of economic processes mentioned with reference to issues of value and amounts in the short passage above is remarkable, and it is indicative of the scope of the problem of equivalencies: distribution (in marketplaces), storage (of corn), exchange (of gifts), the organization of productive resources (land). Moreover, the idea that "less is more"—expressed as, "That half may be worth more by far than whole"—can be interpreted as resistance to greed and accumulation. These notions are reinforced by the second quotation from Moses Finley, a specialist in ancient economies (Finley 1973) and a member of the Polanyi group at Columbia University in the 1950s. From a scholarly vantage point, Finley also grappled with the problem of equivalencies in the form of such questions as "How much iron is the equivalent of one cow?" He emphasized the negative valence of gain in exchange in Homer's time and pointed to "equality and mutual benefit" as the "abiding principle."

In the nearly forty years since Finley and Polanyi wrote, the problem of equivalencies has received very little systematic attention. Two possible exceptions can be found. The first occurs in the work of Robert J. Foster (1990), whose recent article, "Value without Equivalence: Exchange and Replacement in a Melanesian Society," is treated later in this essay; the second appears in the work of Arjun Appadurai, who, in the course of editing *The Social Life of Things* (1986), also deals with the problem of equivalencies. However, they do not refer to it as such. Since equivalencies are fundamental to the operation of all economies and all economic processes, the almost total failure of economic anthropologists to attend to equivalencies has hampered and rendered superficial our understanding of a whole host of economic processes, particularly those of distribution, trade, and exchange.

PART I. EQUIVALENCIES
AS A GENERIC PROBLEM

The problem of equivalencies is a generic economic problem. In fact, one might even consider it to be *the* generic problem for understanding economies across cultures, because equivalencies play a part in all processes of material-means provisioning in cultural systems. Regardless of the particular cultural context, all processes of production, distribution, and consumption involve setting equivalencies that indicate how much of a particular good or activity is appropriate in a given situation. As we shall see, however, appropriateness does not necessarily require that transactions involve equal amounts or values. In this sense, the term equivalencies is misleading. All material-means provisioning processes in all cultural systems, small-scale as well as large, require that participants know how much of what sorts of goods and labor is expected to meet an obligation. Equivalencies are as critical to the operation of foraging systems in small-scale polities as they are to systems of tribute and long-distance trade in large and complex polities. But equivalents are not, by any means, identities; nor do they necessarily involve equal amounts of anything. In fact, all sorts of things can be transacted without any balance or equilibrium between the parties being achieved. In most cultural contexts, equivalencies are fraught with complicated social and political overtones. Even at the band level, equivalencies are complicated indicators of status: kinship, gender, and age.

The matter of equivalencies becomes greatly complicated in post-industrial economies with large informal sectors. In these economies, equivalencies are, for the most part, indicated by prices, but these often operate in tandem with other kinds of arrangements. In addition, the arrangements that set the prices are highly variable. For example, local marketplaces, bazaars, grocery stores, and stock exchanges all use prices in one way or another. However, the principles determining price can be as varied as the goods themselves. The reasons are both simple and complex. Different institutional arrangements shape prices differently; marketplaces (depending upon the contexts within which they occur) determine prices in ways different from market systems; customary prices, administered prices, and prices of many other varieties all operate depending upon their institutional contexts. For example, local marketplaces are actual geographical locations to which buyers and sellers come for the purpose of exchanging goods. While such marketplaces can be found all over the world, they vary enormously in their size and organization and in their relationship to other institutional arrangements such as the market system. This latter is not a geographical place at all, but rather an abstract system in which an "invisible hand" operates to set prices according to the behaviors of suppliers and demanders who sell and purchase goods individually and at will, but who could never be found in one geographical place. Thus we can speak of the world capitalist (market) economy.

Exchange systems that operate without prices—that is, with other devices and mechanisms for setting and measuring equivalencies—include the large majority of equivalency-formation processes in the cross-cultural record. Systems of bridewealth, for example, may or may not involve prices or money. Food distribution systems in small-scale tribal systems all operate with rules of sharing that can be understood as rules that set equivalencies.

The Importance of Context

Equivalencies operate both within and between economic units. We might postulate that, in most instances, what I will call "internal equivalencies" (those operating within economic units) are of longer duration than "external equivalencies" (those operating between economic units). For example, households in state systems maintain internal equivalencies that are geared to household maintenance. Externally, however, the relationships between households and the state vary.

The importance of the context must be emphasized, since households in pre-capitalist states will operate differently from households in capitalist states.[1] In pre-capitalist states, households will be linked to the state through some form of redistributive system (often one operating periodically, as in tribute payments required several times per year) that links the state center and the communities and households at the periphery. In capitalist states, however, households and communities will all be involved in some way with market(system)-determined prices, and the market system permeates all economic processes at every level of the state system. In pre-capitalist states, households at the periphery can be insulated to some degree from state demands by local and regional officials. The only way in which households can escape the world capitalist system is to resist it in some way; the effectiveness of resistance depends upon a variety of factors, among them, the location of the household in a rural or urban area, the degree to which it is cash dependent, and the nature of its resource base. For example, if a household grows and processes most of what it requires for subsistence, it will be less dependent on the capitalist system than households that must use cash. Also, if households can generate cash in the informal economy, whatever its form, they will not be dependent upon the capitalist wage labor system.

Equivalencies that cross cultural boundaries become especially critical for the analysis of trade between people in economies with qualitatively (as well as quantitatively) different forms of organization. For instance, when band-level hunter-gatherers trade with sedentary agriculturalists, some common ground must be established (Schrire 1984).

Equivalencies can operate within units or they can connect units that are organized by different institutional arrangements. In this respect, equivalencies can be bridges between qualitatively different economies. I should emphasize that conceptualizing equivalencies as a generic problem is different from saying that the problem of equivalencies is universal and can be understood in similar ways in all economies. Equivalency-formation processes exist in all economies, but the processes by which equivalencies are formed will vary in different institutional contexts.

Equivalencies and Polanyi's Generic Model of the Economy

Understanding equivalencies as a generic problem requires that this problem be plugged in to the generic model of the economy and to the larger institutional paradigm. As I have emphasized throughout this book, Polanyi's primary scientific concern was to develop a model (a set of analytical tools, or concepts) for understanding the generic (substantive) economy—defined as the (organized, "instituted") processes of provisioning social systems with the material means of livelihood. Such a generic model enables economic processes to be identified, analyzed, and compared without imposing any culturally or historically specific categories.

From the point of view of understanding equivalency-formation processes, it is important to emphasize that the generic model of the economy is hierarchically organized. It begins with a set of general concepts and terms that can be used with equal appropriateness for all economies, capitalist and non-capitalist, pre- and post-industrial, including mixed economies with combinations of capitalist and non-capitalist institutional arrangements. At lower levels of abstraction, that is, for more and more specific kinds of economies or categories of economic processes, the concepts become more particular and thus more restricted in their applicability. In all cases, however, the purpose of the concepts is to understand the organization of economic processes and their variability.

Different types of equivalencies can be found at different levels of generality and in different institutional contexts.

Since, according to the generic model, the combinations of locational and appropriational movements constitute all of the logical possibilities for understanding the relationships among the material elements in cultural systems, these movements must be considered important in the discussion of equivalencies.

The two kinds of movements, locational and appropriational, encompass different dimensions of equivalency-formation processes. Locational movements involve ecological, physical, and logistical dimensions; appropriational movements involve the social and institutional dimensions of equivalency-formation processes. To illustrate, Pomo trade feasts (Vayda 1967) involve moving goods between two groups—staples in one direction, beads in another. These physical movements are locational. How many beads move and what drives the movements are appropriational problems.

As the reader will recall from chapter 3, locational movements are movements in space, changes in the positioning of people, goods, and resources. Polanyi talked about locational movements as "changes of place" and appropriational movements as "changes of hands." The latter are more difficult to pin down, however, because they involve changes driven by institutional arrangements, with or without changes in positioning. Appropriational movements consist of organizational changes or transfers of rights that are difficult to observe "on the ground." An artifact can move from point "A" to point "B" (a locational movement) without a change in the principles governing the movement (appropriational movement) and possibly without a change in its equivalency. A shift from communal land tenure to private property, however, changes the equivalency rules.

All locational and appropriational movements involve equivalency-formation processes. It is important to recognize, however, that while the distances that goods travel do indeed relate to the ways in which equivalencies are formed, locational movements alone do not involve changes in the principles governing equivalencies. The principles behind the movement of a good, whether it is an obsidian blade, a ceramic vessel, a bushel of wheat, or a jade figurine, cannot be determined by examining the locational movement only. Rather, relationships between the parties involved are the key determinants of equivalency-formation processes. Locational movements do not, in and of themselves, necessarily imply any change in the organization of rights and obligations vis-à-vis a particular item; they also do not tell us everything that is essential for understanding equivalencies. Appropriational movements are necessary for a change in the principles governing equivalencies. It is true, however, that the greater the number and kind of locational and appropriational movements, the more complicated equivalency-formation processes become.

Forms of Economic Integration and Equivalency-Formation Processes

At a second level of generality, Polanyi's forms of economic integration—reciprocity, redistribution, market exchange, and householding (see chapter 5)—are models within the generic model of the economy, which encompass different kinds of locational and appropriational movements and different equivalency-formation processes. The forms of economic integration are ideal models approximating patterns of movements within and among certain kinds of institutional arrangements. An understanding of the forms of integration is clarified by a discussion of the problem of equivalencies. The question of how much of what kinds of goods and resources or the number of units of one kind that can be substituted for units of another kind in economic processes is a critical element, if not *the* critical element in the forms of economic integration. These forms of integration are neither categories for classifying economies nor labels for pigeonholing economic formations. They were designed by Polanyi as formal (ideal) models for accommodating variability. He referred to these models as patterns and placed them in an historical framework:

> *Broadly, the proposition holds that all economic systems known to us up to the end of feudalism in Western Europe were organized either on the principles of reciprocity or redistribution, or householding, or some combination of the three. These principles were institutionalized with the help of a social organization which,* inter alia, *made use of the patterns of symmetry, centricity, and autarchy. In this framework, the orderly production and distribution of goods was se-*

cured through a great variety of individual motives
disciplined by general principles of behavior.
(1944:54–55)

Formally, the central feature of reciprocity as a
mode of economic integration is symmetry, which Polanyi understood
as an institutional pattern with variable forms:

> The striking "duality" which we find in tribal sub-
> divisions lends itself to the pairing out of individ-
> ual relations and thereby assists the give-and-take of
> goods and services in the absence of permanent re-
> cords. The moieties of savage society . . . turned out
> to result from, as well as help to perform, the acts of
> reciprocity on which the system rests. Little is known
> of the origin of "duality"; but each coastal village on
> the Trobriand Islands appears to have its counterpart
> in an inland village, so that the important exchange
> of breadfruits and fish, though disguised as a recipro-
> cal distribution of gifts, and actually disjoint in time,
> can be organized smoothly. In the Kula trade, too,
> each individual has his partner on another isle, thus
> personalizing to a remarkable extent the relation-
> ship of reciprocity. But for the frequency of the sym-
> metrical pattern in the subdivision of the tribe, in the
> location of settlements, as well as intertribal rela-
> tions, a broad reciprocity relying on the long-run
> working of separated acts of give-and-take would be
> impracticable.
> (1944:48)

Empirically, reciprocity can take many forms. For example, reciprocity can involve generalized sharing between and among members of
extended-family groups in a variety of cultural systems, or it can involve
more formalized exchanges between symmetrically related kinship
groupings (Lévi-Strauss 1949). In the former, the equivalency ratios are
more or less equal, but no accounts are kept; in the latter, equivalency

ratios are also more or less equal, but accounting figures importantly in all ongoing transactions. In other institutional contexts—e.g., in stratified village societies in which reciprocal transactions between patrons and clients are at issue—equivalency ratios are controlled by the patrons, who have the power to decide how much land, credit, or other resources must be exchanged for requisite amounts of goods or services, especially labor. Inequalities are built into equivalency-formation processes between patrons and clients.

REDISTRIBUTION

The mode of economic integration that Polanyi referred to as redistribution is predicated upon the institutional pattern of centricity. Formally, redistribution involves collection of goods into a center and then movement out from that center. While, again, redistribution takes many institutional forms, Polanyi associated redistribution systems with different kinds of political centers:

> We find, as a rule, the process of redistribution forming part of the prevailing political regime, whether it be that of tribe, city-state, despotism, or feudalism of cattle or land. The production and distribution of goods is organized in the main through collection, storage, and redistribution, the pattern being focused on the chief, the temple, the despot, or the lord.
> (1944:52)

It is important to note here that redistribution encompasses the production as well as the distribution of goods.

Equivalencies in predominantly redistributive systems operate according to principles that are related to but different from those in predominantly reciprocal systems. The center, whatever form it may take, has much greater power over equivalency-formation processes than does the periphery. Households in state-financed tribute systems (Inca, Aztec) are subject to politically mandated equivalencies (Carrasco 1978; Earle and D'Altroy 1982). The following example, taken from Earle and D'Altroy (1982), illustrates several points. First, the case indicates that the concept of equivalencies is very much alive in contemporary archaeology. Secondly, it illustrates several components of equivalency-formation processes that are redistributive in form—among them, not only the form and amount of equivalencies but also their timing. The Inca state polity centrally controlled the form, amount, and timing of inputs to the state coffers. The state also controlled the outputs for purposes of financing state operations. Earle and D'Altroy use archaeologically identifiable storage facilities to describe the operation of prehistoric redistribution, one general form of politically mandated equivalencies. Using Polanyi as their point of departure, Earle and D'Altroy describe staple finance in the Inca state:

> Redistribution is rather a system of finance used to mobilize goods from subsistence producers either as a fraction of their production or as the produce from reserved lands worked by the commoners. Goods collected in this way are then used to pay for the full range of elite and governmental activities. In essence, the development of this rudimentary tax-tribute system underwrites the development of the chiefdom and early state superstructure.
> (1982:266)

This necessary support is typically accomplished by what Polanyi (1968:186–187, 324) has called staple finance, which is a finance in kind with defined accounting units. The staples, typically grains and livestock, are collected by the central government, stored, and paid out in return for state services. Polanyi (1968:321) calls staple finance a "submonetary device" that is associated with standardized values for key staples. A producer therefore gives to the state, either directly or indirectly, measured amounts of the main staples. These are then used to pay individuals working for the state. Here, we see state-mandated values for key staples—in short, equivalencies. Earle and D'Altroy (1982:266–267) also note that these staples were locally produced agricultural products. From the available evidence, then, the Inca state used locally available goods as "financial units" (read, equivalency units) and was not coordinating exchange in subsistence goods among specialized local economies.

LONG-DISTANCE TRADE: EXTERNAL EQUIVALENCIES

Long-distance trade, another form of extra-community or external equivalencies, involves different equivalency-formation processes than redistributive forms of tribute. If the latter (e.g., staple finance) involve redistributive equivalencies, the former involves negotiated equivalencies between two polities. In the Andean case, Earle and D'Altroy say the following about long-distance trade:

> *Craft goods produced by attached specialists and special agricultural crops grown on governmental lands are traded externally for foreign goods. In most instances, these foreign products are valuables used in elite exchanges such as political gifts to establish alliances, to validate offices, and to mark ties of dependence. It is possible, however, that foreign goods could also serve as payment by the state. Providing foreign goods to local populations thus may be important in some "redistributional" systems, but even in those systems it seems likely that the foreign goods would represent only part of the total goods used in payment.*
> (1982:267)

We can see here that the two forms of external equivalencies, redistribution and long-distance trade, are related empirically but separable analytically. The main point for our purposes is that these equivalency-formation processes operate between and across units of economic organization, rather than within them.

INTERNAL EQUIVALENCIES

Internal equivalencies in household and community economies, by contrast, will operate with kin-organized subsistence as their primary goals. Equivalencies will be formed in such a way as to maintain the reproduction of residential and/or kinship groups. Drawing on the work of John Murra (1980), who was also greatly influenced by Polanyi, Earle and D'Altroy emphasize the self-sufficiency of subsistence processes (and the related equivalency-formation processes) for local subsistence economies within the Inca state:

> *The subsistence economy of a local, highland Andean community was generalized and organized to incorporate as wide a range of economic activities as possible.*

> *Community boundaries were laid out to crosscut eco-*
> *logically diverse zones and, in certain circumstances,*
> *were extended by colonization to more distant, eco-*
> *nomically significant zones. The apparent ideal was*
> *to integrate the vertically distinctive economic zones*
> *of the Andes within a single community to provide*
> *access to localized products through autonomous recip-*
> *rocal exchange among community members. Where*
> *feasible, this circumvented the need for an intercom-*
> *munity market exchange and for state-administered*
> *regional exchange. In essence, the subsistence econ-*
> *omy of these Andean communities was largely self-*
> *contained and required no direct state intervention to*
> *organize specialized production and exchange.*
> (1982:269)

Here, we are back to a reciprocally organized economy at the local level. Earle and D'Altroy emphasize the distinctiveness of the state economy from the community economy:

> *The state economy was distinct from the community*
> *economy in form and function. The state mobilized*
> *staples, and to a lesser degree valuables, from the lo-*
> *cal community to finance the operation of the empire.*
> *As Murra (1956) has described, this was accom-*
> *plished by an elaborate labor tax. The Inca empire*
> *asserted ownership over all lands and herds, and a*
> *community's access to subsistence resources derived*
> *from the state in return for community labor on state*
> *projects. The household—as the elemental unit of as-*
> *sessment—provided labor for state and church lands,*
> *for public-works projects, and for special duties such*
> *as weaving. The products of this labor were then col-*
> *lected by the state; the staples were stored locally and*
> *the special products, such as fine textiles were mainly*
> *shipped to the capital at Cuzco.*
> (1982:270)

Redistribution here operates in a corvée-like fashion not unlike that operating in Mexican *ejidos* (Halperin 1975), where labor on public works is required in order to maintain access to *ejido* lands. This form of redistribution is related to but different from the staple finance form.

The important points here are: (1) that we recognize the formal features of the generic model of the economy, especially the heuristic properties of concepts such as the forms of economic integration, i.e., reciprocity, redistribution, exchange, and householding; and (2) that we understand how the forms of integration provide the models for recognizing equivalency-formation processes. The forms of economic integration are concepts designed to understand the variability in economic processes—in this case, equivalency-formation processes. They are, in effect, models that operate at a different and lower level of generality, such that patron–client relationships, for example, can be understood in terms of a combination of two forms of economic integration, reciprocity and redistribution. The generic model of the economy not only provides guidelines for identifying the relevant variables for analyzing particular kinds of movements in specific kinds of cultural contexts, but also provides a series of submodels. As submodels, the forms of economic integration are not labels, but rather heuristic devices that can be used to understand pattern and variability in economic processes in a variety of cultural contexts.

The generic model begins at the most abstract level, with the concepts of locational and appropriational movements. It is a formal model of economies that can be used cross-culturally; it should not be understood, however, as the only (in the sense of universal) model. Out of the primary, general model, we can generate subsidiary models for analyzing particular kinds of problems—such as the problem of equivalencies—in different kinds of cultural systems. Here, the forms of economic integration become critical parts of the generic model at a lower level of abstraction. Equivalency-formation processes work differently for different forms of economic integration.

PART II. QUANTITATIVE AND QUALITATIVE DIMENSIONS OF EQUIVALENCIES: ETHNOGRAPHIC EXAMPLES

Because equivalencies affect all economic processes in all cultural systems, the problem of equivalencies is a generic problem with both quantitative and qualitative dimensions. Questions such as how much of something (a good, a service, a symbolic entity or medium such as money) is moved (locational movement) or designated (appropriational movement) in exchange or in substitution for something are quantitative considerations. Questions about the kinds of goods used as equivalencies, especially questions relating to the appropriateness of substituting certain kinds of goods for others, involve qualitative dimensions. In complex, state-level systems, the problem involves establishing standards of value, measures, weights, etc. Polanyi (1977:63) indicated his awareness of the arbitrary (in the sense of culturally defined) nature of equivalency-formation processes by saying, "Equivalents as such are merely devices by which quantitative relations are set up between goods of different kinds, like a measure of corn and a jar of wine (one to one), or big and small cattle (one to ten)."

In small-scale, preliterate societies, equivalency-formation processes involve complex qualitative dimensions. The Netsilik Eskimo, for example, distribute particular parts of a butchered seal to specific categories of kin. The !Kung San of the Kalahari Desert of Botswana always give water for the asking, but the quantities of water are ecologically constrained, depending upon the season (dry or rainy) (see Dowling 1968). As long as subsistence resources are varied and plentiful, traditional sharing patterns can be maintained and equivalencies will remain stable. Culture contact, especially in the extreme form of state takeover of hunting lands and confinement of formerly nomadic populations on reservations, creates chaos for the traditional expectations surrounding food equivalencies especially. For instance, once confined to government reservations, the !Kung must rely on government rations of "mealie mealie" or use cash to obtain food. Sharing becomes very difficult for those who have any resources at all because their supply is insufficient to go around (Marshall 1980; see also Peterson 1984).

RAFFIA CLOTHS AS KIN-BASED EQUIVALENCIES

The famous raffia cloths of the Lele have never been discussed as equivalencies per se. We can see, however, that Mary Douglas (1967:112–113) clearly conceptualizes these cloths as a form of equivalency because she presents both the quantitative and the qualitative considerations that enter into Lele exchange processes. She also notes the absence of prices, even traditional ones, in the Lele economy. Instead of prices, she talks about "acknowledgment fees" of one or two raffia cloths for the use of ordinary domestic objects. The equivalency-formation processes for the Lele are shaped by kinship relationships. Without kinship ties, a person is effectively barred from exchanging. Douglas writes:

> Baskets, fish traps, fur hats, cosmetic bowls, dishes, cups, loom, mortar—the producer of those things is likely to receive no more than one or two (raffia) cloths from a kinsman, in recognition that both parties acknowledge their relationship.
>
> I had great difficulty trying to buy ordinary domestic objects with francs. They had no traditional price, as they usually changed hands on kinship lines, with an "acknowledgment fee" of one or two cloths. My friends, mistaking this fee for a price equivalent to the value of the goods, tried to persuade reluctant sellers that they ought to part with their things for 10 or 20 raffia cloths. However, even if I doubled the number of francs, they were still not willing to sell. For raffia cloth they would have sold willingly.
> (1967:112–113)

Here we see several different equivalency-formation processes arriving at an impasse. Raffia cloth functions quite effectively as a medium of exchange for ordinary items among Lele kin. For outsiders, however, raffia cloth cannot be used to obtain items. Mary Douglas herself, who presumably had established some close ties with the Lele, could not obtain goods by using Western money (in this case, francs), but had she had access to raffia cloth, she could have obtained goods easily. Such access is not simple, however. Raffia cloths take quite a long time to manufacture, and obtaining raffia cloth requires kin ties in the first place.

TIV SPHERES OF EXCHANGE: THE BOUNDARIES OF EQUIVALENCY-FORMATION PROCESSES

Related to Mary Douglas' (1967) discussion is the concept of spheres of exchange (Firth 1939; Bohannan 1955). The Tiv, subsistence agriculturalists in northern Nigeria, have a ranked hierarchy of spheres or categories of exchangeable commodities. Here, note it is the categories of objects that are critical, not the categories of people exchanging the objects. While the Bohannans' material (1968) is over thirty-five years old, it nonetheless points to issues about the problem of equivalencies that have yet to be addressed. Among these are the boundaries of exchange processes (social and geographical), restrictions on exchangeable items, and hierarchical relationships that order the domains or spheres of exchange.

The three main categories or spheres of exchange among the Tiv are, in order of hierarchical importance: kinship (rights in human beings other than slaves, especially women), prestige (including slaves, cattle, cloth, and metal bars), and subsistence (foodstuffs, chickens, and goats, as well as household utensils such as mortars, grindstones, calabashes, baskets, pots, and tools). Services and labor operate outside of these spheres of exchange and are part of the age-set, kinship, and domestic group structure (Bohannan 1955:63). Land is also outside of the spheres of exchange. As Bohannan says, "Land is, to Tiv, the spatial aspect of social organization; land rights are conditions of agnation. . . . No Tiv can control more land than he can use" (1955:63).

The hierarchical relationships between the three spheres are described by Bohannan as follows:

> *The hierarchical nature of the values involved in the three main categories of exchangeable goods provides a basis for investment and economic endeavor in Tiv society. The drive toward success leads most Tiv, to the greatest possible extent, to convert food into prestige items; to convert prestige items into dependents— wives and children. Tiv say that it is good to trade food for brass rods, but that it is bad to trade brass rods for food; that it is good to trade your cows or brass rods for a wife, but very bad to trade your marriage ward for cows or brass rods. Seen from the individual's point of view, it is profitable and possible to invest one's wealth only if one converts it into a higher category; to convert subsistence wealth into prestige wealth and both into women is the aim of the economic endeavor of individual Tiv.*
> (1955:64)

Tiv exchanges within a category (e.g., subsistence) are different from exchanges between categories (e.g., subsistence and prestige). Bohannan calls the former exchanges conveyances, and the latter, conversions. Bo-hannan is careful to point out that equivalency-formation processes operate differently for conversion (exchanges between categories) than for conveyance (exchanges within the same sphere):

> *Conversion, unlike conveyance, is not mere exchange of equivalent goods. Because there is a definite moral dimension to conversion, it forms a strong source of motivation to individual action. It is in the light of such motivation that we must evaluate the fact that a very high percentage of autobiographies collected from Tiv contain variants of this story: "When I was a very small child, my kinsman gave me a baby chicken. I tended it carefully and when it grew up it laid eggs and hatched out more chickens; I exchanged these chickens for a young nanny goat, who bore kids, which I put out with various kinsmen until I could exchange them for a cow. The cow bore calves, and eventually I was able to sell the calves and procure a wife." Every successful man considers such a story one of the most important sequences of his biography; it proves that he has been successful.*
> (1955:65)

In the Tiv system, bridewealth is one kind of conversion—perhaps the most important kind, since it is near the pinnacle of the hierarchy of exchange categories.

Equivalencies vs. Equivalents

In a recent article based on research in Melanesia (Foster 1990) the author argues that exchange value (what Polanyi called equivalencies) need not imply a transfer of equivalents (equalities or identities). Foster argues that both the social relations of exchange and the culturally defined properties of the terms of the exchange require us to understand that exchange value (equivalencies) must be construed as a relationship of significant difference rather than one of mensurability. Even though Foster uses the terms equivalencies and equivalents to mean two different (and opposite) things, his argument is perfectly consistent with a cross-cultural concept of equivalencies; the Melanesian case study touches upon Polanyi's concept of equivalencies by examining transactions associated with mortuary feasting.

The particular exchange described by Foster (1990) involves the exchange of cooked pigs and shell discs. "Feast-givers display and disburse their productive capacity in the forms of consumable pigs and food while acquiring shell discs, icons of lineage durability" (p. 56). Foster relies on a concept of value that emphasizes differences in the terms of the exchange. Foster says:

> Exchange in this view becomes a process in which actors construct their differential value to each other— instead of the equal value or equivalence of their objects—through the circulation of specific items in specific contexts. This perspective accordingly requires close consideration both of the social relations of exchange and of the significant properties and qualities of the terms or objects of exchange.
> (1990:56)

He then adds, "The value of the exchange objects, however, refers not to a relationship between commensurables or equivalents [read, equalities] but to one of complementary differences in the project of lineage replacement." Foster's conclusion reemphasizes exchange in terms of accepted equivalences (in Polanyi's sense of what is exchanged for what), and he clearly argues that it would be ethnocentric to project the principles of commodity exchange (in a market economy) onto the Melanesian case—again, an argument consistent with Polanyi's cross-cultural approach to economic processes. Foster goes on:

> In interpreting the "meaning" which Melanesians ascribe to their "exchanges," it cannot be assumed that "exchange" always establishes a measurable relation of equivalence (equalities) between the objects exchanged. To do so would be to attribute one of the definitive "meanings" of commodity exchange to Melanesian understandings. . . . In the case of lulu am bo the exchange of shell rings and cooked pigs defines "durability" and "consumability" as the com-

plementary attributes of an encompassing social rela-
tionship. Depending upon the particular enactment of
lulu am bo, either of these attributes can be identified
with either of the parties to the exchange; each party
is the source of both attributes relative to the other
party. Invariably, however, the exchange establishes
and communicates the difference between these attri-
butes through the iconic signification of shells and
pork.
(1990:66)

This example illustrates some of the complex social and ideological structures that condition equivalencies. That things are not exactly as they seem and that the point of the exchange may be to emphasize differences rather than similarities or identities are only two of Foster's points.

Trade and Equivalency-Formation Processes

The relationships between systems of trade and equivalency-formation processes have been assumed rather than analyzed systematically in the literature of economic anthropology. The examples below provide some illustrations of variations in trade systems that can be understood by examining variations in equivalency-formation processes in different kinds of contexts.

TRADE IN A COLOMBIAN CHIEFDOM

Using a world-systems approach as his starting point, Langebaek (1991) has shown that the unequal trade between Highland center and Foothill periphery in 16th-century Eastern Colombia played a significant role in the development of Highland chiefdoms. In his very rich description of the Highland chiefdoms, Langebaek (1991: 329) delineates each as having been divided into *capitanías* (probably matrilineages) which formed nuclear villages, each commanded by a *capitán*. Among other public structures, each village had a communal storehouse, which became the repository of goods (blankets, seashells, gold) received by *capitánes* and *caciques* (chiefs). When there was a surplus, these goods were distributed to the producing community as indicators of the prestige and status of the leaders. Ungenerous leaders ran the risk of having their communities disown them and establish ties with other political leaders (1991:329). The system of internal equivalencies in the Highlands was related to the fact that the Foothills supplied exotic goods (cotton, coca, tobacco, lumber, slaves, feathers, honey, beeswax, unrefined gold) to the Highlands in return for cotton blankets, emeralds, and gold ornaments.

Langebaek uses indirect evidence to suggest that the quantities of gold and cotton that came from the Foothills to the Highlands were substantial. He estimates that 100,000 blankets entered the storehouses of Highland chiefs each year. The chiefs required raw materials from the Foothills in order to maintain their prestige with their followers.

In this example of equivalencies operating within a chiefdom, we can see that rather significant inequalities prevailed. Trade functioned to feed and clothe the chiefly centers, almost in a state-like fashion. In fact, the similarities between the redistributive pattern described by Langebaek (1991) for the Colombian chiefdom and that found by Earle and D'Altroy (1982) for the Inca empire are striking. In both cases there is a powerful center that collects resources and then redistributes them to the periphery. In both cases, the center controls equivalencies. In Langebaek's case, however, prestige is more of a factor in the exchange than it is in Earle and D'Altroy's. The staple finance system described for Peru by Earle and D'Altroy clearly involves some brute force, not the subtle forms of compliance that operate at the chiefdom level. Equivalencies are more negotiable at the chiefdom level than they are in the Inca state as well as more advantageous to those at the periphery.

POMO TRADE FEASTS

In Pomo intervillage trade feasts, we see another slant on chiefly involvement in equivalency-formation processes (Vayda 1967). Vayda's detailed descriptions provide material on trade and equivalencies that is rare to find in the ethnographic record. He tells us that once Yokaia village chiefs accepted the invitation to a fish feast from the Lake chiefs, they requested the men of the village to contribute as many beads as possible to a common fund. Lake chiefs (the hosts) fed the Yokaia guests and the Yokaia men freely used the lake facilities (sweat houses and gambling). Vayda describes the consummation of the deal by making it clear that the chiefs (operating in a collective manner in council) decide equivalencies. The quantifiable units are important to note, as is the exchange of bulky perishables for the portable and durable beads. Vayda writes:

> *In finally consummating the deal, the host chief divided the presented beads into strings of hundreds. The Lake chiefs then determined in council how much produce they would give for each string of beads. After the beads had been laid upon the ground in some prearranged spot, the several family representatives of the Lake people went to their respective stores and each returned with measures of produce to the value of one string. The giver of the fish, after he had left a measure of produce on a common pile, went to where the strings of beads had been placed and took the string of a hundred beads to which he was entitled. This transaction of piling up the fish and taking the beads was kept up by the fish givers as long as they continued to desire to make the trade, or else as long as the beads held out.*
>
> *When the fish were all piled up, the chief of the guests took possession. Up to this point, the Yokaia people had not been involved in the transaction but had merely waited to take what was offered without making any effort to haggle. The Yokaia chief now allotted to each family a basketful or other equal portion of fish, going around as many times as the pile afforded. He kept for himself whatever remained when there was no longer enough to go around once more in the same proportion.*
>
> *Some variations in these trading practices are reported from Morgan Valley, where the Lower Lake visitors traded beads not directly for fish but rather for the right, following a great feast, to go fishing in the creek belonging to the Margan Valley hosts. This creek contained certain species of fish not found in the waters of the Lower Lake.*
>
> (1967:497–498)

While Vayda emphasizes that variations in the production and availability of subsistence goods from one place to another allowed members of a community to temporarily "bank" a surplus of food with members of other communities, it strikes me that chiefly control over equivalency-formation processes and over the actual distribution of food and beads was what allowed this banking to occur in the first place. Chiefs both offered and accepted invitations to feasts involving the sharing of fish and acorns. They controlled both the timing and the occasions for the feasts and, thus, the distribution or spreading out and equalization of consumption of subsistence goods (Vayda 1967:499).

By accepting an invitation to a trade feast, the Pomo villagers who had previously "banked" food would be getting food back, and they might be doing so at a time when they were more in need of food for consumption than they had been previously when they had traded food earlier to other communities (p. 498). One can begin to see that beneath the surface were conditions of trade between groups that hinged on a variety of factors, only one of which was consumption needs. Were there conditions under which more or fewer beads were required by groups in exchange for the same quantity of food? In other words, did the equivalency ratios vary at all, and if so, how? Also, what happened if a group was in need of food and had already cashed in all of its trade beads?

The fact that trade beads were also items of prestige adds to the complexity of the equivalency-formation processes, because prestige factors highlight the variable principles operating within and between groups. Vayda writes:

> These beads were prized mainly for the prestige which their possession and, even more, their generous expenditure bestowed. When the chiefs of a village accepted an invitation to a trade feast they called on the men of the village each to give as many beads to the common fund as he could spare. Every man must have given as liberally as possible, since therein lay prestige; therefore, a community that had received a "superabundance" of beads through its trading may be expected to have disposed of that superabundance when it in turn was invited to a trade feast. It should also be recalled that the chief of the host village arranged for distribution of the beads according to the

amount of food that each of his people contributed, but
the visitors' chief allotted the food with no regard for
the amount of beads furnished by the several members
of his community. Thus it seems that the Pomo trade
feasts served to convert inequalities in subsistence into
more or less temporary inequalities in the possession
of beads not only between communities but also
within communities.
(1967:499)

The fact that we see both internal (inequalities within communities) and external (inequalities between communities) equivalency-formation processes at work in the Pomo case is quite amazing, if only in the sense that it is rare to find these recorded for a single case.[2]

Equivalencies in Peasant Societies

In peasant societies, the problems of equivalencies are extremely complicated and are subject to constant change. Equivalencies operate both within local (village) systems, which are strongly oriented towards subsistence processes, and between local systems and the outside. At the same time, local-level equivalencies are always, to some degree, set by the outside because peasant societies are parts of larger (state) systems. Within the local peasant economy, the livelihood of the subsistence unit—whatever that unit may be (household, family network, or some combination thereof)—is primary and sets the parameters of equivalency-formation processes. Equivalencies associated with production, distribution, and consumption are all affected by subsistence orientation.[3]

THE CHINESE FARM FAMILY

Martin Yang's (1945:73–76) description of work equivalencies for the Chinese farm family (circa 1920) illustrates some of the ways in which equivalencies based on age, gender, and skill divide the labor for production among members of the extended family:

A farm family is a unit unto itself in production. The
family members produce collectively and they produce

for the family as a whole, not for any individual members. This holds true for everything.

The work, in the field, on the threshing ground, in the vegetable garden, and at home, is divided among persons according to experience and physical ability. For example, the father is assigned to plant the sweet potato vines, since he is the experienced one. He knows which is the upper end and which the bottom end of the vines and can put them in the right positions. He knows how deep the vines should be planted and also the proper distance between every two plants. Others may also know these things but as yet cannot put them into practice as efficiently. The elder son is asked to carry water from a distant place because he is the strongest in the family. The younger brother and sister are put to pouring water into the small holes because this does not require much experience or strength. Finally, the work of covering the vines and of accumulating earth to support the young plants needs some experience but not much physical strength, and that is why the mother and the elder sister are assigned to these tasks.

Equivalencies are derived from institutions involving communal property and kin-based (extended family) production units (see Pasternak 1972:208–213). The cooperative principles manifested in the planting process carry over to the harvesting of sweet potatoes and to domestic work as well as to the distribution of earnings. If a son goes to work for wages on another family's farm, he hands his earnings over to his father or to the family. Yang (1967:336) makes it clear that deviations from this (householding) pattern are considered abnormal in the extended-family subsistence unit:

In an old-fashioned family . . . everyone works or produces for the family as a whole, be he a farmer, a mason, a cloth weaver, a merchant or what not. It goes without saying that those who work on the family's farm work for the whole family. If someone keeps a part of his wages, he will be condemned by the

*family head and suspected by all the other members of
the family as being untrustworthy. A merchant who
has to do his business outside may spend what he had
made for his living expenses and according to his own
judgment, but he must turn over all the rest and re-
port what he has spent to the family head. If some of
his expenses are found to have been unnecessary, he
will be questioned about them in detail.*

In this Chinese case, the family head keeps a tight hold on equivalencies. Note, however, that this family-based equivalency system is
not at all centralized or run in an authoritarian manner. Rather, the rules
are well understood; to violate them is to place the entire family in
jeopardy.

The following excerpts from a recent Japanese case illustrate that time
can be the key to local equivalency-formation processes. Bernstein
(1983:66) writes:

*Haruko resented the time her husband spent on the
administration and accounting side of the reforms. He
devoted hours of work to keeping careful records that
were audited regularly. Figuring costs was a tedious
chore for him. There was the cost of the community's
bulk purchases of fertilizer, for example, to be shared
according to each family's land holdings. There was
also the shared cost of paying the machine operators
to be determined, not by the time actually spent in
working each family's holdings, but by the time the
families themselves would have spent in working the
holdings.*

Here, we can see that the traditional economy (before mechanization)
still figures importantly in determining payments for a mechanized operation. Some notion of time saved is apparent here, since the payment is
not for the time the machines spend doing the work, but rather, for the
time that would have had to be used were the machines not available.
We can begin to understand some of the complexities of equivalency-
formation processes. One element clearly is time, but the time that a
family would have spent depended on its size, its age structure, the dis-

tance of its fields from the house, competing time demands, and a whole host of other factors. (See chapter 8 for an extended discussion of "Time and the Economy.")

Since, by definition, peasants exist in the rural and subordinate parts of state systems, their relationships to higher levels of the state stratification system figure importantly in equivalency-formation processes and in perceptions of them. James Scott (1976) describes occasions in which the balance of exchange (read, equivalencies) between landlords and peasants actually remains the same but is experienced as "vastly more oppressive." He says:

> Peasants in nineteenth-century China, for example, found their customary rents suddenly intolerable when the handicraft employment, which had hitherto provided a margin of safety, evaporated. Landlords were not taking any more, but the effect on subsistence of what they took was now catastrophic. The loss of common grazing land or a business depression that at one blow eliminates subsidiary employment may similarly make insupportable tenure arrangements that were in the past supportable. We must ask, as the peasant surely does, not only how much elites extract from him but what effects their claims have on the constituent elements of his life.
> (1976:178)

This last case, from Scott, brings us through a range of rural economies at different levels of state systems. We began the section on equivalencies in peasant societies with a family-based equivalency system in China—one that emphasizes the self-sufficiency of the production and consumption units. All equivalency-formation processes there are geared to the maintenance and reproduction of the extended family unit. By contrast, Scott's case, also from China but from a different century and from a different level of the state hierarchy, involves equivalency-formation processes that operate between two different levels of the state (landlords and peasants). Here, the elimination of the cushioning effects of the handicraft industry, which enabled subsistence producers to generate cash, rendered previously acceptable rents totally intolerable and repressive. Thus, it is not necessary to change the terms of the exchange, but simply its context, to alter peasant subsistence patterns or the viability of existing land tenure arrangements.

PART III. THE PROBLEMATICS OF EQUIVALENCIES AS "THE SOCIAL LIFE OF THINGS"

The problem of equivalencies has surfaced recently in exchange theory. Appadurai's (1986) edited book, *The Social Life of Things*, deals with equivalencies in terms of commodities. While many of the book's themes parallel Polanyi's discussion of equivalencies, *The Social Life of Things* (especially the chapters by Appadurai and Kopytoff) manages to inject some difficulties into the discussion of equivalencies. The difficulties concern both a confinement of the concept of equivalencies to exchange processes and a generalizing about things as commodities that blurs some critical distinctions regarding the institutional (social and cultural) contexts within which "things" are, presumably, carrying on their social lives.

APPADURAI

Appadurai (1986:13) begins by rejecting the distinction between commodities and "other sorts of things": "Let us approach commodities as things in a certain situation, a situation that can characterize many different kinds of things, at different points in their social lives." For Appadurai (1986:13), all things can be conceptualized as commodities ("commodity potential"). Appadurai breaks with the Marxian view that places commodities primarily in production processes and emphasizes commodities' "*total* trajectory from production, through exchange/distribution, to consumption" (1986:13). In fact, he does not emphasize a total trajectory of any sort; rather, he emphasizes exchange over production, proposing "that the commodity situation in the social life of any 'thing' be defined as the situation in which its exchangeability (past, present, or future) for some other thing is its socially relevant feature" (1986:13).

He proceeds to delineate the formal features of "commodity-hood." For example, what Appadurai refers to as "the commodity candidacy of things" is a conceptual feature that "refers to the standards and criteria (symbolic, classificatory, and moral) that define the exchangeability of things in any particular social and historical context" (1986:13–14). Appadurai approaches Polanyi's view of equivalencies in his discussion of "regimes of value." He (1986:14–15) deals with exchange between two culturally and institutionally disparate systems as follows:

> *We may speak, thus, of the cultural framework that defines the commodity candidacy of things, but we must bear in mind that some exchange situations, both inter- and intracultural, are characterized by a shallower set of shared standards of value than others. I therefore prefer to use the term* regimes of value, *which does* not *imply that every act of commodity exchange presupposes a complete cultural sharing of assumptions, but rather that the degree of value coherence may be highly variable from situation to situation, and from commodity to commodity. A regime of value, in this sense, is consistent with both very high and very low sharing of standards by two parties to a particular commodity exchange. Such regimes of value account for the constant transcendence of cultural boundaries by the flow of commodities, where culture is understood as a bounded and localized system of meanings.*

For Appadurai, commodities operate in a variety of social arenas, market and non-market. He is concerned with the ways in which commodities can be exchanged, even when they originate in contexts that are culturally disparate. Again, this is another way of stating what Polanyi called the problem of equivalencies. Appadurai even uses some of Polanyi's examples, such as silent trade, to illustrate the exigencies of equivalency-formation processes between two different cultural and social systems. He writes:

> *Dealings with strangers might provide contexts for the commoditization of things that are otherwise protected from commoditization. Auctions accentuate the commodity dimension of objects (such as paintings) in a manner that might well be regarded as deeply inappropriate in other contexts. Bazaar settings are likely to encourage commodity flows as domestic settings may not . . . the commodity context, as a social mat-*

ter, may bring together actors from quite different cul-
tural systems who share only the most minimal un-
derstandings (from the conceptual point of view)
about the objects in question and agree only about the
terms of trade. The so-called silent trade phenomenon
is the most obvious example of the minimal fit be-
tween the cultural and social dimensions of commodity
exchange.
(1986:15)

Appadurai then proceeds to establish a continuum based on degrees of commoditization. In a post-modern mode of analysis that places the cultural (ideological) ahead of the institutional, Appadurai argues directly with Marx:

Thus, commoditization lies at the complex intersec-
tion of temporal, cultural, and social factors. To the
degree that some things in a society are frequently to
be found in the commodity phase, to fit the require-
ments of commodity candidacy, and to appear in a
commodity context, they are its quintessential com-
modities. To the degree that many or most things in a
society sometimes meet these criteria, the society may
be said to be highly commoditized. In modern capital-
ist societies, it can safely be said that more things are
likely to experience a commodity phase in their own
career, more contexts to become legitimate commodity
contexts, and the standards of commodity candidacy to
embrace a large part of the world of things than in
non-capitalist societies. Though Marx was therefore
right in seeing modern industrial capitalism as entail-
ing the most intensely commoditized type of society,
the comparison of societies in regard to the degree of
"commoditization" would be a most complex affair
given the definitional approach to commodities taken
here . . . the capitalist mode of commoditization is
seen as interacting with myriad other indigenous so-
cial forms of commoditization.
(1986:15–16)

For Appadurai, distinctions of kind give way to considerations of degree. Presumably, one might be able to measure degrees of commoditization, but there remains the problem of how to distinguish between capitalist forms of commoditization and "indigenous social forms." Appadurai proceeds with what is essentially a formal typology of commodities, but this typology strips the goods of their institutional contexts and treats all goods in the same category as comparable. An exchangeable item in a band-level, hunting-gathering society would therefore be comparable to one in a state system. Appadurai divides commodities into four types:

> (1) commodities by destination, that is, objects intended by their procedures principally for exchange; (2) commodities by metamorphosis, things intended for other uses that are placed into the commodity state; (3) a special, sharp case of commodities by metamorphosis are commodities by diversion, objects placed into a commodity state though originally specified protected from it; (4) ex-commodities, things retrieved, either temporarily or permanently, from the commodity state and placed in some other state. (1986:16)

Despite his sidestepping of what are, to my mind, some critical distinctions having to do with the institutional arrangements within which goods are produced and distributed (exchanged), Appadurai does provide some insights into the problem of equivalencies. The most useful way to view these insights, however, is in terms of hypotheses that remain to be tested under different institutional conditions. For example, Appadurai points to the close historical links between rulers and traders, which might partly stem from their roles in the social regulation of demand. He says further:

> Whereas merchants tend to be the social representatives of unfettered equivalence, new commodities, and strange tastes, political elites tend to be the custodians of restricted exchange, fixed commodity systems, and established tastes and sumptuary customs. This antagonism between "foreign" goods and local sumptuary (and therefore political) structures is probably the

fundamental reason for the often remarked tendency of primitive societies to restrict trade to a limited set of commodities and to dealings with strangers rather than with kinsmen or friends. The notion that trade violates the spirit of the gift may in complex societies be only a vaguely related by-product of this more fundamental antagonism. In pre-modern societies, therefore, the demand for commodities sometimes reflects state-level dynamics, or, as in the kula *case, the hinge function of status competition between elite males in linking internal and external systems of exchange.*
(1986:33)

This last comment, on the Trobriand *kula*, is significant because it alludes to the political importance of the *kula* as the coordinating mechanism for a complex island resource system in which coastal and inland products must be moved where they are needed. Chiefly distribution of yams, for example, is a form of internal exchange; so are the control functions of the garden magician over agricultural production. The *kula*, on the other hand, links interior and exterior parts of different islands in the Trobriand archipelago.

KOPYTOFF

Igor Kopytoff's paper, "The Cultural Biography of Things," echoes Appadurai's argument. Bloch and Parry's (1989:15) summary is useful here: "For Kopytoff, the crucial attribute of a commodity is its exchangeability, a commodity exchange is a feature of all societies." Bloch and Parry go on to point out that the problem of equivalencies would essentially disappear in a perfectly commoditized world, because everything would be exchangeable for everything else. By the same token, logically, the opposite would be true in an uncommoditized world—for everything would be "singular, unique, and unexchangeable" (1989:15). Kopytoff does highlight the problem of equivalencies, however, by recognizing that the *sine qua non* of all economic processes is to establish some way of comparing unlike things, whether for purposes of exchanging, producing, or consuming. My difficulty with Kopytoff's argument, however, is that it is driven by the technology of exchange. For him, lower levels of exchange technology lead to lower degrees of commoditization (Kopytoff 1986:87):

> *There are no perfect commodities. On the other hand the exchange function of every economy appears to have a built-in force that drives the exchange system toward the greatest degree of commoditization that the exchange technology permits. The counterforces are culture and the individual, with their drive to discriminate, classify, compare, and sacralize. This means a two front battle for culture as for the individual—one against commoditization as a homogenizer of exchange values, the other against the utter singularization of things as they are in nature.*
>
> *In small-scale uncommercialized societies, the drive to commoditization was usually contained by the inadequacies of the technology of exchange, notably, the absence of a well-developed monetary system. This left room for a cultural categorization of the exchange value of things, usually in the form of closed exchange spheres, and it satisfied individual cognitive needs for classification. The collective cultural classification thus constrained the innate exuberance to which purely idiosyncratic and private classifications are prone.*

For Kopytoff, organizational features—institutional arrangements structuring exchange—are irrelevant.

To summarize, my main point is that the extraction of things from institutional contexts leads Appadurai and Kopytoff to make assertions that are problematical at best. To talk about the social life of things is to approach economic processes and social life in the wrong order. Things exist in social life. They operate in institutional contexts, and not, as Appadurai and Kopytoff would have it, in an institutional vacuum. Without these contexts, the very definition of exactly what constitutes a "thing" or a commodity, for that matter, is subject to question. It was these very contexts that became the focus of Polanyi's discussion of equivalencies.

Polanyi's Generic Model and Equivalencies

Polanyi's concept of equivalencies is much more fundamental and, at the same time, much more encompassing than Appadurai's and Kopytoff's notions of things as commodities. Polanyi designed the concept of equivalencies for understanding variability between and among economic processes that often crosscut systems. For Polanyi, the concept of equivalencies is critical to understanding production processes, for example, movements (locational and appropriational) of resources and people as well as of goods and things. More importantly, though, because it was conceived in the context of his generic model of the economy as a set of "instituted processes," Polanyi's concept of equivalencies permits an understanding of equivalency-formation processes in terms of the varieties of institutional arrangements that shape them. His concept of equivalencies emphasizes context, such that the complexities of equivalencies can be understood not only in pre-capitalist contexts but also in mixed economies.

Polanyi's concept of equivalencies can tackle the problem of goods (generically conceived) moving in and out of different institutional contexts without making any prior assumptions about their exchangeability or nonexchangeability. In many contexts, the goal of the operation may be to create "goods" that are nonexchangeables or noncommodities, or both. State polities often set aside both land and labor for special purposes, such that it is nonexchangeable in commodity form. The postrevolutionary Mexican *ejido* system is a case in point. These public communal lands cannot be sold; they must be allocated by local officials who are, of course, linked to higher levels of state and national government. Non-commodity forms of land are easier for elites to control. Family labor systems, such as those found in many rural agrarian parts of state systems, keep labor out of the market by resisting wage labor or by using it only to maintain the family-based subsistence system (Annis 1987; Halperin 1990). It is important to be able to distinguish (1) the contexts within which labor is exchanged for other labor, (2) the contexts within which labor is exchanged for capitalist wages, and (3) the contexts within which labor is exchanged for non-market-determined cash or goods. Each of these contexts represents different institutional arrangements with different principles for determining equivalencies. Polanyi's concept of equivalencies can accommodate these and many other kinds of variability.

PART IV. THE CONCEPT OF EQUIVALENCIES IN POLANYI'S THOUGHT

By tracing the development of the concept of equivalencies in Polanyi's thought, we can begin to understand some theoretical and practical problems facing ethnologists and archaeologists that would otherwise remain hidden. Polanyi mined many different kinds of sources for his ideas about equivalencies, among which are Malinowski's Trobriand material, social and economic theory, and data on ancient civilizations. My analysis draws on Polanyi's unpublished as well as published work.

In the course of examining Polanyi's explorations, formulations, debates with colleagues and, finally, his mature statements, we begin to understand how difficult it is to create concepts that are not culture-bound. Formulating generic concepts is a long, arduous, and tedious process of weighing ideas and generalizations against empirical data and vice versa. Polanyi's formulations of the concept of equivalencies depended upon the problem he happened to be addressing. In *The Great Transformation*, for example, the question of the origin of the market (capitalist) system dominated his discussion of equivalencies. In *Trade and Market*, his concerns were much broader and his discussions reached into ancient history, prehistory, and ethnography. This kind of breadth was possible because most of the topics covered in this 1957 book had been worked out preliminarily in his seminars at Columbia University held in the early 1950s. Members of the seminar addressed specific problems about equivalencies by collecting and developing and analyzing specific case materials from the historical, archaeological, and ethnographic records.

Equivalencies in The Great Transformation *(1944)*

The problem of equivalencies is only implicit in *The Great Transformation* (Polanyi 1944), but it was extremely important nonetheless. Polanyi's discussion of currency and the gold standard certainly involved the concept of equivalencies, even though he dealt with the problem there primarily in terms of prices and money, financial yardsticks, inflation, and real incomes. For example, early in *The*

Great Transformation, Polanyi (1944:24) wrote of the 1920s and 1930s in Europe:

> *Currency had become the pivot of national politics.*
> *Under a modern money economy nobody would fail*
> *to experience daily the shrinking or expanding of the*
> *financial yardstick; populations became currency con-*
> *scious; the effect of inflation on real income was dis-*
> *counted in advance by the masses; men and women*
> *everywhere appeared to regard stable money as the*
> *supreme need of human society.*

Polanyi did not write about the general problem of equivalencies in *The Great Transformation* but, as indicated in the passage above, he did communicate a sense of the problem and its importance for all people. He went on to talk about belief in the gold standard as a kind of religion, and in this context he hinted at a problem of equivalencies (1944:25):

> *Belief in the gold standard was the faith of the age.*
> *With some it was a naive, with some a critical, with*
> *others a satanistic creed implying acceptance in the*
> *flesh and rejection in the spirit. Yet the belief itself*
> *was the same, namely, that bank notes have value be-*
> *cause they represent gold. Whether the gold itself has*
> *value for the reason that it embodies labor, as the so-*
> *cialist held, or for the reason that it is useful and*
> *scarce, as the orthodox doctrine ran, made for once*
> *no difference.*

In concrete terms, Polanyi wrote about "equivalent amounts." The concreteness is important here, for Polanyi had not yet identified the general problem, merely the fact that equivalent amounts are transacted in the processes of bartering in primitive societies. Again, we must keep in mind that the major question for Polanyi in *The Great Transformation* was the origin and evolution of the market system. Polanyi did, however, note the workings of traditional equivalencies in Tikopia, on which he (1944:25) quoted Firth (1939:347): "As a rule, he who barters merely enters into a ready-made type of transaction in which both the objects and their equivalent amounts are given. *Utu* in the language of the Tikopia denotes such a traditional equivalent as part of reciprocal exchange." The Tikopian parties to the transaction knew how much to exchange for what because equivalents had been set by tradition. This means that people knew automatically what the proper amounts were to exchange. It also means that these amounts had been in existence for a considerable period of time and that they were, in the context of traditional Tikopia society, essentially unchanging (Polanyi 1944:61).

Equivalencies at the Columbia University Seminars

As a general concept, the idea of equivalencies first appeared in the Columbia University Seminar transcripts (1950–1953) in a discussion of the organization of the eighteenth-century trade between European trading companies and indigenous people on Africa's Guinea Coast—two very disparate cultural and economic systems. The transcripts reveal dimensions of Polanyi's concept of equivalencies that are not apparent in published form. Polanyi often worked from example to generalization and then back again. The debates sharpened the concept. They also sharpened the abilities of scholars to collect and analyze data on economies in a cross-cultural framework, i.e., non-ethnocentrically and without projecting the assumptions of the market economy onto the data.

Polanyi's concept of equivalencies was developed and used in connection with Rosemary Arnold's research on the organization of the Guinea Coast trade. Her paper, "Administered Equivalencies in the Guinea Coast Trade of the Eighteenth Century," was discussed in detail by all members of the seminar. In attendance were: Conrad Arensberg, Robert Dorfman, Leo Oppenheim, Karl Polanyi, Frank Tannenbaum, William Vickery, Walter Neale, and Harry Pearson.

Below, I have reproduced a segment of the University Seminar discussion in which Rosemary Arnold presented an alternative to market-determined equivalencies by discussing the politically administered prices in the Guinea Coast trade. The discussion reflects the rigor of the seminar and indicates how ideas were refined in the course of debate. The reader should notice that, while conventional terms such as "price" and "monopoly" were used, these terms often carried different meanings than they would in a market-system context. The discussions indicate how difficult it is for people to avoid conventional economic terminology and to substitute terms that carry fewer ethnocentric assumptions.

Conrad Arensberg's role is particularly interesting, because he was most vocal in his challenges on theoretical matters. As the primary anthropologist for the group, his questions reflected a concern for cross-cultural comparisons and for particularities of specific, culture-bound economic processes. He also pressed the group to understand the culturally specific rationales for arrangements such as administered prices.

The most important substantive point to be gleaned from these transcripts concerns the shaping of equivalencies by political institutions. The major processes forming equivalencies are administrative; in the case described by Arnold, the king and his officials set prices. These are nonmarket prices.

The following are excerpts from the transcripts of late 1953.

Arensberg begins with the term "price" and is quickly corrected by Arnold, who uses "administered trade" as a substitute of sorts. She emphasizes that prices are officially (administratively) set:

> **Professor Arensberg:** How is the native desire to set prices phrased?
>
> **Mrs. Arnold:** The whole situation reflects the administered aspect of the trade. The whole activity is politically organized and enforced. In Wydah it is the king's officials who set the price and enforce it.
>
> **Professor Arensberg:** What is there in this trade that is of theoretical interest to the economist?
>
> **Professor Tannenbaum:** Doesn't the king have a monopoly on the trade, and then could we not deal with this in terms of bilateral monopoly?
>
> **Mrs. Arnold:** It is true the king sets the "price" and here there may be much bargaining. In fact there are stories of the king coming to the ship and bargaining for weeks. But after the "price" has been fixed all may trade. Rather

than call it monopoly I would simply say it is highly administered.

The definition of trade itself is raised by Arensberg:

> **Professor Arensberg:** Why call this trade at all? Couldn't this be better understood in terms of prestige exchange between different dignitaries?
>
> The term "prestige exchange" is awkward, but it certainly is more precise.
>
> **Professor Polanyi:** But there is a real difficulty here. The king first expects a gift and he gives a countergift even if there is no bargain made. But this must be separated from the trade interest involved. On the native side there is a burning interest in imports.

Arnold talks about the relationships between administered trade and reciprocity, again with an emphasis on how economic processes are organized. The idea that there can be more than one type of administered trade is important.

> **Mrs. Arnold:** This is *one* kind of administered trade where there is also much gift and countergift. It is definitely trade, but organized in a certain way.
>
> **Professor Dorfman:** Then we can say that prestige enters the negotiations, but how much of it is shrewd bargaining?

Polanyi emphasizes the importance of "statecraft" in the formation of treaty terms.

> **Professor Polanyi:** There *is* hard bargaining over the terms of the trade treaty, and matters of prestige and status attest this, of course. But these negotiations represent highly sophisti-

cated statecraft with 1,000 years of diplomacy behind them.

In his true fashion, Arensberg brings the discussion back to theoretical issues—he seeks the explanation for such highly administered trade. It is not sufficient merely to describe it.

> **Professor Arensberg:** Isn't the theoretical problem why there is only one price here and why the whole activity is so highly administered? In other words, what is the need for fixed prices?

And now Arnold introduces the idea of equivalencies and their importance in allowing the trade to take place while at the same time keeping the internal economy (redistributive) of the kingdom in one piece.

> **Mrs. Arnold:** This is the *precondition* for trade in this situation. The equivalencies which are established by treaty after negotiations allow the trade to take place, and yet keep the internal organization of the native kingdom intact. The king's measure, e.g., is bigger than that of the commoner, and by means of such devices the revenues from the trade are distributed according to status differences . . .

Note here that Rosemary Arnold's approach to the problem of equivalencies and administered trade was very sophisticated. The number of issues she mentioned in her brief statements was considerable, and these issues anticipated problems that economic anthropologists are just beginning to address. The distinction, for example, between the exchange processes involved in the internal economy of the kingdom itself and those involved at the interface between the two different types of economies is beginning to be addressed by archaeologists, especially (Ericson and Earle 1982; Sabloff and Lamberg-Karlovsky 1975; Hirth 1984). There is also the question of how the revenues from the trade are distributed within the internally stratified kingdom according to status differences. If we think of the implications of such questions for interpreting the archaeological record, we can begin to see the need for refining concepts such as equivalencies, and, for that matter, the concept of trade itself.

Tannenbaum then introduces his concern for understanding changing equivalencies, which he refers to as changing prices. Arnold makes it clear that prices do not fluctuate, that rates are set by administrative means.

> **Professor Tannenbaum:** Do the prices ever change, and if so why? It seems to me that either there are customary prices or changing prices. In Mexico, e.g., the rate of wages has remained the same for nearly two centuries. This is customary price.

> **Mrs. Arnold:** Prices may change according to the situation, but they are not fluctuating prices. There is *a* rate set by the king.

> **Professor Polanyi:** It must be emphasized that his is a treaty price. In principle, if the treaty is made by a great king, the price is fixed forever. But, of course, if he dies, a new treaty is made with new prices, etc.

> **Mrs. Arnold:** During the treaty negotiations no goods change hands. The bargaining is over the setting of the rates, and this activity is limited to the top people in the society.

Here, Rosemary Arnold is getting at the role of elites in setting equivalencies.

> **Professor Tannenbaum:** But all of this may also be true of commercial trade, as, e.g., with cartels, etc.

Note Pearson's attention to specific words and terms.

> **Mr. Pearson:** The word "commercial" is ambiguous, for the distinction here is between market trade and administered trade. In market trade prices move the goods. A cartel arrangement would really be administered trade.

Mr. Neale: Does interior production in the native kingdom depend upon the rates or "prices?"

Mrs. Arnold: The rates of the European goods are fixed by the Europeans, and these are accepted by the natives. The haggling takes place over the assortments.

Professor Polanyi: The European trader trades on a real invoice and he makes a standard profit of 100%. The items to go into the sorting depend on native demand, but the 100% profit is not affected.

Note that Neale's question was not answered. He was interested in what determined the amounts that the natives produced and its relationship to the rates that were set by the king.

Mrs. Arnold: Operationally it works like this: if one blue baft equals two shillings, then it is equal to four shillings to the native, and this is so for each item in the sorting.

Professor Polanyi: And the actual exchange is made possible as the result of treaty-made equivalencies. Thus if a sorting, including the 100% profit, is worth four pounds, this then is equated with gold, say one ounce, which is equal to a slave. Thus the European trader cannot lose on price, but if the sorting is not correct his "customer" may go away.

Professor Tannenbaum: Suppose the European trader *has* the right cargo. Would there be any bargaining?

Professor Polanyi: I suspect that there is no real bargaining in this type of trade, but that the whole activity is determined by social custom.

Professor Dorfman: Does bargaining arise because non-treaty goods enter?

Mrs. Arnold: This is one reason for bargaining.

Professor Tannenbaum: Then, if the Europeans make a treaty with an old, well-established king, and no new items enter, the trade goes off with ease?

Professor Polanyi: Yes, I know of no delays.

Having established how goods became involved in the trade, the discussion returned to the concept of equivalencies per se, but we should notice how tempting it was for some of the participants (in the instance below, Professor Tannenbaum) to revert to defining equivalencies in negative terms. Rosemary Arnold replied with a positive definition of the situation, however.

Professor Tannenbaum: Is the concept you wish to illustrate here trade without price?

Mrs. Arnold: Not trade without price; rather trade where the equivalencies are determined not by bargaining, but set by administered means. The word equivalencies is used rather than "price" so as not to give the connotation of a supply-demand-price mechanism.

The discussion then returned to Neale's question about the relationship between the organization of external trade and the organization of the internal economy.

Professor Arensberg: Is this example of administered trade linked to a redistributive internal organization?

Mrs. Arnold: Well, this is offered only as an example of administered trade, but to understand fully we would have to look into the native society for its organization of distribution, etc.

Mr. Neale: Isn't this a supply-demand-price mechanism with bargaining after all? The native wants as much as he can get, the trader wishes to give as little as he can get by with. They know the supplies available and they strike a bargain.

Professor Polanyi: The trader is not interested in price. He makes a standard 100% profit. To be successful he must know how many pounds are equal to a slave. His interest is in turnover at standard rates, not in price. After the treaty, price became a secondary matter.

Professor Tannenbaum: Does the chief want to get as much as he can in trade?

Mrs. Arnold: Yes, in terms of goods. His interest is in kind and quality of goods. His is an import interest.

Professor Dorfman: From the native viewpoint, does the trade turn pretty much on guns?

Mrs. Arnold: Yes, although they also want cowrie.

Professor Polanyi: Without cowrie, they cannot buy on the local market.

Professor Oppenheim: Who brings the slaves to be sold?

Mrs. Arnold: In Dahomey the king's traders and big men are authorized to have slaves. One cannot trade without slaves, but you must be authorized to hold slaves. The traders may keep the items they get from trade, except the guns which go to the king.

One is struck by many things in this Seminar transcript: the diversity of topics covered, the temptations to go off in many different directions, and the dual role Polanyi played as questioner of the presenter—mainly, for facts—and as the analyst who set the discussion back on its theoretical course when it tended to wander into the realm of detail for its own sake.

What do these transcripts tell us about equivalencies? First, there is constant tension between conceiving equivalencies in a market-system framework and conceiving of them more broadly. Arensberg set the tone of the discussion by asking about how people talk about equivalencies: "How is the native desire to set prices phrased?" In other words, the question is, how do we (the analysts) or they (the indigenous peoples) develop terms that are alternative to prices. Arnold's interest in economic organization comes through, but she seems to have skirted the terminological problems by resorting to talking about economic organization when she said: "This is one kind of administered trade where there is also much gift and countergift. It is definitely trade, but organized in a certain way."

Even though Polanyi and Arnold persisted in presenting alternative forms of economic organization and, thus, alternative ways of rendering equivalencies, they had a difficult time countering the conventional economic models that are designed for understanding equivalencies in a market system. For example, Tannenbaum persisted in using the term "price" instead of equivalency, but he modified "price" with words such as "customary." Even Arensberg, the anthropologist, used "price," while Arnold maintained her use of "equivalency." In fact, ethnocentric terminology abounded. Dorfman, for example, used terms such as "negotiating" and "bargaining" in such a way as to imply individualized self-interest, to which Polanyi replied that the negotiations operated in a very deep historical context. Polanyi countered the implied ethnocentrism; he did not come up with an alternative terminology, however—a terminology that is sorely needed for economic anthropology. He said only that he suspected "that there is no real bargaining in this type of trade, but that the whole activity is determined by social custom."

What is most important to note, however, is that the discussion of equivalencies above is couched in a comparative framework. The case study presented by Arnold clearly called for alternative concepts and terms that could be generated only after additional comparable cases were analyzed.

Equivalencies *in* Trade and Market in the Early Empires *(1957)*

The problem of equivalencies became a major topic in *Trade and Market in the Early Empires* (1957). Here, Polanyi used the term equivalency as a concept, that is, as a general term. "Price" was now only "that form of equivalency which is characteristic of economies that are integrated through (market) exchange" (Polanyi 1957:268–269).

A rather abstract but brilliantly stated summary of the University Seminar's discussion of Rosemary Arnold's materials appears in Polanyi's discussion of administered trade in his famous essay, "The Economy as Instituted Process." I reproduce the paragraph below in full because it is equally about trade and about equivalencies, or what Polanyi referred to as "rates" or proportions of units exchanged. It also contains other elements, such as a discussion of the relationship among trade, equivalencies, and the internal domestic economy. Polanyi emphasizes the political nature of equivalencies:

> *Administered trade has its firm foundation in treaty relationships that are more or less formal. Since on both sides the import interest is as a rule determinative, trading runs through government-controlled channels. The export trade is usually organized in a similar way. Consequently, the whole of trade is carried on by administrative methods. This extends to the manner in which business is transacted, including arrangements concerning "rates" or proportions of the units exchanged; port facilities; weighing, checking of quality; the physical exchange of goods; storage; safekeeping; the control of the trading personnel; regulation of "payments"; credits; price differentials. Some of these matters would naturally be linked up with the collection of the export goods and the redistributive sphere of the domestic economy. The goods that are mutually imported are standardized in regard to quality and package, weight, and other easily ascertainable criteria. Only such "trade goods" can be traded. Equivalencies are set out in simple unit relations; in principle, trade is one-to-one.*
> (1957:268–269)

In three subsequent paragraphs, however, Polanyi extended the concept of equivalencies considerably beyond that of the University Seminar. He related this concept to forms of economic integration and provided a considerable number of examples from different kinds of economies. Polanyi used a discussion of price as a form of equivalency as a starting point for discussing equivalencies in general. He gave considerable importance to the element of quantification and to the relationship between the form of equivalency and the form of economic integration:

> "Price" is the designation of quantitative ratios between goods of different kinds, effected through barter or higgling-haggling. It is that form of equivalency which is characteristic of economies that are integrated through exchange. But equivalencies are by no means restricted to exchange relations.
> (1957:268–269)

Having dispensed with equivalencies under a market exchange form of integration, i.e., price, Polanyi went on to discuss relationships between redistribution and forms of equivalency:

> Under a redistributive form of integration equivalencies are also common. They designate the quantitative relationship between goods of different kinds that are acceptable in payment of taxes, rents, dues, fines, or that denote qualifications for a civic status dependent on a property census. Also the equivalency may set the ratio at which wages or rations in kind can be claimed, at the beneficiary's choosing. The elasticity of a system of staple finance—the planning, balancing, accounting—hinges on this device. The equivalency here denotes not what should be given for another good, but what can be claimed instead of it.
> (1957:269)

Polanyi's lapse into using the economists' term "elasticity" in the above is a surprise, given his quest for more generic terms. We can see here the origins of Earle and D'Altroy's discussion of staple finance in Peru. We can also see that Polanyi's discussion of redistributive equivalencies leaves plenty of room for elaboration. His discussion of equivalencies under reciprocity follows after that of redistribution. Reciprocity as a form of integration received short attention in connection with forms of equivalency:

> *Under reciprocative forms of integration, again,*
> *equivalencies determine the amount that is "adequate"*
> *in relation to the symmetrically placed party. Clearly,*
> *this behavioral context is different from either ex-*
> *change or redistribution.*
> (1957:269)

Following this relatively simple discussion of relationships between forms of economic integration and forms of equivalencies, Polanyi switched gears into an historical/evolutionary frame. His framework now contained several more variables, some operating in several dimensions (layers of equivalencies). He wanted to examine the relationships between different kinds of equivalencies as they are associated with different forms of economic integration as both of these dimensions change over time. "Price systems, as they develop over time, may contain layers of equivalencies that historically originated under different forms of integration" (1957:269).

He continued by providing some examples that indicate relationships between forms of integration and forms of equivalencies. He showed that redistribution shapes equivalencies in certain definite ways in different historical and cultural contexts. Polanyi jumped easily from Greece in Hellenistic times to the Bible, and to Soviet redistributive equivalencies. In all of these discussions, what Polanyi called an "institutional history" (the way equivalencies have changed as their institutional arrangements change) was of critical importance. He begins by asserting an historical connection between redistributive equivalencies and prices in Hellenistic marketplaces. He also traces Soviet redistributive equivalencies to their origins in nineteenth-century world markets. Thus, he does not argue for non-market forms of equivalencies necessarily preceding market (system) forms.

> *Hellenistic market prices show ample evidence of*
> *having derived from redistributive equivalencies of*
> *the cuneiform civilizations that preceded them. The*

thirty pieces of silver received by Judas as the price of
a man for betraying Jesus was a close variant of the
equivalency of a slave as set out in Hammurabi's
Code some 1,700 years earlier. Soviet redistributive
equivalencies, on the other hand, for a long time ech-
oed nineteenth century world market prices. These,
too, in their turn, had their predecessors. Max Weber
remarked that for lack of a costing basis Western capi-
talism would not have been possible but for the medi-
eval network of statuted and regulated prices, custom-
ary rents, etc., a legacy of guild and manor. Thus
price systems may have an institutional history of
their own in terms of the types of equivalencies that
entered into their making.

This last sentence is particularly important because it raises the question of the origins of price systems. By writing of types of equivalencies
that contributed to the "making" of price systems, Polanyi gave us a
sense of one type of equivalence changing into another until price systems were formed. Equivalencies, then, are not static entities, nor do
they simply fluctuate by going up or down. Rather, they evolve in complex ways, not always in a unilineal fashion. The form equivalencies take
may become sidetracked, diverted, or arrested for awhile. Forms may
also disappear for a period of time and then resurface.

Types of Equivalencies: The Livelihood of Man (1977)

Chapter 6 of *The Livelihood of Man* (1977) is
"Equivalencies in Archaic Societies." There, Polanyi developed a typology of forms of equivalencies. He assumed that economies, as we
know them historically and ethnographically, have used many forms of
equivalencies, and he proceeded to create a way of analyzing the wide
"scope of equivalencies" (1977:64). Polanyi created two types: (1) substitutive equivalencies and (2) exchange equivalencies. Empirically, the
two types are related. Analytically, they can be separated.

Substitutive equivalencies indicate how much of one kind of good
may be given in lieu of goods of another kind. Polanyi's example was
that of "large-scale staple finance," in which "an exchange system of

goods is arranged between central government and citizens" (1977:64). Here, Polanyi was referring to all cases of large-scale staple finance and was creating a formal model (set of propositions) to indicate how equivalencies must work in these systems. Polanyi defined the common feature of all these cases: "there is a need for reckoning with goods of different kinds, replacing one by the other or, as the saying goes, 'adding up apples and pears.' Established ratios are the only possible device for these operations" (1977:64). His examples included the taxation systems of the ancient Near East, in which payment of a fixed amount per unit of land and the need for different items (barley, oil, wine, wool) to be substitutable for one another was very important. Systems of taxation in which taxes were paid in kind could not rigidly insist on payment in definite produce. They had to establish ratios of goods that were substitutable for other goods. In a summary statement, Polanyi said of systems of state finance: "Hence, at the basis of state finance we find a system of equivalencies that allows for the complexities of taxation with tithing, along with the fixing of ratios by means of a point system" (1977:65).

Below, Polanyi (1977:65) uses the term "administrative exchange" to indicate the strong role of the state in setting equivalencies:

> An administrative exchange of goods between farmers and palace was practiced in Babylonia, for example. From a document concerning cancellation of debts under Hammurabi it appears that farmers were free to list surplus produce they wished to exchange against palace goods. These goods might be assumed to be either foreign imports or tax goods from other regions or even manufactures of the palace. Inevitably, much uncertainty attached to the transaction before it could be carried into effect. The total value of the goods offered by the farmer and those received in exchange from the palace would eventually have to be equal. . . . To the mediating official would fall the intricate task of adjusting the palace goods to the goods desired by the farmer. . . . All in all then, when there was such exchange between the government and farmers, substitution between the items on either side's list was regulated through equivalencies. On both sides, "apples and pears" would have to be added up before totals could be equated.

For Polanyi, substitutive equivalencies were validated by custom or law, not by the forces of supply and demand, for the concept of substitutive equivalencies was designed to analyze processes (transactions)—in this case, administrative exchange in "marketless economies."

Polanyi's discussion of exchange equivalencies is somewhat difficult to decipher but, from his examples, it does appear that exchange equivalencies involve transactions between individuals. Here, the critical distinction for Polanyi seems to have been that between "administrative exchange," which is compulsory, and ordinary transactions, which are voluntary, between equals or at least people who interact regularly. Polanyi (1977:68) used the peasant-farmer as an example of an individual economic actor who might be likely to use exchange equivalencies:

> *Exchange equivalencies are of special importance for the independent peasant farmer: they help to tide him over in an emergency whether the neighbor is bound to lend him the necessaries he needs or to exchange them against the equivalent.*

In the above passage, Polanyi is using exchanges between neighbors to illustrate two things. First, as I have noted above, he is talking about two individuals who can engage in one or several transactions involving what Polanyi called substitutive equivalencies. Secondly, he is saying that there are two possible transactions between these neighbors, both of which can involve substitutive equivalencies. One possible transaction involves a loan of the needed items from one neighbor to another— presumably one that will be repaid in some form. The other possible transaction is one in which one neighbor provides the necessary goods to the other in exchange for equivalent goods (or even labor). Polanyi elaborates:

> *In case of a crop failure or other emergency, a house- holder could thus count on his neighbor to supply him with a minimum of the necessaries, though no more. The transaction is incumbent on the latter: 1. in re- gard to all the basic staples, 2. to the amount neces- sary in the circumstances, but definitely no more, 3. against an equivalent amount of other staples, and 4. with the exclusion of credit.*
> (1977:69)

It is relatively rare to find discussions of the workings of exchange equivalencies in the ethnographic literature on peasants, but anyone who has lived and worked in such cultures has seen them going on—probably on a daily basis. Food handed out (usually at the back door) by people occupying higher rungs of the village stratification system to those less well-off is an extremely common occurrence in peasant villages. Storekeepers who provide people with goods in exchange for payment (in money, in kind, or in labor) at some future time are engaging in transactions involving exchange equivalencies.

Polanyi summarized his discussion of substitutive and exchange equivalencies as follows:

> But the range of equivalencies is then by no means limited to goods such as foodstuffs, precious metals, or raw materials. Any dealing in the sphere of the substantive economy that involved what we would regard as a transaction stood under the law of equivalence. Only equivalents were exchangeable, whether the notion referred to land or labor, goods or money, or a combination of these; whether it involved ownership or use only, or even conditional items such as surpluses still to be achieved.
> (1977:67–68)

This was one of Polanyi's most general statements on equivalencies. In it, we can see that the concept of equivalencies was meant not only for the so-called world of goods, but for the world of work in general and of production processes in particular. Thus, equivalencies are just as important for discussions of land tenure, for example, as they are for discussions of money stuffs. Furthermore, an understanding of equivalency-formation processes can help identify different forms of land tenure, from land that is available to producers only for use to land that is alienable as private property.

In a section in *The Livelihood of Man* called "The Sociology of Equivalencies," Polanyi dealt with the question of "the manner in which equivalencies were established and formulated." He cited Thurnwald (1932) and said that, in primitive societies, the equivalency is mostly a matter of custom and tradition (1977:70). Polanyi did not stop at this, however. He said that the problem of origins "includes the types of transactions that assume equivalency and the manner in which the equivalency is institutionalized." His example was from Nuzi society of fifteenth century B.C., in which one of the main transactions was

> the free exchange of the use of land, persons, cattle, money, vehicles, or other goods, against any of these goods, on the assumption that the use of the two parties can be regarded as equal. Ownership is not transferred; use alone is. Neither party is supposed to make a profit. In principle, the exchange, since it refers to use only, is limited in time.
> (1977:70–71)

Polanyi then proceeded to discuss the concept of "just price" as an equivalency and as a precursor of price. He began with a very general statement that sounds tautological but which is, in fact, only a way of saying that equivalencies are socially constructed and formed and that they reproduce themselves: "Equivalencies between the units of different goods were meant to express proportions that both resulted from the conditions existing in that society and contributed to the maintenance of those conditions." He became more specific:

> Far from being the expression of a pious hope or of an uplifted thought irrelevant to "economic realities," as the orthodox economic classics tended to believe, the just price was an equivalency, the actual amount of which was determined either by municipal authority or by the actions of the guildsmen in the market, but in neither case according to determinants relevant to the concrete social situation. The guildsmen who refused to sell below a price that would endanger the standard of his colleagues, and equally refused to accept a price that would secure for him a revenue higher than that approved by his colleagues, cooperated to create the "just price" as effectively as the municipal authority that could be called upon to fix the price directly in order to uphold these very principles.
> (1977:71–72)

SUMMARY

As we can see from the foregoing discussion, much of what Polanyi had to say about the concept of equivalencies was suggestive of further elaboration and analysis in the context of the full range of institutional arrangements that organize economic processes. Polanyi's project was, in the main, historical. That is, Polanyi was interested in the role of equivalents—more precisely, in my terms, equivalency-formation processes—in the emergence of the supply-demand market system. He constantly juxtaposed non-market and market arrangements:

> *Non-market trade—this is the crucial point—is in all essentials different from market trade. This applies to personnel, goods, prices, but perhaps most emphatically to the nature of the trading activity itself. The traders of the karum of Kanish were not merchants in the sense of persons making a living out of the profit derived from buying and selling . . . [they] were traders by status, as a rule by virtue of descent or early apprenticeship, in other cases maybe, by appointment. . . . The goods were trade goods—storable, interchangeable and standardized . . . Apart from standard cloths, the chief staples were metals—probably silver, copper, lead and tin, all goods reckoned according to their silver equivalent. Silver, besides functioning as a standard, was also, up to a point, a means of payment. The role of gold was much more restricted in both these uses. "Prices" took the form of equivalencies established by authority of custom, statute or proclamation . . . In principle there was always a "price," i.e., the equivalency at which the trader both bought and sold. But rules regarding the application of equivalencies were hardly the same for monopoly goods, consignment ware and "free" goods. The numerous qualifying adjectives which accompany the term equivalency refer to the various rules and their effects. The equivalency for copper, "a monopoly," was fixed by treaty over a long term. Copper mining, as organized by the natives, would in-*

*volve assurances by their chiefs that at least a part of
the equivalencies, presumably in goods coveted by the
people, would be forthcoming in definite amounts. As
to consignment ware, mainly fine cloths manufactured
in Assur and imported lead (or tin?), prices were
similarly fixed and the goods bought and sold at that
"price." "Prices" for free goods are especially important, for eventual departures towards market trading
were likely to originate from here; in other words, the
present meaning of "price" might have developed
from equivalencies for "free" goods.*
(1957:20)

In many respects, Polanyi's discussion of equivalencies was profound
in its breadth of vision; in other respects, however, it was schematic,
incomplete, or wrong. His discussion of the sociology of equivalencies,
for example, began with the manner in which equivalencies were established in primitive society. Matters of custom and tradition were said to
be primary, and the manner in which the equivalency was institutionalized was central. He introduced confusion when (1977:63) he talked
about equivalencies as institutions, however. Equivalencies are not institutions of any sort. Rather, they are a result, an outcome, of different kinds of institutional arrangements. Indeed, it is difficult to discuss
equivalencies in an institutional vacuum, that is, outside of specific institutional contexts.

What Polanyi was really trying to achieve was an understanding of the
relationships between forms of equivalency and forms of economic integration—the latter being the central concept for understanding types
and varieties of economic institutions. He was interested in the internal
organization of economies in the context of his discussion of equivalencies. He was also, as the seminar discussion surrounding Rosemary
Arnold's material indicates, interested in the problems of establishing
equivalencies between two societies whose internal economies are organized very differently. In short, he was interested in how equivalencies are established in trade relationships. Polanyi used his discussion of
equivalencies to describe different kinds of transactions and the nature of
economic institutions, including a rather elaborate discussion of credit institutions among equals and among superiors and subordinates in local-
level stratification systems (1977:68–69). His major point was that equivalencies operate differently under different institutional arrangements:

The concept of price, then, might in comparative economies be conveniently replaced by the term "equivalency," which is neither restricted to market rates, nor does it imply fluctuation. While all prices are then equivalents, not all equivalents are prices. Also, equivalents were not primarily intended to express rates of exchange, but rather of substitution—a very different matter.
(POLANYI N.D.A.:16–21)

Establishing prices by means of a supply-demand mechanism is one way of solving the problem of equivalencies, but not the only way. Prices are a kind of equivalency. In fact, Polanyi and his colleagues created the word "equivalencies" to be used instead of "price." The important point is that the problem of equivalencies is universal, in that it affects all economic processes from the marshaling of productive resources, such as labor, to the distribution and consumption of the products of labor. This is true whether we are dealing with the sharing of meat among band-level hunter-gatherers, or with the extraction of surplus from workers in highly stratified state-level societies. In 1958, Polanyi wrote: "Neither reciprocity nor distribution is workable without 'rates' [equivalencies] that are valid as between different goods" (n.d.b.:9, "Money and Related Institutions in Early Societies" Box 10; brackets mine).

The implications of Polanyi's notions of equivalencies are wide-ranging. They have particular immediacy and currency in light of the resurgence and elaboration of informal economies and modes of resistance to capitalism in post-industrial states.

Five

HOUSEHOLDING: RESISTANCE AND LIVELIHOOD IN RURAL ECONOMIES

Householding is one of Polanyi's most important and, potentially, most widely applicable concepts. As a form of economic integration, it has the capacity to deal with complex economic processes and combinations of economic processes, especially with the articulation of different institutional arrangements organizing units of production and consumption in stratified, state-level societies— pre-industrial, industrial, and post-industrial. Householding is not designed for small-scale economies in so-called primitive, stateless societies. Rather, the concept is designed potentially to handle complexity, change, and resistance to political and economic elites in cultural systems where there are constant tensions between the demands of elites and the material and cultural requirements of people who stand on the lower rungs of state stratification systems. Examining the relationships between Polanyi's concept of householding and contemporary anthropological thinking about forms of colonialism, informal economies, and peasant resistance reveals aspects of complex economic organization that otherwise might remain hidden. I have in mind, specifically, the various non-capitalist forms of economic organization that persist and grow in the midst of capitalist and post-capitalist economies.

The concept of householding and its relationship to the organization of rural economies in state systems has not been well understood. In comparison to the concepts of reciprocity, redistribution, and market exchange, householding has received relatively little attention from scholars interested in the organization of economic processes. The term itself is unfortunate because the relationships between householding, as a form of economic integration, and actual households is highly problematical.

As shown in the analysis below, householding is not confined to households, nor does it require them.

Polanyi's published work shows that he equivocated on whether householding was to be considered a form of economic integration. Householding figures importantly as a form of integration in *The Great Transformation* (Polanyi 1944), but it drops out of *Trade and Market in the Early Empires* (Polanyi et al. 1957). Polanyi's unpublished writing, however, shows that householding is an extremely important form of economic integration that has the capacity to combine market and non-market forms of economic organization as well as different non-market forms that operate at various tiers of state stratification systems.

In this chapter I will argue that:

1. householding is best understood as a model with formal properties;

2. as a strategy of self-sufficiency and family autonomy, householding is the primary form of economic integration for working class people in a region of northeastern Kentucky;

3. within and, most probably, among cultural systems, householding takes many forms and involves different kinds and combinations of institutional arrangements, capitalist and non-capitalist;

4. the forms and units involved in householding change historically and geographically in relationship to urbanization and proximity to urban centers;

5. householding is the primary means for rurally based, three-generational extended families to resist domination by and capitulation to industrial capitalism in the northeastern Kentucky region analyzed here.

The analysis presented here should be regarded as a case study in householding, or perhaps as one of many possible test cases of the concept of householding. It may be that this analysis is applicable to rural people in many nation states, as long as they can sustain direct, long-term access to the means of production and as long as the extended family remains intact. In short, householding is a concept with great comparative potential.

Householding and the Substantive Economy

Polanyi defines the substantive economy as the material-means provisioning process in cultural systems (Polanyi 1944, Ch. 4; Polanyi et al. 1957, Ch. 13). Since all societies "possess" economies, the central question for Polanyi is to understand the forms that economies take in various times and places, that is, both historically and evolutionarily. The key concepts in Polanyi's generic model of the economy are those of locational and appropriational movements—briefly, "changes of place," as in the physical movements of goods or labor from one geographical area to another (locational movements), and "changes of hands," as in transfers of rights to land or labor (appropriational movements). Appropriational movements may or may not involve physical (locational) movements. In the example of land transfers, there is no locational movement. Locational movements are certainly more visible, and, often, more dramatic in that long distances may be covered or elaborate ceremonials may be involved, but they do not necessarily imply a change in appropriational movements (Halperin 1989). The important point is that, together, these two kinds of abstractly conceived movements constitute all of the logically possible kinds of movements in any and all economies.

HOUSEHOLDING AS A MODEL

Polanyi's forms of economic integration—reciprocity, redistribution, market exchange, and householding—are patterns of locational and appropriational movements. These forms must be understood as models with formal characteristics: *symmetry*, in the case of reciprocity; *centrality*, in the case of redistribution; *random movements* by pairs of buyers and sellers, in the case of market exchange; and *circularity*, in the case of householding. That the forms of integration were intended by Polanyi to operate as models has not been recognized sufficiently in the literature of economic anthropology. By "model" here, I refer to a set or sets of idealizations. The process of model-building involves establishing a series of expectations postulated under known or assumed conditions and then using these expectations as basic guidelines against which the data at hand can be measured. Formal models enable the analyst to compare an artificial or an ideal order with a set of facts. Of course, these models also shape the kinds of facts we collect (Plattner 1975).

The model of householding can be further elaborated if householding is understood as the provisioning of a group by means of circular flows of resources, goods, and services. Goods and services move in ways that articulate different patterns of economic organization, that is, different economic institutions. For example, people work in factories for wage labor, they work for direct subsistence on their own family farms, and they bring goods produced in family gardens to sell in flea markets, where they also buy and sell used goods from a variety of sources (family goods, garage sale items, goods from other marketplaces) alongside of goods that are produced by the capitalist factory system and bought by vendors as seconds or rejects.

Family goods are themselves of different varieties. Some are pure gifts, given freely with no expectation of a return; other family goods are given (usually by older to younger family members) with the expectation that a portion of the selling price will be returned to the giver. In any case, goods move among members of a family network rather than back and forth between two points (reciprocity) or in and out from center to periphery (redistribution). It will be seen that householding, like the other forms of economic integration, must be understood as a principle with formal features. It is in this formal aspect that householding, along with the other forms of integration, must be understood as a model. The purpose of the model is to understand a certain range of variability in economic processes. There are many forms of householding, just as there are many kinds of reciprocity, redistribution, and market exchange.

The actual construction of formal models, however, cannot be done responsibly and usefully without reference to some set of data, large or small, quantitative or qualitative or both. There are highly complex (feedback) relationships between model and data, which require appropriate modifications in concepts and data as part of the critical process of model formation and data analysis. The important point is that, if models are built in a vacuum, they may be logically consistent and elegantly parsimonious, but they may also contain unwarranted, or downright wrong, assumptions, concepts, and variables (Kaplan 1968; Halperin 1988).

All models must set priorities among features and variables. For the model of householding, the coordination, timing, and scheduling of economic activities (production, distribution, and consumption) by people who move in and out of differently organized economic institutions are the key features of the model. In the Kentucky case analyzed below, coordination involves dealing with seasonal cycles and with cycles of employment and unemployment, as well as with the vagaries of state supports and subsidies for the prices of cash crops. Coordination requires dealing with a variety of institutional arrangements in state systems: market and non-market, rural and urban, domestic and public, agrarian and industrial, formal and informal, etc. Regionally based kin networks are the units of analysis.

THE CONCEPT OF HOUSEHOLDING IN POLANYI'S WRITING

In *The Great Transformation*, Polanyi (1944:53) defines householding as follows: "The third principle, which was destined to play a big role in history and which we will call the principle of householding consists in production for one's own use," that is, "production for a person's or a group's own sake." According to Polanyi, householding appears historically after reciprocity and redistribution but before market exchange (price-setting markets). Polanyi says in *The Great Transformation* that householding, as "the practice of catering for the needs of one's household, becomes a feature of economic life only on a more advanced level of agriculture; however, even then it has nothing in common either with the motive of gain or with the institutions of markets" (1944:53). We have only to read between the lines to discern that Polanyi conceived householding to operate in complex sociocultural contexts ("a more advanced level of agriculture") with, we can assume, relatively high population densities and complex sociopolitical structures. Yet, householding is primarily a non-capitalist form of economic integration, precisely because it has "nothing in common either with the motive of gain or with the institutions of markets." Notice, however, that Polanyi does not preclude the possibility of householding's operating within capitalist contexts.

Polanyi goes on to describe householding in rather abstract, formal, and general terms, that is, as a pattern that can be organized by different arrangements:

> *Its pattern is the closed group, whether the very different entities of the family or the settlement or the manor formed the self-sufficient unit, the principle was invariably the same, namely, that of producing and storing for the satisfaction of the wants of the members of the group.*
> (POLANYI 1944:53)

The institutional arrangements that organize householding can be as varied as the patriarchal family, the village settlement, the seigneurial manor, the Roman *familia*, the South Slav *zadruga*, or the average peasant-holding of Western Europe. In fact, Polanyi (1944:53) emphasizes that "the nature of the institutional nucleus is indifferent." The internal organization of the group does not matter, and the overall context within which the group operates is also variable. As we will see below, in the Kentucky case, householding as a form of economic integration operates in both community and regional contexts.

It is in Polanyi's unpublished writing, however, that the concept of householding is most clear. Householding is the key form of economic integration for the rural parts of state systems. "Historically, the third form of integration (after reciprocity and redistribution) to come into dominance is householding . . . it is the background of rural organization" (Polanyi n.d.c.). By rural organization, Polanyi means the rural parts of state systems.

Formally speaking, householding is not, then, redistribution writ small, for there is no requirement of centrality. Polanyi clearly differentiates the formal features of householding from those of reciprocity and redistribution. In fact, he emphasizes the formal features of householding for the precise purpose of setting it off from reciprocity and redistribution:

> Householding as a form of integration of economic activity embodies the principle that action is directed by the interest of the group which runs the household. How egalitarian or oligarchic, enlightened or narrow minded the outlook of the planner is indifferent. We are stressing here the formal characteristic of the method of integration which is essentially different from that of reciprocity or redistribution.
> (POLANYI N.D.C.)

In some contexts, supply-demand markets may be involved in the larger economy within which the group is operating. In others, a state-run socialist economy may be dominant, although these are becoming more and more rare in the contemporary world economy. Nonetheless, householding is a form of integration capable of coordinating capitalist and non-capitalist provisioning processes for the benefit of groups at various tiers of state stratification systems, regardless of how the state or the local economies within it are organized.

The problematical relationship between the principle of householding and actual households deserves some mention. The operation of the principle does not require actual households. It may, for example, involve several individuals or pairs of individuals as well as pairs or groups of households. Concomitantly, actual households may or may not be provisioned by the principle of householding. As we will see, the model of householding allows us to understand the limits of households as provisioning units (Netting et al., 1984; Parry 1989:85).

Householding in Northeastern Kentucky

In this section I make explicit the concept of householding as it will apply to the northeastern Kentucky case analyzed below. In order to do this, the historical and social organizational contexts within which householding has functioned must be given some attention.

Historically, rural Appalachian economies have consisted of sets of family-based subsistence farms designed to provision the family group with the material means necessary for their survival. From the time of Euro-American settlement, the primary units involved in householding have been family-based subsistence farms. In 1880, Appalachia contained a greater concentration of noncommercial family farms than any other area in the nation (Precourt 1983:91; Batteau 1983). The primary purpose of these family farms was to meet the direct consumption needs of the family, not to generate a profit. When goods were sold by family members, the aim was to use the cash to maintain the family farm and to sustain the family unit.

While householding operated in rural Appalachia within both large and small units that had various residence and settlement patterns, in different environments, mountainous and nonmountainous, the aim of householding remained the maintenance of the family. Scholars (Eller 1982; Billings et al. 1986) have emphasized different elements of householding. For example, Eller's description of householding in the mountains emphasizes self-sufficiency and the dominance of family units, meaning that householding was the principle organizing the family economy at the local levels of the state system. The landed base of householding is also clear; private property in the form of land is the key productive resource for the family economy. The other productive resource is family labor. Eller (1982:92) writes:

Each mountain homestead functions as a nearly self-contained economic unit, depending upon the land and

the energy of a single family to provide food, cloth-
ing, shelter, and the other necessities of life . . . the
family not only functioned as a self-contained eco-
nomic unit, but it dominated the economic system it-
self. The mountain farm was a family enterprise, the
family being the proprietor, the laborer, and manager:
the satisfaction of the needs of the family was the sole
objective of running the farm.

Field research in this northeastern Kentucky region began in 1983 and continued until 1988. The research area consisted of ten counties, seven Deep Rural ("the country" in folk terms) and three Shallow Rural (a rural part of the region between "the country" and "the city," with no folk term of its own). The agrarian holdings in this region are, and have always been, small. During the period of fieldwork, only 2 percent of the farms in the region were larger than 500 acres. The average farm size in the region is 121 acres. The agrarian units are themselves diverse, however. Some are small, family farms with a few acres devoted to cash crops (primarily burley tobacco) and one to two acres planted in livestock feed. Other agrarian units are simply households located on small holdings with subsistence gardens. Still others are combinations of farms, gardens, and workshops (welding, crafts, furniture, appliance repairs, etc.). The agrarian holdings provide the baselines from which people move back and forth from their wage labor jobs in factories in the Shallow Rural part of the region.

The Shallow Rural is the most analytically problematic, as well as the most interesting, part of the region. It is an unstudied, unnamed, and uncategorized gray area between country and city that contains an intricate mix of livelihood strategies. A rotating, periodic marketplace system and the factories for temporary wage labor are located in the Shallow Rural; so, too, are small farms and rural homesteads with gardens. This Shallow Rural middle ground also exhibits a complex infrastructure of highways, as well as considerable numbers of factories, shopping malls, housing developments, and mobile home parks. People who live in the Shallow Rural are migrants from the Deep Rural parts of the region. A person who speaks "country English" is not at all conspicuous in the Shallow Rural; in the city, he or she may be labeled a "hillbilly." By the same token, speakers of "city English" are conspicuous as outsiders in the factories and marketplaces of the Shallow Rural parts of the region.

In the Shallow Rural, the pattern of householding utilizes three settings, each of which constitutes a different set of livelihood strategies, with different resources, labor requirements, and organizational principles. These three settings are: (1) residential settings such as hamlets, which are the sites of small farms and rural homesteads with subsistence gardens; (2) the periodic marketplace system, which is an arena for generating cash as well as a source of inexpensive necessities ranging from food and clothing to farm tools and garden equipment; and (3) the wage labor sector. This latter consists primarily of light industry factories, most of which are located in an industrial park in the Shallow Rural, but also includes work in fast foods or in small shops.

Taken together, these three economic arenas provision the three-generational family networks. The arenas themselves are complex, and the fact that people use all three arenas and frequently move between arenas simply points to the intricacy of the system of householding. While the gardens clearly represent a non-capitalist form of economic organization using exclusively family labor, the marketplaces represent a mix of capitalist and non-capitalist elements. Family labor is used to work the vendors' booths, but the goods sold in the marketplaces enter by a variety of capitalist and non-capitalist paths. Some of the new goods are simply the seconds and castoffs of the capitalist system, for example, Levi jeans with uneven stitching or bottles of salad dressing with dates that have expired. Other goods sold in marketplaces are the products of non-capitalist productive relations of many sorts, from old clothing to the craft products of unpaid family labor.

The rotating marketplace system is extensive and elaborate. Major markets are quite large; one is now located in a former tobacco warehouse. These major markets, of which there are three in the region, are located as far apart as fifty miles along an interstate highway. Major markets meet only on Saturdays and Sundays; other markets meet once a week. Intermediate and minor markets tend to cluster near major markets and are often accompanied by auctions. These smaller markets are located on county and local roads.

DEEP RURAL: COMMUNITY-BASED HOUSEHOLDING

The Deep Rural is the area which the folk in northeastern Kentucky call "the country." Brick County, a typical Deep Rural county, had a total population of approximately 7,500 in 1985. Its county seat had 700 people, down from 800 in 1952, when the county population was 8,468. Soil is fertile; bottom land is, of course, the most fertile. In this county, the chief cash income is from burley tobacco, but cash can also be generated in other ways—beef cattle, sheep, poultry sales, and dairy farms. Enough hay is grown to satisfy local needs. Ninety-six percent of the 131,840 acres (206 sq. miles) in Brick County is farm land. In 1950 there were a total of 1,364 farms averaging 92.8 acres. In this same year, there were approximately 225 farm wage laborers in the county and 500 unpaid farm family workers. By 1978, there were only 803 farms.

The Deep Rural parts of the region are the locations of family land for the small subsistence farms with substantial kitchen gardens. People own family land in the manner of a landowning peasantry. Land is private property, and land ownership confers independence as well as a sense of place. Owning land renders a landowner "beholden to no one" (Foster 1988:169). Burley tobacco is the major cash crop, but all cash cropping in the region is done on an extremely small scale. In recent years, falling tobacco subsidies at the federal level and rising costs of mechanization have caused people to pursue other cash-generating strategies.

Householding in the Deep Rural takes the following form: people marshal their family resources—primarily land and labor, but also tools, information, transportation, goods, and services—to piece together a livelihood that serves to maintain the members of the family network. The Deep Rural part of the region contains communities that are much like those described for mountain areas of classic Appalachia where coal mining was absent. The famous "Beech Creek" community in southeastern Kentucky is a case in point (Brown 1952; Schwarzweller et al. 1971). Small, family-run subsistence farms, operating relatively self-sufficiently, with the large majority of agricultural products consumed by the producers is the dominant pattern (Schwarzweller et al. 1971; also see Pearsall 1959; Stephenson 1968; Bryant 1981, 1983).

Householding operates primarily in community contexts in the Deep Rural. Homesteads composed of several households develop out of extended-family life course patterns. As children marry, ideally they establish households on the family land. All children inherit on an equal basis; it is not uncommon, however, for a brother or sister to sell his or her parcel of land to a sibling. Households rarely contain two generations of adults (Foster 1988:55).

Before 1950, most families in the Deep Rural were quite large. A typical nuclear family with four to six children would commonly reside in the same hamlet with relatives on both the mother's and the father's side.

These residents of a typical hundred-acre farm raised almost everything that they consumed. Butchering five hogs in fall to tide the family over until spring was not uncommon. Entire families worked in the fields hoeing tobacco, tending vegetables, and minding stock. Adult men and women participated in farm tasks, depending upon the season. Elderly people and children participated as well. The women of the household mended, washed, and ironed clothes, using homemade starch.

The fields of family members often were adjacent to one another. Work arrangements involved passing tasks around from one family member to another, depending upon the task and according to the age and sex of the family members. Whether the tasks involved the planting, weeding, and harvesting of crops or household maintenance and child care, everyone—male and female, young and old—contributed some work. Traditionally, extended families gathered after church for Sunday dinner. While these dinners were primarily social events, they also provided the opportunity to coordinate labor and to arrange for goods and services to be distributed among the family members. For example, during the highly labor-intensive tobacco harvest season, relatives freely offered labor to one another.

Although nuclear families usually maintained separate households, the economic support provided by relatives was essential for the maintenance of these households. Kin were expected to help one another as needed. When people required cash in addition to that generated by the sale of cash crops, they sold garden products or else they sold their labor by working at some form of off-farm employment. Hiring oneself out as a farmhand and performing odd jobs (repairs, minor building projects, etc.) were some of the ways people contributed additional cash to the general maintenance of their families. People had multiple sources of food as well as multiple sources of cash in the Deep Rural. Such sources included the gardens and livestock of nuclear families, as well as those of members of their kin network. The hunting of deer, rabbit, and quail and the gathering of nuts and berries in season were also significant sources of food. Cash sources included earnings from the sale of cash crops and garden produce as well as earnings from wage labor and odd jobs.

Taking these institutionally diverse provisioning processes together, the pattern that emerges is the form of economic integration that Polanyi called householding. The pattern of householding consists of multiple and interconnected livelihood strategies associated with diverse capitalist and non-capitalist economic institutions. The strategies operate under different institutional constraints; for example, the price of cash crops is driven by price-making markets, whereas the labor inputs on family farms are unpriced. The ways in which kin relations structure and organize the various components of rural economies—the complex economic links among kin, especially the economic components of intergenerational ties—are very common throughout Appalachia. Indeed, these patterns of householding typify many rural economies. Various combinations of agricultural labor (both for subsistence and for cash purposes) and wage labor are also common. Families combine their resources and allocate them in intricate ways. As analysts of rural economies, we must translate the folk categories of livelihood—expressions such as "we do things 'the Kentucky Way'" and "we are close-knit"—into analytic categories such as householding that can be used to understand pattern and variation in rural agrarian economies, not only in Appalachia but in other parts of the world as well.

THE REGIONAL BASIS OF HOUSEHOLDING IN THE SHALLOW RURAL

In the Shallow Rural we see a shift from a pattern of community-based householding in the Deep Rural to a pattern of regionally based householding. It is important to keep in mind that the Shallow Rural is still predominantly rural in the sense that people own small amounts of land and maintain kitchen gardens. Some have small amounts of livestock, as well. The Shallow Rural features a rather elaborate infrastructure of interstate highways, and its population density is much higher than in the Deep Rural. Since the Shallow Rural is also the location of the rotating, periodic marketplace system and an industrial park with factories employing temporary wage laborers, it provides ready access to many more options for livelihood. Its geographical proximity to the city also affords opportunities for earning cash that are not easily available in the Deep Rural.

The average homestead in Shallow Rural hamlets occupies one acre of land that includes, in most cases, a subsistence garden plot tended by family members. The composition of the homesteads is varied. In some cases, the entire extended family can be found in a cluster of households on a homestead. In most cases, however, people in hamlets interact economically in complex ways with kin who live dispersed throughout the region. An intensive study of one Shallow Rural hamlet revealed some kin residing in a mobile home park that is a ten to fifteen minute drive from the hamlet; other family members live elsewhere in the same county, and still others live in the Deep Rural areas. People raise fruits, vegetables, and other farm products for consumption by devoting considerable effort and planning to their subsistence gardens. When necessary, they recruit the labor of family members from throughout the region to help with all stages of garden work—from clearing and planting, to weeding and harvesting, to processing for storage and consumption.

The economic activities observed in Shallow Rural hamlets are diverse, and provide a picture of activities that are typical of the region as a whole. Selling goods in the periodic marketplace system is an important activity for many of the people who live in hamlets. The marketplaces are sources of necessary cash as well as goods and food. People buy goods at local garage sales and auctions to sell in marketplaces. By the time they reach adulthood, most people have had some experience in the wage labor sector. Other means of generating cash in the hamlet include small, family-owned, and family-run businesses. Many of the men in the hamlet perform odd jobs or handiwork both within and outside the town and the hamlet. Pairs of related males will commonly work together. In addition to working at these tasks, people in hamlets contribute to one another's livelihood by exchanging home-canned produce, vegetables, and used household items as well as labor for a variety of purposes, including childcare. Hamlet residents pass around goods when they have an excess or when they want to trade goods and services.

HOUSEHOLDING AND THE
SMITH FAMILY NETWORK

The following case of one kin network illustrates the regionally based pattern of householding in the Shallow Rural area. Part of the network is located in one Shallow Rural hamlet; other parts are elsewhere in the Shallow Rural; still another part of the network is in the Deep Rural. The unit of householding is the bilateral kin network. Householding coordinates multiple institutional arrangements and productive activities: farming, gardening, hunting, gathering, wage labor, and marketplace buying and selling. The network is typical of those in the Shallow Rural, with regard to its residence pattern, its complex of livelihood strategies, and its patterns of coordination. While the case is written from the vantage point of a hamlet in the Shallow Rural part of the region, the same patterns emerge if one takes the marketplaces or the factories as one's vantage point (Halperin 1990). Most importantly, the pattern of householding revealed in the Smith family network provides an understanding of rural economic organization and its possibilities for enabling people to resist dependency on the system of temporary wage labor.

Harry and Ilene Smith live on the main road running through a hamlet in the Shallow Rural. They have one daughter, Sue, who is married to Nathan (a carpenter), has two children and lives in the mobile home park about six miles from the hamlet. On a typical fall weekend, the following activities must be coordinated. Harry will commonly have two or three odd jobs, such as housepainting and/or house renovating, to finish before the weather turns cold. Harry and Ilene are regular vendors in the periodic marketplace system, and in autumn, they are anxious to sell out the goods they have accumulated over the summer from garage sales and auctions. The best days to sell at major marketplaces are Saturdays and Sundays. In autumn, Ilene is also always concerned with "putting up" her beans and cucumbers for the winter. If she does not process them in time, both of these vegetables will grow too large and tough.

On one particular fall weekend, Ilene's sister, Kate, who lives on a farm in the Deep Rural part of the region, has taken ill, and Ilene must bring her some cooked food during the weekend. Ilene and Harry decide to sell at one of the major marketplaces on Saturday, the busiest day. They take their grandchildren with them. Sue and Nathan, who work as temporary wage laborers in a nearby factory, will harvest Ilene's beans and cucumbers and prepare food to take to Ilene's sister after their shift on Saturday. They work six days each week on varying shifts. Sometimes they work double shifts. Nevertheless, Sue feels responsible for her parents' well-being. She has said many times that she always makes sure that Mom and Dad have a pot of soup or stew on the stove "ready to go." (This means that the soup is ready to consume on the spot or that it can be brought to a needy relative.) On Sunday they will all go to Sue's aunt's farm "in the country" (Deep Rural) for Sunday dinner.

Harry was born in 1920. He grew up on a family farm in a nearby Deep Rural county. There, the Smith family farm consisted of 300 acres of land with 300–400 head of sheep. It was a self-sustaining subsistence farm with a large garden. The family sold the wool from the sheep, a strategy that reflects their Scottish roots dating back to the nineteenth century. Harry's siblings were a sister, Emerald, ten years younger than he, and a brother who died at the age of twenty-one of a "burst" appendix. Emerald is an extraordinarily vigorous woman who lives in the region. She works with her husband, who owns a garage, and spends most of her time driving a truck to bring spare auto parts to the garage. On her excursions around the region, she stops to visit kin, to exchange news, and to contribute what she can to her family network. She often brings medicine in exchange for cooked food. She has purchased a new house by the river, on good bottom land that benefits from the fertilizer and soil washed down from higher ground. She maintains a large garden.

In 1940, Harry married Ilene Rowan, who was from the same Deep Rural county. Ilene was born in 1919, one of seven children. Ilene's parents were tenant tobacco farmers. Her paternal uncle, Kale, lived with the family. Everyone worked in the tobacco fields. Ilene herself was known as an extremely organized and energetic person. From the time she was seven, she worked consistently in the household, cleaning, straightening, and caring for small children. At the age of nine, Ilene began raising turkeys for cash. She used the cash to buy bolts of cloth for dresses. Ilene also trapped rabbits with her male siblings and sold them to a middleman. She was an excellent shot, but she would not hunt because she enjoyed watching wildlife, especially birds. Since the boys provided plenty of meat for the table, Ilene did not see any reason to waste meat by producing a surplus. She loved to go out with her uncle because he knew a great deal about wildlife.

Upon their marriage, Harry and Ilene left their Deep Rural county and came to "town" in the Shallow Rural. They chose to live in one particular town because a bus line went directly to their Deep Rural county. Every Friday afternoon for many years, Harry and Ilene went home to Brick County. They alternated visits to his parents and hers along with other relatives. The visits always included Sunday dinners. Harry and Ilene were expected to help with farm chores and with the overall maintenance of the family farm.

In his early years, Harry walked from the town in the Shallow Rural, across the Ohio River to the Coca Cola plant. He held this job for seventeen years, driving and delivering. Harry has worked at many different tasks throughout his life, some simultaneously. His persistence and his success at finding work have allowed him to contribute to the maintenance of different segments of his and his wife's kin networks. After his employment at Coca Cola ended, his wage labor jobs included working a water station in his home county. He also stripped furniture, painted houses, repaired typewriters, and raised "bird dogs" for sale. These are beagles that are used for hunting rabbits, squirrels, and quail. Harry has taken great care to pass on many of his skills to his nephew, Mike. Since Mike's father (husband of Emerald, Harry's sister) is a small businessman who, with the exception of his river-bottom garden, has little interest in the outdoors, Harry has always made sure to include Mike in his hunting and fishing trips. Because Harry visited his sister's homestead quite often, Mike developed a very close relationship with him. Mike's son, now age eight, is already a rather accomplished marksman, and he accompanies Mike regularly on deer hunting trips. Mike, in turn, provides Harry and Harry's daughter and son-in-law with venison (thirty pounds in summer 1987) in the form of hamburger, steaks, and roasts.

When Ilene was first married, she worked for a florist in a Shallow Rural town in Kentucky. She later traveled to the city to work as a receptionist in a dentist's office. Her mother cared for their only daughter. Ilene worked for the dentist for thirty-five years.

Ilene's family network is quite extensive. Her sister, Linda Marks, is employed in a craft supplies store in the city. She also operates a home crafts business and, in addition, produces paintings, ceramics, wreaths, refrigerator magnets, etc. Linda can purchase craft items that have been reduced for sale at her place of employment. She also uses her employee discount privilege to purchase goods such as cloth flowers, baskets, etc. Ilene combines these items with dried wild flowers for the flower arrangements she fashions to sell in the marketplaces. The arrangements consist mainly of dried wildflowers and ferns, which she collects and processes regularly. Ilene has a knack for combining a few "store-bought" things with items she has acquired at auctions and garage sales or from relatives who contribute pressed flowers, baskets, and vases for her arrangements.

Linda's daughter, Sally, is employed at the Goody Company (a pseudonym) in Cincinnati. She regularly takes crafts her mother produces to sell at work. The employees of the Goody Company, especially those in management positions, often commission Linda to make special items such as flower arrangements. Linda then calls on Ilene to produce extra arrangements. At the same time that Linda started her business, Lou Ann Rist, Ilene's sister-in-law, began a retail business in a well-to-do town in the Shallow Rural. Lou Ann commissions Linda to make crafts for her shop. Ilene also makes pillows, bittersweet wreaths, and flower arrangements to sell at Lou Ann's shop. Linda herself exchanges her crafts with Ilene for fresh garden produce.

Throughout their adulthood, Harry and Ilene raised a large garden and, until recently, kept an orchard of pear, plum, peach, cherry, and apple trees. They also grew grapes. The fruit was used for their own consumption and, in summer, they sold about half of it; much of it was "put up" for the winter in mason jars. Their daughter and son-in-law could always count on a steady supply of apple butter, jams, and preserves. Sue and Nathan collect wild raspberries and blackberries in the summer to contribute to the supply of fruit used for sale, home consumption, and canning. Sunday dinners in the wintertime are not complete without biscuits and fruit spreads. In 1970, Harry and Ilene moved to their current (smaller) homestead. They gave up the orchard, but they maintain their garden. Recently, they began growing large quantities of tomatoes. They sell enough tomatoes to a local restaurant to buy sugar to put up the wild berries for jam. Harry has continued to paint both the interiors and the exteriors of houses in the county in which he now lives. Harry's son-in-law, Nathan, a carpenter who has also had several jobs as a temporary wage laborer, is becoming increasingly involved in Harry's repair work.

Harry and Ilene are also regular vendors in the marketplace system.[1] They began selling in 1979. Most of the time, they attend the major marketplaces on the weekends. Throughout the week, they collect goods and process them (repairing, mending, cleaning) for sale. They devote Fridays to acquiring goods from yard sales and from any relatives who may want to rid themselves of "old things." Ilene has a talented eye for bargains, and she can transform an old and dirty set of dishes or picture frames into valuable "antiques." Recently, Harry has begun to specialize in used guns and knives. These are popular items, but they require a much higher cash outlay to acquire than do the other used items sold by either Harry or Ilene. He previously sold lower-priced used goods, such as tools, and trinkets, and his present concentration on guns represents specialization for Harry and a selling plateau. He now makes more money than ever before in the marketplaces. He can risk the high initial expenditure on guns and knives because he is an experienced seller who has a network of people from whom he buys guns cheaply. He also has established a reputation for being an honest seller, and people come to him to buy or trade guns.

Their kin network is absolutely critical to Harry's success. People in the network inform him about "hot" markets (i.e., those in which goods are moving fast). They also bring him buyers. On average, Harry and Ilene can count on $1,000-$1,200 per month in cash generated from market sales. This is a major way for them to generate cash and to provide their daughter, Sue, with "luxuries" she cannot afford. Recently, Harry bought Sue an expensive coat from a fashionable clothing store. She confessed that she was embarrassed by the coat's obvious cost, but she was pleased to receive it for Christmas.

Harry's success is linked to his son-in-law Nathan's ability to keep the wage labor system "at arm's length." After several years in the wage labor system, Nathan and Harry have become "partners." They perform "odd jobs" obtained through Harry's extensive regional network. Now that Harry is "getting up in years," Nathan can keep Harry going by performing the heavy work. Nathan expresses great dislike for all facets of the factory system and he uses it selectively—only when he is in need of a steady source of cash. Nathan, age twenty-eight, was born on a farm in southern Indiana. From the age of fourteen, he worked as a carpenter's apprentice. At twenty-one, Nathan moved to Cincinnati, where he worked as a permanent wage laborer for a wholesale food company. When the food company went out of business, he went to work as a temporary wage laborer for the Goody Company, a large manufacturing firm, where he held a similar kind of job maintaining machinery, operating a forklift truck, etc. He obtained this temporary job from an agency in suburban Ohio. While working for the Goody Company, he met his present wife, Sue, also now age twenty-eight. Nathan and Sue were married in December 1986. Since her temporary employment had ended one month before, both of them renewed their job search. Sue quickly found another temporary job at the Rinterline (a pseudonym) plant. About one month into Sue's employment at Rinterline, she learned of a few openings in the machine recycling area. She told Nathan about these jobs. He applied and was immediately hired because of his experience as a machine operator at the Goody facility. Since both Sue and Nathan were only temporary employees, they could both be hired at Rinterline; a nepotism policy prevented permanent employees from suggesting to their spouses that they apply either for permanent or for temporary work.

Nathan's job in truck part recycling was dangerous and dirty. Grease covered everything in this area of the plant and the floors were extremely slippery. As a temporary employee, Nathan had to furnish and maintain (wash) his own work clothes, a considerable cost in both time and money on Nathan's $4.00/hour wage. A set of clothes lasted two weeks at most. Nathan was also exposed to a variety of toxic substances; the company provided little or no protective equipment, and he experienced a variety of health problems. First, Nathan's back became very sore from several bad falls on the floor. A short time later, since grinding metal was part of his job, the company did provide Nathan with goggles. The metal particles were so small, however, that they still slipped into Nathan's eyes. On one occasion, his cornea was severely scratched and the company physician required Nathan to wear a patch. Nathan's work station remained the same and he became increasingly disenchanted with Rinterline. Sue, his wife, repeatedly said that "Nathan really hated Rinterline." He would look out of the back door and exclaim that the entire area of the industrial park had been converted into "moonscape—all trees plowed down—only concrete and brown grass—factories, not farms on the horizon." Nathan said he "felt dirty, like a peon! I know I can do better for myself."

Nathan walked off the Rinterline job after four months as a temporary wage laborer. He began self-employment as a painter and carpenter. Harry's long-standing social relationships with people in his county greatly helped Nathan to obtain work. Nathan and Harry operated as a team; Nathan could perform much of the heavy work that was becoming increasingly difficult for Harry. Such father/son and father/son-in-law combinations are typical throughout the region. They are part of the pattern of intergenerational ties that maintain family networks throughout the region. Intergenerational ties are critical to the pattern of householding because they coordinate people working in different institutional settings. Nathan's working for Harry involves Nathan's decision to shift his labor from the wage labor economy to a more informal, and safer, arrangement.

RESISTANCE TO DEPENDENCY ON CAPITALISM

People, particularly men, who quit their wage labor jobs, whether temporary or permanent, in favor of odd jobs or who decide to intensify their activities in the agrarian and marketplace sectors, often see themselves as "opting out of the system." Discussions about the dangers of factory work, and the lack of concern for safety on the part of owners and managers, were common throughout the period of fieldwork. People see themselves as resistant to factory work, and their resistance takes many forms. Sometimes criticism of fellow factory workers for not learning how to plant gardens, for wasting time and money on beer and partying instead of spending time with family, became the idiom for householding (the provisioning of the family network) as well as the idiom for resistance to temporary wage labor.

Clearly, people see their investments in kin networks as providing them with economic security and with the option to leave wage labor jobs and establish other combinations of work.

In one sense, these livelihood options were established long ago in response to layoffs and plant closings; in another sense, people have created new options and strategies for generating cash and for provisioning their families with the necessary material means for their maintenance. Older people in the region lament the loss of agrarian skills on the part of younger adults, referring to them as "shut ins"—people who live in apartment complexes without land for gardens. Attitudes about employment and preparation for loss of employment vary according to the extent of one's family network and position in the life course, however. Older workers, many of them in positions of permanent wage labor jobs, express strong sentiments that the wage labor available to them will soon disappear. Many people perceive their jobs in the wage labor sector as fragile, as "soon coming to an end." These older workers are highly dependent on subsistence gardens, about which they speak with great pride; their alternative cash-generating strategies include selling in marketplaces and performing odd jobs. They encourage their younger kin to work the booths in the marketplaces, especially on Sundays when wage workers are free. Younger workers are encouraged "to see for themselves" how a hundred-pound sack of potatoes can be obtained for two to three dollars from a fellow market seller who lives on a farm. These potatoes are commonly distributed to members of the family network. Workers with ties to marketplaces and to agrarian economies are much better equipped to use temporary labor selectively—that is, as part of a system of multiple livelihood strategies but not as a reliable source of income. Most temporary workers regard wage work as a short-term strategy for filling time between jobs and for helping out in "bad times."

Householding as a Form of Peasant Resistance

Peasant resistance has become an increasingly important topic in social science (Scott 1985). The strategies used by rural people to exercise control over their lives and livelihood are now beginning to be documented. Practical skills (food production, processing, storage), knowledge and use of local resources, and maintenance of intergenerational ties through the meeting of family obligations provide people in the region with some measure of control over their livelihood.

Families organize productive tasks and allocate labor and, to some extent, land within the larger context of a mainstream capitalist economy without becoming dependent upon the capitalist economy for their livelihood. They manage to circumvent many of the common constraints of the capitalist system. Their work schedules are flexible, although they often work far more than forty hours per week. Substantial portions of their incomes are not reported to the official tax system. Labor resources seem to move where they are needed to maintain the family network and people use elements of the capitalist economy (often its rejects, seconds, and used goods) to their advantage. Practitioners of "the Kentucky way" go to great lengths to be honest, even to the point that sellers in the marketplaces provide customers with their home phone numbers as a kind of guarantee of the quality of their refurbished goods.

Intrafamilial exchanges are difficult to document, but they are very much present and important. Members of family networks exchange goods and services regularly without attention to record-keeping or reporting. In fact, a great many economic activities do not appear anywhere in employment statistics. People obtain odd jobs through kin connections; these jobs often involve kin as work partners. People's best economic interest is to treat these jobs as occasional, unimportant, and inconsequential; they do this with great vehemence, refusing in some instances to reveal the exact earnings from these jobs. Such treatment by the folk masks the actual economic importance of these non-mainstream (informal) work tasks, both in and out of the marketplaces. These are forms of resistance to the tax system and to nation-state authority.

In addition to the considerable exchanges of labor and goods among kin, there are some extremely subtle ways in which kin relations shape people's economic lives. For example, people who work in factories often do so only until someone in their network provides them another option. People quit their jobs often, and they speak with pride of their decisions to terminate employment in the mainstream capitalist economy. What may appear to outsiders as irresponsibility towards a job may simply be the replacement of a wage labor job with one or a set of work tasks that are safer, offer better pay and more time flexibility, and provide greater independence and sense of self worth. Sporadic employment is only sporadic from the point of view of a system that focuses on individuals' actions and not on the larger cultural and institutional contexts within which such actions must be understood. Young adults become the subjects of concern to their kin (especially their older male relatives) when they choose to remain in the temporary wage labor sector to the exclusion of economic activities in the agrarian and/or marketplace sectors. "Putting all your eggs in one basket" is not considered wise.

In virtually all cases, the cash generated from sales of products or from wage labor is used to maintain members of the kin network—to provide them with the basic material means for their survival. From the point of view of the people practicing "the Kentucky way," cash must be generated for certain purposes: not for accumulation, not for display, but for purchasing those necessities that people cannot produce or obtain in any other way. Private property in the form of land provides the resource base for economic activities aimed at provisioning and at maintaining family networks. Selecting jobs that are harmonious with maintaining kin ties is another form of resistance to capitalism, because it keeps the family provisioning processes going. In the Kentucky case, family provisioning ("family" here being an extended, regionally based kin network) is the essence of householding.

The goal of the familial economy is not to ascend the ladder of social stratification; rather, it is to make ends meet by keeping the kin network intact through everyday, ongoing economic activities, often in seasonal cycles. The kin network becomes an umbrella that protects people from depending upon any single economic sector. Here, occupation is secondary in defining who people are. The family network (who are "my people") defines self and person. "The Kentucky way" (in folk terms), in all of its various forms and manifestations, provides people with an identity precisely because it also enables them to make ends meet. Thus, a family imperative guides people's economic activities. Kinship orders livelihood processes through the pattern of householding. These livelihood processes are connected to geographical and residential places, but the livelihood processes are not bounded by households or communities.

Householding must be understood as a form of resistance to capitalism and to dependency upon the state (Comaroff 1985). The multiple livelihood strategies that are organized by family networks—by practicing "the Kentucky way" in this Appalachian region—are highly structured. That this structure may not be apparent is in part a function of the family's dispersion in the region. Furthermore, the informal nature of the provisioning strategies masks their structure. Flea markets are easy to observe, but they are not easy to understand as parts of a structured system of rotating periodic marketplaces. The fact that the marketplace system is only one element of a complex provisioning process is also not immediately obvious. In this respect, marketplaces are public, open arenas with private, hidden agendas. Members of family networks use the system very carefully; they calculate many variables (seasonality, location, number of people in the network) into their buying patterns, their selling locations, and the timing of both.

The behaviors of individuals—of those who quit their temporary wage labor jobs, for example—also do not appear immediately to belong to a structured system of provisioning relationships that insure the circulation of goods and services. A mother's or a father's few moments of conversation with a wage-laboring son who literally passes through a marketplace can coordinate a large family gathering during which food, information, goods, and services are circulated. Even if no gathering is planned, people can communicate with one another at designated times and at designated places to plan a whole series of activities. These activities encompass both locational and appropriational movements, and they range from coordinating the transportation of goods to the distribution of time, labor, and food.[2] These coordination processes give people a degree of control over their livelihood that enables them to resist becoming dependent upon the capitalist economy.

There is a wisdom here, a rationality that has a logic of its own, a steadfastness and a doggedness that has tremendous resiliency precisely because it is multifaceted and flexible (Weinberg 1975). If people opt out of the family network, they give up householding as a provisioning process, and their powers of resistance are weakened considerably.

SUMMARY

The complex provisioning process described above can be understood in terms of the model of householding. Householding is an example of what I have elsewhere (Halperin 1988) called a formal processual model. Formal models are ideals or sets of ideals against which the data can be measured. Models are heuristic devices designed to give us some ways of ordering data. Formal processual models (in contrast to formal atomistic models, in which the units are individual actors) consist of units that are complicated processes or sets of social relations occurring in a population or set of populations. In the case of northeastern Kentucky, we see a complex of institutional arrangements that are organized by different but, in some cases, overlapping principles of organization: price-making markets for labor, periodic marketplaces, subsistence-oriented family farms with substantial kitchen gardens—to name the major institutional arrangements. House-holding coordinates the economic activities of members of extended family networks as they participate in all of these different institutional arrangements.

Householding can be understood, then, as the analytical term characterizing all of the locational and appropriational movements that allow people to make ends meet "the Kentucky way"—or more generally, to provide the material means necessary for the survival of the members of the groups (in this case, kin networks) that can be found in the lower strata of a post-industrial (and deindustrializing) state. Householding here is not a throwback to a traditional, non-market, kin-based economy. Rather, it is a new form in the sense that it coordinates elements of capitalist and pre-capitalist economic processes. People use "the Kentucky way" to maintain long-term direct access to the means of production, in this case land, whether family farms in "the country" (Deep Rural) or homesteads in the Shallow Rural. By doing so, they control their own labor and can resist becoming dependent upon capitalism.

Six

STORAGE AS AN ECONOMIC PROCESS

S torage, or the setting aside of material things (food, tools, water, seeds for plants) for some future use— whether short- or long-term—is a fact of economic and social life in all cultures, at all times and in all places. All of the processes—such as drying, smoking, manufacturing of receptacles such as pots, baskets, or storage bins—that are associated with, and indeed are a requirement for, setting aside resources for future consumption are storing processes. Yet, storage and storing processes are some of the best-kept secrets of the archaeological and ethnographic records—we know they exist, but we don't know how to think about them as economic processes, and we don't know how they are organized in relationship to processes of production, distribution, and consumption. Part of the reason for this somewhat mysterious situation regarding storage has to do with a set of problematic assumptions about storage, including: its association with the ability of cultural systems to produce a surplus (Adams 1966; Sanders and Price 1968; Smyth 1988); its incompatibility with residential mobility (Testart 1982); and its absence and/or relative lack of importance in small-scale stateless societies.

The premise with which we shall begin is as follows: Storing processes exist in all cultures, albeit in different institutional contexts and environments. The forms taken by storing processes are highly variable, and are not always immediately recognizable in material terms. That is, while all storage has a material referent, the materials themselves, such as food or water, are not always the items that are stored. They may be exchanged, shared, traded, or literally banked in the ground or elsewhere. Storing processes operate both within and between cultural groupings such that one group may hold and consume resources for the eventual use by other groups. To say this in a slightly different way—what may to one group operate as a storing process will be part and parcel of the production and consumption system of a related group. These are some of the reasons why it is so important to understand storage analytically.

Storing processes reflect aspects of economies (of their production, distribution and consumption processes) that might otherwise remain unknown. Having goods on hand, under most circumstances, is clearly better than not having them, unless they are a hindrance to mobility or indicate inappropriate hoarding that may encourage raiding. Again, under most circumstances, stored goods provide certain degrees of flexibility and freedom for individuals and groups. Stockpiles of stored goods can obviate or postpone certain kinds of productive activities, or the stores can be traded or exchanged. The possibility of storage may also allow groups to use available labor effectively. Production or processing of goods for storage when help is on hand can then facilitate use or exchange of those goods at some later time. The availability and control of stored goods can free some people from food production altogether, providing time for other tasks. Timing and scheduling can be critical matters (see chapter 8).

Storage has not enjoyed the status or the attention that has been devoted to other economic processes. Unlike processes of trade and market, and exchange and production, there has been very little written on storage as an economic process (see Smyth 1991). Existing literature often treats storage as an ecologically driven process (Binford 1980; Jochim 1981), or as an independent variable indicating population density, sedentism, stratification, and the like (Testart 1982). Most of what has been written on storage deals with opposite ends of the spectrum of cultural evolution—that is, with hunter-gatherers or with complex pre-industrial states such as the Inca. We know relatively little about storing processes in cultural systems that are between these extremes, although there are bits and pieces of data that can be gleaned from the literature. For example, Herskovits (1952:364) wrote of cattle as stores of wealth. Bohannan (1959) wrote of money as a store of value. Raymond Firth wrote of "the problems of storage" in connection with a discussion of money and implied that storage is a problem for all economies:

> *The existence of money promotes saving, if only because it helps to solve the problems of storage. In a community such as Tikopia, where fish, root crops,*

*breadfruit and coconuts are the staple foods, only the
coconuts can be stored for any length of time without
special preparations of an elaborate kind, involving
much labor. Even bark-cloth and pandanus mats—
which have sometimes been described as "currency"—need special care and periodic unwrapping
for exposure to sunlight to preserve them from mold
and pests. Storage of money avoids most of these
difficulties.*
(1964:23)

The kinds of storing processes that exist in cultural systems remain to
be analyzed, however. This chapter uses Polanyi's generic model of the
economy in combination with some selected archaeological and ethnographic examples to propose some preliminary models for understanding the place of storing processes in economies—the relationships between storing processes and the processes of production, distribution,
and consumption and, thus, the ways in which storing processes can be
understood to vary and to change through time. The locational and appropriational aspects of storage are extremely useful for understanding
storage as an economic process.

Storage among Hunter-Gatherers

The literature contains a considerable amount of
discussion of storage among hunter-gatherers. This literature raises questions about the relationships between storage and sedentism, seasonality
and mobility. Testart (1982) uses the absence or presence of storing processes to distinguish "two radically distinct types of economy" (1982:
523). The first type is based on the assumed absence of storing processes, that is, the immediate use of food resources in environments with
little, if any, seasonal variation and with what Testart calls flexible economies based on "multiple alternative strategies" (1982:523). Examples
include the Bushmen (!Kung) and the Australian Aborigines. The second
type is based on large-scale seasonal food storage such as that found
on the Northwest coast and California. Testart argues that the storing
economy has two main features, both of which derive from ecological
variables. The first is "a conspicuous seasonal variation in the intensity
of food-getting activities." When food is available, food production and
food processing activities for preservation are at their peak (1982:524).

Great labor inputs are required at these times, in contrast to the relative leisure of times of food scarcity, during which stored foods are consumed. Testart proceeds to hinge many aspects of social structure on storage, which functions as an independent variable in his analysis: population, stratification, and other forms of inequality, including private property. Thus, storage takes on evolutionary importance.[1]

Testart's argument has been criticized by many writers, most notably by Ingold (1983), whose analysis of storage rejects ecological determinism. Ingold addresses the assumption that there is little or no storage of food among hunter-gatherers, arguing that storage of subsistence resources is the rule (1983:554). His aim is "to bring out certain ambiguities in the concept of storage itself" (1983:554).

Ingold's first point is that "the extent of storage is not simply determined by environmental fluctuations in the availability of resources for harvesting" (1983:558). Rather, there are numerous other conditions that may obtain in the organization of production, especially labor, that can bring about the need for storage. Ingold points specifically to the relationship between storage and sharing:

> For example, even where a number of resources (X, Y, Z) for which there is a continuous demand are continuously available, if the exploitation of one (X) means breaking off from the exploitation of any of the others (e.g., Z), some storage may be necessary (of both X and Z alternately, though not Y).
> (1983:558)

The time demands and the scheduling of work become critical here. If, for example, an activity requires long periods of unbroken activity, or the activity can be done sporadically, storage can be obviated by the obligations to share. That is, one group or person may rely on another for certain things that it might otherwise have to store. Ingold says:

> Thus, if one man has been concentrating on the exploitation of X and therefore lacks supplies of Z for immediate consumption, he may depend on receiving his needs from others who have been devoting their attention to the exploitation of Z, in his turn sharing with them his supplies of X. This would be impos-

sible were everyone within the community of sharing
engaged at the same time in the work of exploiting X.
(1983:558)

In short, a person or a group may store up obligations in lieu of storing goods. While one might object to this rather broad definition of storage, it does contextualize storing processes in particular kinds of economies and economic processes.

For Ingold, storage is by no means incompatible with nomadic movement. His discussion of storage among reindeer hunters, who are both nomadic and dependent upon a single game species, is an example. He says:

> *Hunting is for survival. It provides not a supplement*
> *but a mainstay to his diet, as well as materials for his*
> *clothing and shelter. For this reason, as we have seen,*
> *he must slaughter more animals than he can possibly*
> *consume in their entirety. Storage over the winter*
> *months is not only possible but vitally necessary. . . .*
> *The Nganasan, for example, obtain virtually a*
> *whole year's supplies from only four months of hunt-*
> *ing (Popov 1966:21 in Ingold 1980:73). The quan-*
> *tities of meat stockpiled during a successful autumn*
> *hunting season are far in excess of the amount that*
> *could physically be consumed in the same period, even*
> *on a festive diet. In short, rather than taking a little*
> *at a time before moving on, Arctic hunters take as*
> *much as they can get before their prey move on, and*
> *then stay put until stocks run out.*
> (1980:73)

The relationship between storing processes and processes of reciprocity and redistribution comes through in Ingold's discussion. He points, for example to the relationship between storage and extravagant consumption that is organized by festive redistribution. Hunters are required to do two things when they return from the hunt: share their meat and set aside provisions for the winter:

> *We find, therefore, that the incidence of generalized*
> *reciprocity tends to peak towards the two extremes of*
> *scarcity and abundance. The communal feast that fol-*

*lows a successful hunting drive involves the same
heightening of band solidarity, and calls into play the
same functions of leadership in the apportionment of
food, as does the consumption of famine rations. . . .
This variation in the range of sharing is reflected in
cycles of band aggregation and dispersal, and in the
extent of dependence upon stored supplies. . . . The
fortunate hunter, when he returns to camp with his
kill, is expected to play host to the rest of the community, in bouts of extravagant consumption. Yet he is
also concerned to set aside stocks of food to see his
household through at least a part of the coming winter. The meat that remains after the obligatory festive
redistribution is therefore placed in the household's
cache, on which the housewife can draw specifically
for the provision of her own domestic group. After the
herds have passed by, domestic autonomy is re-estab-
lished as each household draws on its own reserves of
stored food. The incidence of reciprocity falls, but the
large aggregation persists as long as people are immo-
bilized by their supplies.*

*Once stores begin to be depleted, households must
disperse either singly or in pairs to seek out the now
scattered herds of reindeer.*

(INGOLD 1980:146)

Ingold points to particular kinds of locational movements:

*The movement entailed is often a kind of "fixed-
point" nomadism—a series of moves between pre-
established locations, each conveniently situated for
the exploitation of particular resources during particular periods. These locations may be marked by physical structures of a permanent or semi-permanent nature, including structures intended for storage. . . .
Food may be cached at a great number of different
points, dispersed widely over the landscape, so that
the hunter can travel light and still be sure of finding
something to eat.*

(1983:560)

One thinks immediately of certain Arctic groups. The Netsilik, for example, maintain caches of fish and also store fish as part of their technology in the runners of their sleds in slabs of fish cut lengthwise (Balikci 1970). The Nunamiut (Binford 1978) store caches of caribou meat across the landscape.

Ingold emphasizes that transportation factors (again, locational movements) are important determinants of storage practices and the location of stored goods.

> *The logistics of transport may have a critical bearing not only on whether produce is stored, but on where it is stored. If hunting, for example, involves a continuous period of unbroken activity, we would expect kills to be cached temporarily at the points where the animals were brought down, for subsequent collection and transport to the settlement.*
> (1983:559–560)

One aspect of storage that has not been discussed extensively in the literature has to do with its nonlocational and nonphysical components (in Polanyi's terms, appropriational movements). In this regard, Ingold's discussion of what he calls "social storage" is extremely important:

> *Storage in its quite distinct social sense refers neither to the physical activity of setting stuff aside, nor to the organic accumulations that result, but to the appropriation of materials in such a way that rights over their future distribution or consumption converge upon a single interest.*
> (1983:561, EMPHASIS HIS)

The appropriational dimensions of storage are important for several reasons. First, they indicate the organization of storing processes and the relationships between storage and other features of economic organization. Secondly, it is difficult to get at the appropriational aspects of storage from an archaeological perspective because we can see the movement of goods, or the lack thereof, on the landscape, but the institutional arrangements driving the movements are not so readily apparent. We can begin to see the necessity of combining archaeological, ethnoarchaeological, and ethnographic research. Ingold provides some insights into appropriational movements by talking about the importance of considering "the store" as "property or wealth, and storage as a concomitant of social relations of distribution" (1983:561). He emphasizes the links between physical location and social appropriation. Storing produce in containers that are portable and not tied to specific locations points up the possibility of separating analytically the locational and appropriational aspects of storage.

Ingold's speculations on the significance of food containers are interesting, especially the implications for the relationships between storage and processes of distribution and exchange. Also, Ingold identifies an apparent paradox—the association between portable food containers and relative sedentism among hunter-gatherers. And, as we will see below, Ingold uses the phrase, "change of hands" when he talks about transferring produce and relabeling storage containers. He is aware of the distinction between "changes of place" (locational movements) and "changes of hands" (appropriational movements):

> One is struck by the apparent paradox that, amongst hunters and gatherers, the elaboration and personification of portable food containers appears to be most characteristic of relatively sedentary peoples. This phenomenon may be related to the evolution of complex structures of distribution and exchange. Such structures accommodate regional variations in the supply of different environmental resources through the institution of trade between solidary local groups, rather than through the nomadic flux of personnel. The conduct of trade depends upon the carriage of produce into public arenas which are neutral as regards the personification of space. Where items of produce cannot by their nature be individually identified, the function of identification must be borne by containers, and a change of hands indicated either by transferring the produce from one container to another or by changing the identification of the container— that is, by "relabeling" it.
> (1983:561)

This notion of relabeling, which can be argued to be a result of reduced locational movements and/or reduced mobility, is a perfect example of an appropriational movement. Something may be stored and thus change hands, or it may be taken out of storage and then relabeled, thus changing hands at a different point in the economic process, namely at the point of storage. Ingold also notes the advantages of containers for the measurement and setting of equivalences. Again, we hear echoes of Polanyi:

> *Food containers also allow the measurement of produce in standard units of volume. The significance of this function naturally depends upon the degree to which exchange involves the reckoning of strict equivalences.*
> (1983:562)

The relationship between storage and sharing is a topic Ingold takes on with some vengeance, in part as a disagreement with Testart. For Ingold, storage and sharing are not mutually exclusive, although the emphasis on one or the other may be a key factor in understanding evolving social complexity. Storage may simply hold (reserve) goods that are not available for future sharing and consumption (1983:562–563). Ingold says that the "social store" for the pastoralist is "that particular section of the total animal population on which he can exert a direct claim, as against others in his society" (1983:564).

In sum, we can see that Ingold's foregoing discussion reads very much like Polanyi's generic economy model in which the key elements are locational and appropriational movements, and in which the problem of equivalencies figures importantly.

Tropical Horticulturalists: Storage as Part of Production

One might find it surprising that manioc, which is the most reliable food source cultivated in continuous cropping in the Amazon Basin, involves storage as part and parcel of its production process. The three important manioc products are starch, juice, and fiber. Starch and fiber may be stored for several weeks in holes dug in the plaza, or in baskets kept in family compartments (Hugh-Jones 1979:178).

Starch and fiber may be stored for days or even weeks (1979:179). Storage is part of the second stage of processing which involves liquefying and separating the constituents of the solid roots. The third stage involves first washing, then drying, and finally adding the fiber to starch to make solid manioc bread. After processing the manioc bread is consumed (1979:180). The starch sours in the underground store; the souring is an improvement in Indian eyes (Hugh-Jones 1979:189).

Dufour describes manioc processing as follows:

> Manioc tubers, once harvested and peeled, deteriorate very rapidly. In processing the fluids are removed and the starch separated from the more fibrous part of the root. This is accomplished by grating the tubers, then sieving the grated mass with water to wash out the starch. Both the starch and the fiber are relatively stable, and can be stored for a month or more. Both ferment slightly in storage, and it is in this fermented form, rather than fresh, that they are recombined into bread.
> (1980:6)

She notes that:

> The processing and preparation to which manioc is subjected clearly serve to reduce the level of toxicity, as well as producing more palatable, and storable forms of food.
> (1980:7)

In the Amazon Basin women do not go to the fields everyday to harvest manioc; neither do they process it on a daily basis. The more manioc a woman can store, the greater is her prestige as a good wife, and the greater is her time flexibility. Substantial stores of manioc are also indicators of how much garden area her husband has cleared for her (Jean Jackson, personal communication). It should be emphasized that manioc shows little seasonal variability, but in some cases it has been demonstrated to account for 85 percent of the total caloric intake (Dufour 1980:4). Dried manioc can be stored for considerable lengths of time in the form of dry cassava cakes; Gillin (1936:17) says for as long as three months. Schwerin (1971:15) reports the Karinya claim that dry cassava cakes will keep for up to one year. Cassava cakes are often quite large in their stored form, but they can easily be broken up and carried to the field on hunting expeditions or on extended trips. Schwerin emphasizes storability and portability:

> *The two facts of enhanced storability and utility for travel probably explain why so many peoples willingly undertake the laborious process involved in the elaboration of cassava rather than remaining satisfied with some of the simpler techniques of preparation.*
> (1971:15)

If, in fact cassava cakes can last for up to one year, is it possible that manioc production could be interrupted for long periods of time?

Farinha, a dried flour or meal, is another form of manioc that stores exceptionally well. It is also more easily portable. Farinha may be consumed dry, mixed with water or other food, or boiled up as groats (Schwerin 1971:18). Here processing and storage techniques render food available in different forms for different purposes: portable food for traveling and for hunting and fishing excursions, or for trading trips or for expeditions of war. Schwerin states that "farinha seca" (dry meal) is reported for seventeen aboriginal groups, mostly from the Amazon Basin (1971:18; see also Dole 1960). One might hypothesize that the smaller the group, the fewer producers there are, and the greater the need for a mixed food supply—in this case one food supply that is available in different forms. The fact that manioc exists in several forms, some of which are storable, is in many respects analogous to the multiple food sources of hunter-gatherers. Schwerin argues, in fact, that dried grated manioc is set aside at the end of the first day's labor because of conflicting demands for a woman's time on the second day. It allows a woman more flexibility in deploying her time while maintaining a store of partially prepared manioc pulp which she can be prepare more readily than if she had to start from scratch with the raw tuber (1971:20).[2]

Storage and Agriculture

It has been argued (Cordell 1984) that once agriculture takes hold and begins to spread, food storage practices reinforce sedentism. Given successful crops, stores can be maintained to be used when necessary—throughout the winter, but especially in the late winter and early spring when the availability of wild foods is at the lowest. Corn is a case in point. As long as it is dry and protected from vermin and moisture, it can be stored without much preparation (see Smyth 1991). The labor requirements of corn storage increase as agricultural production grows, since the amount of time needed to prepare and store the crops also is extended:

> As cached food becomes more abundant and more important, it must be guarded effectively from possible human theft in addition to pest damage; therefore, some portion of a population might be left to protect the stores throughout much of the year. If there is an increase in the amount of stored food available, . . . people may remain sedentary much of the year, living on stored food and making periodic trips to gather wild resources.
> (CORDELL 1984:188)

Patricia Gilman's work on the change from pithouse to pueblo has implications for understanding storage in the context of overall economic processes. Vernon Scarborough's work on ceramics and sedentism (1992) in the transitional period (Pithouse-to-Pueblo) village in the American Southwest (south-central New Mexico) complements her analysis of storage. Agriculture became a mainstay during the Pueblo Period with the complex of maize, beans, and squash; agricultural production replaced the earlier strategy of foraging associated with the Pithouse Period villages (A.D. 1–1100) (Scarborough 1992:313).

Pueblos are multiroom (ranging from a few rooms to hundreds) structures of adobe or masonry that occur in aggregated clusters. Pithouses are much smaller and more ephemeral structures. They are semi-subterranean houses that are seldom more than one meter deep (Scarborough 1992). In pithouse villages, storage pits and cists are located both inside and outside dwellings. In pueblos, food storage areas are inside and above ground-level in rooms adjoining habitation rooms (Cordell 1984:231). As Cordell points out, Gilman accepts the basic contention, supported empirically in the Southwest, that population growth entailed increased dependence on agriculture, and argues that the increased dependence on agriculture changed both information networks among groups of people and the timing and character of food preparation and storage activities.

The timing of storing activities, including the processing of foods for storage as well as the construction of storage facilities and storage vessels, is an indicator of the organization of production, particularly labor. Gilman (1987) argues that pit structures are associated with subsistence systems that are at least partly agricultural but that these systems follow a semisedentary settlement pattern that was possibly like that of the Western Apache, who combined agriculture with hunting and gathering. People planted crops in the spring, left the crops to be tended by the elderly, and then returned to them in the fall and winter after pursuing wild plants during the summer. People were thus mobile during the growing season and sedentary in non-growing seasons (1987:553). Scarborough makes a similar argument about locational movements (1992: 309; Binford 1980). Depending upon how long the period of winter sedentism lasted, storage facilities would have looked different. Gilman proposes a continuum with regard to storage facilities:

> Under conditions of less winter sedentism and low stored food bulk, storage facilities may be smaller, less formal, and so less obvious archaeologically than under conditions of increased winter sedentism and greater stored food bulk. . . . Southwestern archaeologists have long recognized that storage facilities may take various forms such as pits, rooms, pots, and baskets, and some investigations have begun to determine the conditions under which different kinds of storage facilities will be used. I would expect the varying degrees of subsistence intensification that probably accompany southwestern pit structures to be related to varying kinds of storage facilities. For example, with less subsistence intensification, shorter winter sedentism, and therefore less food to store each winter, pit structures should be accompanied by less permanent, less labor intensive, and perhaps less archaeologically detectable storage facilities such as baskets, hide containers, and perhaps pottery. With increasing intensification and more food to store for longer winter sedentism, storage facilities might also include storage pits, cists, and definitely pottery. . . . I suspect that interior pits are rarely used for long term food storage

and that food storage in pottery vessels represents special kinds of storage such as short term storage, agricultural seed storage, and oily seed storage.
(1987:554)

Gilman goes on to point out that the subject of storage is not well recorded for many puebloan groups. I continue to quote her at length so that the reader can see exactly how she conceptualizes and describes storage:

With the increasing sedentism of people using pueblos, however, storage should become an even more critical problem than for people using pit structures. Less mobility means that resources must be brought to the habitation site when they are available and potentially much before the time that the resources will be used. Puebloan storage also probably occurs for a longer duration than pit structure storage, because some hunting and gathering options are constrained for a more sedentary group, and therefore that group may not have access to sequentially available resources that a more mobile group can obtain. . . . Because food is stored and used for a longer period each year in pueblos than in pit structures, it appears that the major food resources in use while pueblos are inhabited are stored goods. Stored goods may also be used when puebloan people are living in their alternate settlements such as agricultural field houses or herding shelters, although more ripening agricultural and wild foods may also be available at these times.
(1987:551)[3]

If a population is living for long periods of time on stored foods, the question of what their economies look like becomes critical. The above description by Gilman is not unlike that of Testart's for hunter-gatherers on the Northwest coast where the population size and social organization look much more like that of sedentary tribal societies than that of small-scale nomadic bands. Similar storing processes may thus indicate groups with similar social and political structures, but with different subsistence techniques (see Smyth 1989). The issue of storage facility changes is important as well, for these indicate changes in economic organization (Gross 1992).[4]

Storage and States

STORAGE AND TRADE IN STATE SYSTEMS: THE MAYA

The location of storage facilities in relationship to other economic processes such as trade, subsistence, and consumption is problematic. One cannot assume that storage facilities are necessarily physically adjacent to the sites where most other economic activities take place. Sabloff's and Freidel's discussion of the storage site of Buena Vista is a case in point. Buena Vista is located approximately five hours' walking time from the principal port zone, the port of San Miguel.

Sabloff and Freidel argue that while seasonally available trade items (salt, honey, and cacao) had to be stored, to store them at the port itself would have rendered trade items vulnerable to attack from the sea. Therefore, they continue, it made sense to locate storage facilities inland, where seaborne pirates would not have such easy access to valuable trade goods (1975:375). The need for defensive storage locations outweighed the inefficiency of locating long-term warehousing far from the port of trade (1975:376).

In addition, Sabloff and Freidel propose a working hypothesis that links the Buena Vista storage facility with the activities of the residents of this area:

> We propose a fourth possibility as a working hypothesis: that the nucleated area at Buena Vista was indeed a residential district, but that it was also a major storage area for perishable commodities being transhipped through Cozumel in its role as a trading port. . . . We see the residents of the nucleated area at Buena Vista as active in nonsubsistence service, but, rather than servicing a local population, they were serving the elite of Cozumel by maintaining storage facilities.
> (1975:400)

Sabloff and Freidel see the nucleated population maintaining the storage facility at Buena Vista as a response on the part of Cozumel's elite to

PHOTO 4.   *Maize storehouse. Courtesy Michael Smyth.*

external economic factors that are associated with the trade system that passed through San Miguel, the local port of trade (1971:401).

DOMESTIC STORAGE: THE MAYA

Food and water storage at the local (household and village) level has been important to the Maya for centuries if not millennia. Food and water storage at Sayil, Yucatan, figured importantly in offsetting high population densities, limited water supplies, short growing seasons, and instabilities in rainfall (1991:3). Motivated by a dearth of knowledge about storage, Smyth undertook an ethnoarchaeological study of storage practices in the Puuc region of Yucatan, Mexico. Focusing on Puuc maize agriculture, Smyth identified and mapped maize storage facilities (cribs and bins), storage techniques, and processing areas, and he compared households with different storage facilities. He selected thirty-five households and fifteen communities on the basis of their involvement with traditional subsistence agriculture and maize storage practices.

Maize is always stored in a storage facility, which is not always a storehouse or in a storehouse. Storehouses are freestanding buildings that have either been specially constructed or rehabilitated from previous residences.

Maize storage facilities are either cribs or bins. These are rectangular structures made from wood poles located either within storehouses or dwellings, or standing alone within the patio. Men exclusively build storage facilities (1991:23), and they must plan to build these in conjunction with their other productive activities.

Shelling, husking, and packing are the three important storage techniques, each corresponding to a different period of preservation. These techniques require different amounts of time and labor and they present different possibilities for future production, distribution, exchange, and delayed consumption:

> *Shelled and husked ear maize are stored exclusively in bins and serve the daily consumption needs of the household. Husked ear maize is poorly protected from vermin and the elements and will usually last no longer than six months. Packed ear maize is stored exclusively within crib facilities. These ears, which are protected by the outer husk, are packed individually in a tight vertical position and are aligned in horizontal rows. When arranged properly, packed ear maize produced an ideal storage environment. The open design of the cribs allows for air passage around the facility, thus regulating the temperature of the stored maize. In addition, insects within the tight packing of the ears quickly deplete the limited oxygen supply, thus raising the levels of carbon dioxide. This airtight storage environment serves to discourage insect investigation and bacteria growth. Under these conditions, packed ear maize can be preserved for over three years. When packed ear maize is not required for daily food, it can be converted into cash, used as a banking strategy to guard against crop failure, and/or put aside as seed corn for the next year's planting.* (1991:25)

Smyth indicates that the spending of maize stores must be timed prudently for the long-term economic benefit of the household. If people can hold on to their maize stores for a long period, they can sell at a higher price (1991:59). On the other hand, those who have access only to shorter-term storage techniques may not be able to reap such benefits. As we will see in the final section of this chapter, the different patterns of storage can be modeled in relation to production, distribution, and consumption.

Smyth's analysis proceeds to examine factors that account for variability in domestic storage (1991:31). While he stays very close to storing processes (use and placement of storage facilities, use of permanent vs. temporary storage structures, and size and volume of facilities in relation to family size) his data have wide implications for understanding storage as an economic process. In one instance, for example, a maize crib was built out in the *milpa* because it was over four kilometers from the houselot and was only accessible by a narrow footpath fifteen kilometers from any main road.[5] Smyth notes that given the distance from the house, the relatively small labor pool within this household (two adults), and the high cost of harvest transportation, the most practical way to transport the maize harvest is to store it in the *milpa* and bring portions to the household as needed (1991:35).

Storage structures are also an indicator of local stratification patterns, and/or longevity in the community. Smyth notes that Puuc land tenure systems favor long-term community residents or those who are most closely related to local *ejido* leaders. *Ejidos* are federally instituted (inalienable) public lands that were created by the Mexican Government after the Revolution of 1910. These leadership positions rotate, but are often restricted to certain families over time (Halperin 1975). Those who have the least land, or the land of poorest quality, will have lowest crop yields, but a quick way to identify these families may be to examine the kinds of storage structures associated with them. Less fortunate producers will be unlikely to invest in storehouses as permanent or as separate structures.

INCA STORAGE

The Inca state was a machine—a machine with an unparalleled capacity to mobilize and organize human labor. In the Inca realm, the position of elites in the stratification system was measured neither in gold nor land, but in capacity to mobilize labor.
(LA LONE 1982:295)

> *The major role of the state economy was to mobilize labor to finance state operations. Key state operations included support of the elite population and retainers, support of military and political organizations, and capital investment in such projects as agricultural intensification and the construction and maintenance of roads, administrative centers, and storehouses.*
> (LA LONE 1982:294)

In the Inca case, it is through the analysis of storage that we know how the Inca state operated (Morris 1967). La Lone calls for analysis of state storage systems:

> *Archaeological analysis of the state storage system is of utmost urgency for our understanding of how the central economy worked. Expansion of storage implies that agricultural production in the rural hinterland also increased. This, of course, is not a new revelation, since we know the Inca state promoted intensive cultivation of maize (Murra 1973). In its centers the state controlled not only stockpiles of maize, but also concentrated production of cloth, pottery, and chicha.*
> (MORRIS 1972)

According to Cieza de Leon, 30,000 people "served" the administrative center at Huanuco Pampa alone. The state storage system was critical to the state's ability to absorb and use the greatly increased output of such massive labor mobilization.

Analysis of storage and state finance in the Upper Mantaro Valley of Peru by Earle and D'Altroy deals with some of La Lone's concerns. Staples are organized by the state in a redistributive pattern: the region's dominant staples are collected by the central government from subsistence producers, stored, and paid out in return for state services (1982: 266). In essence, the storing processes associated with staple finance become, in Polanyi's words, "a submonetary device" that is associated with standard values for key staples (Polanyi 1968:186–187; Earle and D'Altroy 1982:266).

Earle and D'Altroy say further that the stored goods maintained their local integrity: "Apparently the Inca state used locally available goods as its financial units and was not involved in coordinating exchange in subsistence goods among specialized local economies. Stored goods, then, were not trade goods but were used to subsidize craft specialization and trade. The staples were, however, used to support craft specialists attached to the Inca elites; crafts were then used in foreign or long-distance trade" (1982:267).

The staples (maize, quinoa, potatoes, etc.) originated at the household level. Laborers from households, organized as community labor on state lands, produced both staples, which were stored locally, and craft products, such as textiles. There were specialists to record all goods moving in and out of storehouses (Earle and D'Altroy 1982). The stores were used to support military and state functionaries. Anyone who worked on state functions and who needed to be fed was maintained from the state stores (Earle and D'Altroy 1982:271).

The scale of storage in the Mantaro Valley is impressive, to say the least. In fact it was massive, with storage volume approaching 122,000 cubic meters, which is equivalent to 3,500,000 bushels of maize, potatoes, and quinoa. The staples of this storage volume are found closely attached to the main administrative center, but a large number of storage sites are found removed from the administrative center (Earle and D'Altroy 1982:278).

Earle and D'Altroy note three features of storage that are worth mentioning:

> (1) Distinct village-level storage was not found in pre-Inca sites and therefore was probably imposed by the state;
> (2) The storage complexes were all apparently constructed according to uniform canons of form and size;
> (3) The storage mechanism was apparently not under direct community control.
> (1982:281)

D'Altroy and Hastorf (1984:335) assume that the Inca state stored its goods at the points of consumption rather than production. The Spanish sources on Inca storage overwhelmingly support a concept of storage organization in which the state concentrated supplies at state centers for consumption nearby (1984:336). They do point to one example of a large storage facility in Bolivia, however, which may have housed agricultural goods produced in the immediate vicinity but intended for consumption elsewhere by the military (Wachtel 1982). D'Altroy and Hastorf point out that differential distributions of foodstuffs or craft items among storage facilities may reflect different state-financed activities at these locations.

The two Maya and Inca examples of state-level storage deal with different economic processes, the first with trade, the second with staple finance. In the case of Cozumel, local production is not an issue. Rather, goods come via long-distance trade networks. In the Inca case, the internal organization of the state at all levels is critical. Since the amount of storage decreases with distance from the administrative center, Earle and D'Altroy interpret this to mean that state-financed activities were performed at local settlements, but that these activities were concentrated at settlements closer to the administrative center. To test this hypothesis, they suggest investigating the location and extent of state-directed production (1982:287–288). The fact that the pattern of storage facilities in the Upper Mantaro Valley contrasts with that found by Morris (1967) for the Inca administrative center of Huanuco Pampa presents some interesting comparative potentials that would be illuminated by an understanding of production systems in relation to storage facilities. At Huanuco Pampa there is an enormous storage complex just outside the center. This was built to supply the Inca military when stationed in the vicinity. Obviously storage is linked to production, but in variable ways (see also Earle and D'Altroy 1989).

SUMMARY

Using Jochim's framework as a starting point (while at the same time rejecting his assumptions about system equilibrium and optimization) we can say that storing processes postpone consumption and are anticipatory strategies (Jochim 1981). All storing processes involve what Polanyi called locational and appropriational movements. These are both physical movements of goods from one place to another (locational movements) and changes in rights of access to goods (appropriational movements) as in designating or labeling resources for use, before and after storage has occurred. All storing processes, like all economic processes, consist of these two components: locational and appropriational movements. Locational movements involve

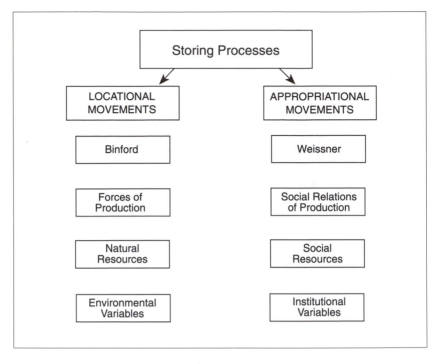

FIGURE 4.   *Aspects of Storing Processes*

forces of production and ecological variables. Appropriational movements involve social relations of production and institutional variables.
Examples of these two approaches to the analysis of storing processes
can be found in Binford (1980), who focuses on the locational aspects of
storage, and Weissner (1982), who focuses on the appropriational aspects
(see chapter 3). Binford deals primarily with the movements of goods
and people over the landscape. Weissner writes of risk reduction strategies which include: prevention and loss, transfer of risk or loss from one
party to another, storage or losses covered by previous accumulation,
and pooling of risk or risk sharing (1982:172–173).

  Jochim has argued for small-scale systems that delayed exchange is a
substitute for storage. Examples include the Pomo trade feasts (Vayda
1967) in which groups that are oversupplied with food exchange it for
the beads of a group with less food. Thus, instead of storing fish, the
Pomo exchange fish for beads. Alternatively, Bronitsky (1984) describes
a situation in which communities convert crop surpluses into durable
items in order to reduce or minimize the effects of future scarcity. As

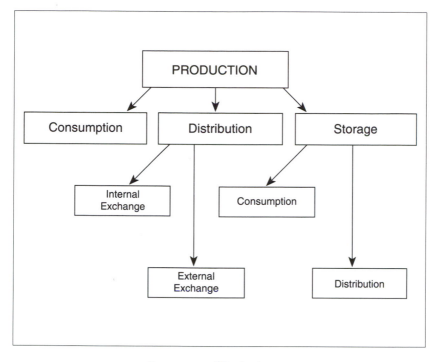

FIGURE 5.   *Components of Production*

Bronitsky points out, what he calls "banking trade" need not be restricted to differentially occurring natural resources. In the Vitiaz Strait region of New Guinea, long distance canoe trading among ecologically comparable localities permitted an efficient local production specialization, rather than the alternative, and comparatively inefficient, strategy of local production diversification as a hedge against crop failure (Harding 1967).

These examples raise some important questions regarding the utilization of labor. For example, which system requires more labor, trading and feasting, or simple processing and storage? Which system is more labor intensive? Are there features of local production that render local systems more or less conducive to storage or trading?

Placing storing processes in the context of other kinds of economic processes is clearly an important first step in any analysis. Storage (storing processes) logically may occur directly after production.

Production → Processing → Storage

Alternatively, distribution may occur directly after production and before processing and storage.

Production → Distribution → Processing → Storage

The relationship between the quantity produced and the quantity stored is problematical. The goods produced may have traveled some distance either before or after they are stored. In addition, the producers and the food processors may or may not be the same people, depending upon the ordering of production, processing, distribution, and storing activities. Of course, one also has to consider a direct line from production to consumption, in which there is no storage at all.

Production → Consumption

From an archaeological perspective, we can ask: which features of storing processes manifest themselves in the archaeological record? Material remains will look different at each point in the material-means provisioning process. Goods may, for example, be aggregated at the point of production. Distribution sites, i.e., sites containing goods that have been moved from the point of production to another place, will look different from production sites. Depending upon where storage comes in the life cycle of a good, understanding storing processes sheds light on the nature of production and distribution.

Seven

A CROSS-CULTURAL TREATMENT OF THE INFORMAL ECONOMY

> *The informal economy is a market-based response of the people to the overweening attempts of bureaucracy to control economic life from above. The social forms capable of succeeding state capitalism are likely to be grounded, at least embryonically, in that response.*
> (HART 1992:223)

This chapter proposes a model of the informal economy that can be used as a heuristic device for dealing with variability, plurality, and change in economic systems across cultures and over time. It is an extension of the institutional paradigm in the sense that it elaborates the concept of informal economy as a general cross-cultural process that is organized differently in different contexts. I explore the potentials of the concept by drawing upon a range of cultural systems—from hunter-gatherer to third-world and post-industrial states.

Most discussions of the informal economy have been restricted to the marginal, hidden, or illegal segments of urban, state-level societies (Arizpe 1977; Babb 1985; Bromley 1978a, 1978b, 1985; Davies 1979; Dow 1977; Gaertner and Wenig 1985; Hoyman 1987; Mattera 1985; Obregon 1980; Peattie 1980, 1982). Whether under capitalism, or in centrally planned economies (Grossman 1988; Sampson 1985–86, 1987; Wedel 1986; Bloch 1985–86), the primary foci have been industrialized societies or the urban sectors of developing countries (Gerry 1987; Hart 1973; Miller 1987; Trager 1985, 1987).

The rural parts of state systems have not received attention from analysts of the informal economy. For the most part, discussions have used ethnographic materials from rural and non-state societies as quaint examples of small-scale systems, or as indications that principles such as kin-based reciprocity (Mauss 1925; Lévi-Strauss 1969; Polanyi 1957; Sahlins 1972) are universal, with variations in different cultural contexts (Gaughan and Ferman 1987). With a few exceptions, exchange processes have been emphasized to the exclusion of processes of production or consumption (Simon and White 1982; Lomnitz 1988; Gaughan and Ferman 1987).

Most importantly for our purposes, these focused treatments of the informal economy have not used their discussions to inform the subfield of economic anthropology as the scientific study of economies across cultures (Halperin 1988). As a result, some confusions are in evidence. For example, the domain to which the concept of the informal economy applies is not at all clear. The concept has been used in both the developed and the underdeveloped world, but with some inconsistencies. The rural parts have been assumed to constitute the informal sectors. If, on the other hand, the rural as well as urban parts of industrial and pre-industrial or industrializing states can be said to have both formal and informal sectors, how should these be considered? A concept of the informal economy that is cross-culturally and historically based will solve some of these problems.

In this chapter, I take a broad-based perspective and attempt to develop a model to explore the utility of the concept of the informal economy as a cross-cultural construct. The wording "explore the utility" is important because our aim here is to examine the potentials of a concept of the informal economy for understanding pattern, variability, and change in processes of production, distribution, and consumption in a range of sociocultural types. That is, I develop the concept of the informal economy as a heuristic device or model—a conceptual tool that can be used to understand aspects of economic processes that would remain hidden without such an analytic instrument. I use the concept of the informal economy to deal with processes of production as well as with processes of distribution—in particular, problems of the organization of the productive resources, land, labor, and credit (Long and Richardson 1978; Illich 1981; Henry 1987). To summarize thus far: (1) we need a concept of the informal economy that can be used across cultures and over time; (2) this chapter is intended to indicate how such a cross-cultural concept of the informal economy can be formulated. Below, I outline a model of the informal economy and present some examples of how the model can be used in different cultural contexts.

Definitions and Assumptions

FORMAL ECONOMY AS MAINSTREAM ECONOMY

First, some definitions and assumptions. If we assume that all economies have both formal and informal components, then, logically speaking, the informal economy can be understood analytically as the opposite of the formal economy. Any treatment of a concept of the informal economy, then, requires a prior definition of what constitutes the formal economy. For definitional purposes, we can say that the formal economy is the mainstream economy. By "mainstream economy" we mean what Polanyi referred to as the dominant mode of economic integration, or, more simply, the major, recognized, and accounted for (by either qualitative or quantitative mechanisms) principles organizing a given economic process or set of processes. The formal sector of the economy also operates in a hegemonic fashion over the informal economy. It is dominant.

The formal economy is both a folk and an analytic concept. In its folk meaning, the formal economy is recognized in a given cultural system as being the officially sanctioned, most accessible to those in power, and the expected way of doing things—in either the normative or the statistical sense, or both. Analytically, the formal economy may be a model that is set up for scientific purposes only, say, as a set of ideals, or as a set of expectations under known or controlled conditions. As will become clear below, the analytical meaning of informal economy can be understood in similar terms. From both folk and analytical perspectives, the formal economy may generally be understood as follows: In state-level economies, the formal economy may be organized by the polity itself in its many pre-industrial or industrial forms, by the capitalist market mechanism, or by some combination of the two. In pre-state societies, kinship principles or principles involving age sets, for example, may dominate the organization of economic processes. Notice that the definition of the formal economy here does not refer only to bureaucratic mechanisms, but includes a range of structures.and institutions, both bureaucratic and non-bureaucratic (Hart 1973).

INFORMAL ECONOMY AS
"ANTI-ECONOMY"

Given the above framework for the formal economy, the informal economy is the opposite of the formal economy, what we will call the "anti-economy." The anti-economy can be defined as follows: locational and appropriational movements outside of the mainstream economy (Polanyi 1957). Remember that locational movements involve physical changes, such as the movement of goods from one place to another; appropriational movements involve changes in organizational principles, primarily the nature of the rights and obligations associated with a given economic process.

The term "anti-economy" is meant to indicate tension between the formal and the informal elements of economic processes, whether the tension takes the form of deviance from the mainstream economy (as in breaking the rules of the mainstream economy by secret or illegal activity), or whether the tension takes the form of alternative economic institutions that operate in parallel to the mainstream institutions. Whatever its form, we can assume that there is always tension between the formal and the informal components of economic processes. In some instances, for example, only some of the folk will have access to knowledge of the workings of the informal economy. Still others may have access to the goods of the informal economy. There is a tug-of-war between the formal and informal economies that operates on several levels. The framework that I am suggesting allows for the fact that what was at one time an informal sector may become formal and dominant; or there may be changes in both formal and informal components of economies such that both change qualitatively and quantitatively.

Defined operationally in this way, the concept of the informal economy is not necessarily restricted to state systems, but can be used across cultures and over time. If we assume that variability in principles of economic organization exists in all economies—that no economy is completely homogeneous—then the advantage of a cross-cultural concept of the informal economy is that it provides an analytical tool for gaining some insight into the nature of the variability. I might note here that, especially for kin-based economies, the assumption that principles of economic organization (e.g., reciprocity) operate consistently and homogeneously is a holdover from British structural-functionalism and has prevented the examination of variability. Malinowski (1922) used terms such as "reciprocity" to describe many different kinds of economic exchanges. Raymond Firth (1929, 1939) followed in his footsteps. Helen Codere (1968) wrote of social economies as organized by reciprocity, and political economies as organized by redistribution. Even Morton Fried (1967), whose framework was evolutionary rather than functionalist, wrote of egalitarian societies having reciprocal economies, but did so without any attention to the variability inherent in these economies and polities. This concept of the informal economy as anti-economy is designed to get at some of this variability.

VARIABILITY WITHIN ECONOMIES

We can use the concept of the informal economy, then, to question conventional canons about economic organization, especially about the homogeneity of small-scale economic systems. In short, a concept of the informal economy, if used heuristically in a cross-cultural framework, allows us to ask certain kinds of questions that are difficult to ask otherwise. For example, the division of labor by age and sex has commonly been thought to operate in all small-scale egalitarian societies in an exclusive and consistent fashion. But what happens if we use a concept of the anti-economy to ask such questions as: What are the conditions under which men and women, young and old, reverse economic roles? What are the economic rituals of rebellion? Who is exempt, either permanently or temporarily, from the conventional economic rules and roles? We find that some very interesting answers emerge. One is that we find deviation and flexibility that, when recognized, lead to a series of other questions: How much informality is allowed? How much deviation from the mainstream economic principles can exist before the system changes radically or falls apart? How many alternative forms of economic organization are possible?

In all cultures informal economic mechanisms can be understood to provide people with time flexibility and with alternative ways of resisting or varying their standard processes of livelihood. A concept of the informal economy as "anti-economy" allows us to examine relationships between different kinds of economic activities, i.e., those organized by different principles. These relationships have been handled in a rather cumbersome manner, e.g., as "articulating modes of production" (Foster-Carter 1978; Taussig 1980).

*Pre-State Societies: The Informal Economy as a
Barometer of Variability, Conflict, and Change*

My basic hypothesis is that, in pre-state systems,
the model of the informal economy can be used as a barometer of variability that may lead to conflict and, ultimately, change.

THE !KUNG AND THE JIVARO

For egalitarian societies, it is difficult to conceptualize or imagine how an informal anti-economy might work except as
a barometer of conflict and change. The inimitable, non-shareable Coke
bottle that falls out of the sky in the film, "The Gods Must be Crazy" is
one very clever, highly symbolic example of what happens when egalitarian cultures become suddenly integrated into nation-state capitalist
systems. The bottle represents exclusivity, indeed, private property, and
cannot, without extremely rapid and radical change in the economic system, coexist in an economy of sharing and generalized reciprocity. Exclusivity can also be imposed from the outside by the nation-state in
ways that cause conflict and, ultimately, cultural disintegration. Once the
!Kung have been placed on a reservation, their sedentary existence renders them reliant upon government rations (the distasteful mealie-
mealie). Since there is a scarcity of this food, and since all food must be
purchased with cash, sharing is very difficult (Marshall 1980). The fact
that the !Kung woman, N!ai, becomes a street beggar who sells her songs
for cash is an example of the development of an informal economy. Her
exclusive access to songs, and thus, cash, creates at least as much conflict
as the Coke bottle.

An example of an informal economic arrangement operating parallel
to the mainstream economy of reciprocity is that of the accumulative
economy of the Jivaro shamans. The five Jivaro tribes, whose population
was estimated to be 7,830 persons in 1956–1957, inhabit the tropical forest of the Ecuadorian and Peruvian Amazon. Their subsistence patterns
include the cultivation of sweet manioc, and a variety of other carbohy-
drates including sweet potatoes and peanuts, in gardens in a manner of
shifting cultivation, or "slash and burn" swidden. They also hunt for
protein. Harner (1973:81) reports that "one's status in a neighborhood is
greatly affected by one's generosity with beer and food." The shamans
exemplify the "anti-economy." They are the only people who are exempt from the dominant, mainstream economy of reciprocity in goods

and labor. They are the only people allowed to engage in accumulation. For example, Harner reports that, for an ordinary Jivaro, a request for a gift cannot be denied without the one refusing "losing face." This makes it difficult for the majority of persons to hoard quantities of possessions (Harner 1973:117). Non-shamans badger one another continually for gifts, but these ordinary people almost never ask a shaman for gifts. The shaman's ability to accumulate appears to be important for political relations with neighboring groups since shamans "frequently use their wealth and social influence to secure specific services from their non-shaman neighbors, including hosting neighbors to help in land clearing" (1973:118). It is interesting to note that according to the ideological system, this acquisition of services with the expectation of a return effort is understood as reciprocal cooperative labor, but, says Harner, "the shaman's neighbors are reluctant to ask him to work for them in turn" (1973:118). In addition, Harner reports several cases in which shamans received daughters in marriage, but were exempt from both bride service and bride price (Harner 1973:118).

Among the many interesting elements in the Jivaro case is the fact that the "anti-economy" is so public and political. It allows the shaman to play both political (alliance-forming) and economic (goods-and-services-obtaining) roles. It is also of note that one out of every four adult men is a shaman, a significant portion of the male population. They cannot be discounted as rarities or deviants. In short, non-mainstream economic activities are not significant. Rather, what we have here is a case in which the concept of the informal economy can be used to indicate heretofore unrecognized variability in an Amazon Basin economy. These economies have conventionally been treated as homogeneous, reciprocal economies.

THE TIV

For the African Tiv, the Bohannans (1968) are much more specific about some of the informal elements of the economy. Women's work, which is informally organized, stands in contrast to the more formally organized men's work. The formal rules of work organization consist of the following: (1) brothers tend to work together; (2) co-wives work separately, unless they are attached to senior wives.

Ordinarily, work groups of women tend to be smaller and more circumscribed than those of men. Women's work groups are composed of a senior woman, those junior wives who are "put into her hut," and her daughters-in-law (1968:70). According to the Bohannans, the important facts about such female groups are as follows: (1) the optimal, day-to-day size of a working group of women is three to four women (1968:71); (2) if there are more, they tend to form two groups; (3) women who find themselves in an uncongenial group leave their husbands.

There is one condition under which women deviate from this pattern. This is for weeding. The Bohannans describe what is involved in extremely tentative terms, to indicate irregularity:

> All of the women of one compound, or of several nearby compounds, may band together two or three times a year for a hoeing party to weed the fields of each of them. Such a hoeing party is "called" by a senior woman, who supplies food and beer. . . .
> These groups are usually composed of between fifteen and twenty women, but there may be as many as thirty-five. The important point is that this is the major form of agricultural cooperation among women; other forms are rare.
> (1968:73)

In contrast to the irregular and sporadic nature of large cooperative work groups for women, men cooperate regularly, systematically, and in a formal manner:

> Cooperation in agricultural tasks is more formally developed among men and has no equivalents among women. . . . When hoeing mounds (of yams) in large groups each man makes a diagonal row of mounds, but all work together in a single vertical row. This enables them to mound the field with regularity. As soon as a man's diagonal row reaches the side of the field, he goes to the other end of the line. Between forty and fifty men mounded about five acres of yams in two days.
> (1968:73 – 74)

It is difficult to know how many groups of this type have similar combinations of formal and informal arrangements of large-scale cooperative labor. One suspects that such informal ways of organizing work are quite common. Ethnographers tend to deal only with the dominant forms of work organization, however, and do not look for the variability. In the

Tiv case, it is possible to contemplate a whole range of deviations from the clearly articulated forms of production and particularly exchange. The systems of conveyances and convergences, described in great detail by the Bohannans, can be, and probably are, subject to a variety of irregular forms.

We can begin to see one important point from the Tiv example, a point that will be further elaborated below: the institutional context determines whether a given form of organization is informal or not. In one institutional context, large groups of workers, organized along kinship lines, may be dominant and, therefore, represent the mainstream (formal) economy. In others, household–based groups are dominant. Deviations from the dominant form constitute the informal elements of the economy. The point at which informality in work turns into deviance, pure and simple, is another important issue.

State Systems: The Informal Economy as a Barometer of Pluralism and Change

In state systems, the informal economy is not only a barometer of variability and change, but also of pluralism. By "pluralism" we mean numerous economic sectors and activities operating simultaneously. Complicating the systems at the state level is the fact that the informal sector itself is heterogeneous, with many different types of economic activities, e.g., street vendors, small market traders, and small shops, as well as many different categories of workers (Trager 1987). The importance of the overall institutional context in determining the informal economy will become even more clear. We will use three examples to illustrate the utility of a cross-cultural concept of the informal economy as the "anti-economy" outside of the dominant capitalist contexts and in rural and non–bureaucratic settings: the first involves centrally planned economies; the second treats stores and storekeepers in a rural Appalachian community; the third considers marketplace systems in rural Kentucky as they interact with other modes of distribution.

CENTRALLY PLANNED ECONOMIES

The utility of first defining the informal economy as the "anti-economy" and then using the concept as a heuristic device is nowhere made more clear than in the case of centrally planned economies in the former Soviet Union and Eastern Europe. In this context, there are several anti-economies operating simultaneously both in conjunction with and in opposition to the mainstream, centrally planned economy. We draw here on the work of Steven Sampson because he deals with varying forms of the informal economy, from

> *capitalist entrepreneurship: the peasant who cultivates her private plot and sells the produce on the free market, speculative trading, middlemen fees, renting property, money, lending, and operating a private firm . . . [to] producing or selling illegal goods such as narcotics or providing illegal services such as prostitution; pilfering from the workplace, . . . conducting unregistered or untaxed trade; and paying off police or inspectors to ignore such activities . . . [to] second economy activities that are neither typically capitalist nor universally illegal . . . underground factories; paying bribes or tips in order to buy something in a store or to induce planners and controllers to revise plans; buying and reselling goods obtained from shops for foreigners; and selling scarce or rationed goods taken from the state.*
> (1987:121)

Sampson argues that these second economies must be understood within the context of the total economic system: "The second economy is an integral part of the official, planned economy, sometimes complementing it, sometimes hindering it directly, sometimes competing with it" (1987:122). A cross-cultural definition of the informal economy is essential for dealing with this variability. All of these are forms of the informal economy, but to define the informal economy only in terms of exchange and not production, for example, rules out underground factories. To define the informal economy as only those activities that are illegal rules out all of the alternative forms that are legal, but non-mainstream. Clearly, today the situation in the former Soviet Union is reversing itself. Private entrepreneurs are coming to dominate the mainstream.

A RURAL APPALACHIAN ECONOMY

The operation of informal mechanisms in rural, non-bureaucratic settings is often quite secretive and always full of subtlety and nuance. In this essentially kin-organized subsistence economy, storekeepers engage in certain kinds of informal economic arrangements which produce tension in the system. The rural Appalachian community under consideration here is that of Little Laurel, described by George Hicks in the book *Appalachian Valley* (1973). Little Laurel is a community typical of many in the Appalachian region: it is small (population 1,300 at the time of fieldwork) and its economy is oriented to subsistence farming combined with daily and weekly, as well as seasonal, migration to towns and cities for factory-based wage labor. Loyalty to kin is a primary principle of social and economic organization and store patronage is patterned along kinship lines. Trade in both livestock and other goods has existed for at least a century.

Storekeepers in Little Laurel are the intermediaries between the subsistence and the cash economy. They control the flow of goods and cash both into and out of the rural community. Storekeepers also compete with one another for clientele. For example, galax, a fern gathered in Little Laurel by men, women, and children alike, and used as background greenery in flower arrangements, is sold to florists outside of the community for cash. Storekeepers distribute galax to the outside by obtaining galax from clients and converting it into credit against a person's account. As Hicks describes it, when a galacker who is known to be a regular customer of store A, in which his galax would be converted into credit only, wants cash for his galax in store B, storekeeper B must not reveal this cash transaction to store owner A, to whom the galacker owes money. This secret economic transaction is part of the informal economy in this small community.

Storekeepers also have other sorts of knowledge about economic matters. While Hicks notes that the secrets are often short-lived, there is a short-run economic advantage for the people involved. For example, Hicks reports:

> Locations of good patches of galax, prices paid for land and livestock, the whereabouts of individuals at various times, and the income of families are all matters about which storekeepers have a great deal of

> knowledge. *They find it to their own advantage not*
> *to spread their knowledge too freely.*
>
> *Indeed, the successful operation of a store in the*
> *Little Laurel depends very much upon the storekeep-*
> *er's adeptness in controlling the flow of information*
> *among himself and his customers. Privy to many se-*
> *crets, he can choose what part of them to put into*
> *circulation. . . . By protecting his customers—keep-*
> *ing wives from knowing what husbands are doing or*
> *government officials from knowledge of certain illegal*
> *activities in the valley—he earns their gratitude and*
> *attaches them more firmly to his store. Information*
> *about the plans and activities of his competitors' busi-*
> *nesses is, thus, in appreciation for past favors, taken*
> *in and used to financial advantage.*
>
> (1973:87)

Here, mechanisms of kinship and friendship are part of the informal economy, but the consequences of violating kinship obligations, a distinct possibility where multiple stores are used by clients, are unclear. This example raises questions about the relationships between informality, secrecy, and even corruption, and the position of a person or group in the local and the regional stratification system.

A PERIODIC MARKETPLACE SYSTEM IN EASTERN KENTUCKY

Periodic marketplace systems can be the primary and dominant mode of extra-community (non-local) distribution; this has been true in much of the pre-industrial third world. Examples from China (Skinner 1964) and Mexico (Cook and Diskin 1976; Malinowski and de la Fuente 1982) are common. On the other hand, periodic marketplace systems can be the key components of the informal economy. Our work in eastern Kentucky illustrates this point. At the rural urban interface the periodic marketplace system is a major source of cash as well as an outlet for locally produced goods. The marketplace system is, however, only one component, albeit an important one, of a system of multiple livelihood strategies that consists of three factors: (1) the informal (periodic marketplace) sector; (2) the formal (market economy) sector; (3) the subsistence sector, which is neutral from the point of view of formal and informal principles of economic organization (Halperin, 1990).

The example of the informal economy in eastern Kentucky raises some important points associated with our hypothesis that informal economies are barometers not only of variability, but also of pluralism and change in the organization of economic systems. First, the system of marketplaces has grown enormously during our six years of fieldwork. The numbers of vendors in each major marketplace, and the number of actual marketplaces, have increased markedly. In one of the major marketplaces, for example, the number of stalls, both interior and exterior, grows on a weekly basis. When we first began the fieldwork, there were several empty aisles inside the converted tobacco warehouse; now all booths are occupied and the marketplace has expanded. Ironically, perhaps, it is located in an area adjacent to a large shopping mall in which many identical items are sold for as much as ten times the price. Many of the vendors in the market are themselves owners of stores and shops in both urban and rural areas. It could be argued that the existence of such an alternative system of distribution is what makes it possible for the large numbers of light industry factories. Alternative sources of distribution for goods are essential in this context; otherwise people would either have to retreat back to the Deep Rural areas or move to the cities and become totally dependent upon cash from low-level jobs or welfare. The fact that the interface provides so many livelihood alternatives, and that people utilize multiple strategies, is an indicator of pluralism that appears on the increase and, for the near future, likely to remain. The point should be underlined, however.

SUMMARY

I have argued here that if we define the informal economy as the "anti-economy," then all economies have informal components (institutional arrangements). In this framework, the concept of the informal economy is a heuristic device designed to handle variability, pluralism, and change in economic systems.

Informality is not necessarily "a residue of traditionalism" (Lomnitz 1988:42). Informal components may represent the newest economic form, or at least a sophisticated set of adaptations at various levels of local, regional, and national economies. What is informal, or even corrupt, at the local level may simply be normal and regular in the upper echelons of the state bureaucracy. The abilities of local elites in Mexico to monopolize resources by using their ties to the state come immediately to mind.

It is clear that, as an analytic tool for cross-cultural analysis, the concept of the informal economy tells us different things in different types of economies, capitalist and non-capitalist, state and non-state. The informal components of economies are organized; they are instituted in complex and changing ways. In this framework, informal economies are not marginal, but represent variability and alternativity across cultures and over time.

Eight

TIME AND THE ECONOMY: A SUBSTANTIVE PERSPECTIVE

All great theories are expansive, and all notions so rich in scope and implication are underpinned by visions about the nature of things. You may call such visions "philosophy," or "metaphor," or "organizing principle," but one great thing they are surely not— they are not simple inductions from observed facts of the natural world.
(GOULD 1987:9)

The test of any organizing principle is its success in rendering specifics, not its status as abstract generality . . . time's arrow and time's cycle is, if you will, a "great" dichotomy because each of its poles captures, by its essence, a theme so central to intellectual (and practical) life that Western people who hope to understand history must wrestle intimately with both—for time's arrow is the intelligibility of distinct and irreversible events, while time's cycle is the intelligibility of timeless order and lawlike structure. We must have both.
(GOULD 1987:15–16)

Time is a dimension of economic organization in all cultures. All processes of material provisioning—production, distribution, and consumption—involve time and timing. Time is also implicit (even explicit) in some of the traditional topics in economic anthropology, such as periodic marketplace systems, seasonal production regimes, or cycles of crop rotation. Yet time, in all of its dimensions, has either been treated very narrowly,[1] or has been largely assumed or ignored by economic anthropologists. It is still relatively rare, for example, to find a group or a village studied ethnographically at more than one point in time.[2] By the same token, all ethnographic studies, including economic ones, have been filled with images and concepts of time, whether these are subtle and implicit, or the subjects of chapter headings. How did concepts of time affect the study of economies? What kinds of temporal categories, if any, came out of these perspectives?

I use a handful of cases, classic and contemporary—including Evans-Pritchard's classic *The Nuer* (1944)—to begin to provide some substantive perspectives upon the time frames within which economic processes are organized and within which they change. I also examine some of the time concepts that are embedded in Polanyi's work and some of the potential uses of a processual concept of time (chronotype) for refining and elaborating a general theory of the economy, especially the forms of economic integration. While this chapter begins by going back to the discussion of householding and its timing introduced in chapter 5, we can appreciate that processes of reciprocity, redistribution, and exchange, as well as householding, will vary depending on the time frames within which they are carried out and organized. Historical and evolutionary time, linear and cyclical time (Heidegger 1982), seasonal time (Mauss and Beuchat 1968), and life course (Lambek 1990) are some of the frameworks to keep in mind. Whether or not economic processes such as resource allocation, and production itself, occur over long or short time periods, or whether exchange processes can be delayed or prolonged, all figure in to the shape of economic organization. In all economies, productive work must be scheduled and resources allocated and placed in definite order. There are periodicities to production and distribution processes, just as there are rhythms to storage and consumption. Do similarities in time and timing tell us anything about similarities in economic organization? How can we understand and use different time frames to model economic processes? (See Halpern 1992.) The archaeological record is particularly important in this regard, because the choices of time frame are legion.

Johannes Fabian's book, *Time and the Other* (1983), an essay on the uses of time in anthropological discourses, is the springboard for this chapter. In a manner perhaps unintended by Fabian, his book stimulates questions about the temporal dimensions of the economy that can be addressed using a substantivist perspective. Given the traditional archaeological concern with time, and given the absence of time considerations in the classic (British structural-functionalist) ethnographies of economic anthropology, it is appropriate to introduce time as a critical component of economic processes.

This chapter begins with a discussion of time and the substantive economy. It then turns to the timing of householding in two cases, Kentucky and Guatemala, both viewed as rural economies within states. These are alternative time frames for simultaneously using and resisting capitalism. Evans-Pritchard's discussion of time in his chapter in *The Nuer*, "Time and Space," follows. The next part of this chapter deals with a case of African horticulturists as described by Jane Guyer (1991). The last section focuses specifically on the issue of time and the economy in one archaeological case.

The anthropological literature has seen a recent flowering of interest in the analysis of time in cultural systems (Munn 1992; Bender and Wellbery 1991). With only a few exceptions,[3] however, the analysis of time has been connected to symbolic systems, not to material ones, and the question of time and the economy in concrete, everyday life has not really been addressed from an institutional perspective. Also time has been dealt with primarily in relation to action and actors (Munn 1992: 94)—or, in Giddens' terms, with an emphasis on agency rather than on structure. Munn emphasizes the methodological individualism in Bourdieu's treatment of time and the economy. Among other things, Munn notes (1992:106) that Bourdieu "frames time through an agent-oriented lens." She says also that "the temporality of action is integral to Bourdieu's theory of practice." Interestingly, Munn (1992:107) points out that when Bourdieu examines calendric rhythms and periodization (1977, 1964), his "agent-oriented lens tends to disappear in the more conventional focus on the multiple rhythms of different production activities" (Bourdieu 1977). She is critical, however, of the fact that in *Outline of a Theory of Practice* he "does not follow these 'incommensurable islands of duration' into the microlevel of daily life where situated actors, operating in the light of expectations and past references . . . strategically develop the sequences and tempos of work. Instead, he pursues the symbolic homologies that relate the different task cycles in a general 'logic of practice'" (Munn 1992:107). In short Munn is saying that he switches from methodological individualist to symbolic anthropologist. He does, however, go back to methodological individualism in his discussion in *The Logic of Practice* of the interactional models of games and exchanges (Bourdieu 1990), and Munn says (1992:107): "In these contexts one encounters Bourdieu's actor strategically manipulating time."[4]

This chapter takes a very different tack. We are not interested in temporality as illuminated in economic processes, but rather in the timing of economic processes per se—that is, what attention to time and temporality tells us about pattern and variation in economic processes. How do people in cultural systems construct sequences of economic processes? The concern here is not with the timing of economic action, but with the timing of economic processes.

Polanyi's concerns for economies in both history and anthropology, his ideas about the historical development of the market economy, and his strong "transformative" emphasis, most explicit in *The Great Transformation* (1944) (but also present elsewhere in his work), suggest that his models of the economy (from the most general and abstract to the most specific) contain concepts about time that have not been explicated. For example, locational and appropriational movements all involve duration as well as sequencing. These concepts need to be made explicit with respect to time if the full benefits of his cross-cultural, comparative approaches to economic organization are to be realized and used by archaeologists, ethnohistorians, and ethnographers. By the same token, it is not sufficient to confine our discussions of time and the economy to Polanyi, for we are now at a point in economic anthropology where we can elaborate Polanyi's models beyond what was possible in the 1950s.

Fabian's essay, *Time and the Other*, begins with an economic analysis (in the form of a quote from Charles Dickens's *Hard Times*) of time. Specifically he is talking about people knowing or not knowing the value of time—time concepts being a way of differentiating people from one another—in effect a stratification pattern:

> *"You see, my friend," Mr. Bounderby put in, "we are the kind of people who know the value of time, and you are the kind of people who don't know the value of time." "I have not," retorted Mr. Childers, after surveying him from head to foot, "the honour of knowing you—but if you mean that you can make more money of your time than I can of mine, I should judge from your appearance that you are about right."*
> (AS QUOTED IN FABIAN 1983:IX)

We can see in this quote some of the assumptions about time that capitalism has created—that time is indeed something to be valued in monetary terms and that it is indeed quantifiable according to the measuring rod of money. The assumption here is that time is a possession; it is something one does or does not have, again in definite quantities and with certain trade-offs for individuals. Similar kinds of assumptions about time have been projected onto a whole range of economies—small and large, simple and complex—in ways that resemble the aforementioned time allocation studies, but also in ways that may mask what we actually know about these economies if we broaden our notions of time.

I began to suggest some alternative time frames in chapter 5 on householding, but I did not give this full attention. Similarly, in chapter 6 on storage, time was certainly implicated in the entire discussion, but not addressed directly. We know that many hunter-gatherer groups, both small and large, simple and complex, engage in sometimes rather elaborate storage processes. But storage processes, especially among hunter-gatherers, that prolong the time period for which goods are available are only beginning to be examined. How then do we as analysts conceptualize time in order to begin to account for these kinds of realities and variations?

Time and the Substantive Economy

If we read Polanyi's essay "The Economy as Instituted Process" (1957), we learn that there are notions of time implicit in his generic model of the economy (this is what Polanyi here calls the substantive definition of the economy). The substantive economy is situated in both time and place. The formal economy, by contrast, operates in a time and space vacuum. When Polanyi says that the formal economy derives from logic and the substantive economy from fact, he is acknowledging the rootedness of the substantive economy in historical circumstances. This, of course, is a Marxian notion.

Polanyi's model of the substantive economy is designed to investigate a range of economies understood in historical and evolutionary frames:

> It is our proposition that only the substantive meaning of "economic" is capable of yielding the concepts that are required by the social sciences for an investigation of all the empirical economies of the past and present.
> (1957:244)

Polanyi is really constructing an argument which shows that the market economy is an historically particular form of economic organization. The market economy is not one that has existed in all times and places. As Polanyi says:

> But the anthropologist, the sociologist or the historian, each in his study of the place occupied by the economy in human society, was faced with a great variety of institutions other than markets, in which man's livelihood was embedded.
>
> (1957:245)

The economy "as instituted process" has two key components or concepts: "process" and its "institutedness" (1957:248). Polanyi states that "process suggests analysis in terms of motion." Since I have dealt with Polanyi's concepts of locational and appropriational movements in chapters 2 and 3, I will not dwell on them here. I will say, however, that Polanyi's use of the term "motion" here is a code for the words history and change. What he is really saying about economic processes is that they change over time. One might even go so far as to say that economic processes work dialectically, and this requires some complex concepts of time—concepts that Marx suggested but did not elaborate.

Polanyi's notion of "institutedness" is a difficult one, but it is one in which time plays a critical part. Actually, "institutedness" refers to the cumulative properties of culture (J. Halpern, personal communication). First Polanyi makes a claim for the stability and continuity of economic processes in society (cultural systems) over time:

> The instituting of the economic process vests that process with unity and stability; it produces a structure with a definite function in society; it shifts the place of the process in society, thus adding significance to its history. . . . Unity and stability, structure and function, history and policy spell out operationally the content of our assertion that the human economy is an instituted process. . . . The study of the shifting place occupied by the economy in society is therefore no other than the study of the manner in which the eco-

nomic process is instituted at different times and
places.
(1957:249–250)

Over time economic organization takes different forms. This is what he means by "the shifting place occupied by the economy." The forms of economic integration are designed to provide some ways of ordering the variable forms of the economy found in the past and the present. Built in to Polanyi's models, which he calls forms of economic integration, is a notion of continuity of form over some fairly long period of evolutionary time. Therefore, by arguing that the behaviors of individuals alone do not add up to a form of economic integration, Polanyi is not only rejecting a form of methodological individualism, he is also making an argument for the longevity of certain forms, albeit with variations. In other words, institutional arrangements do not crop up overnight; neither are they a one-night stand. They develop over time and they must persist at least to the point of achieving some stability before they can be considered as forms of economic integration. Polanyi writes of the structures that are essential in order for the forms of economic integration to exist:

> *Hence our forms of integration and supporting structure patterns.*
>
> *This should help to explain why in the economic sphere interpersonal behavior so often fails to have the expected societal effects in the absence of definite institutional preconditions. Only in a symmetrically organized environment will reciprocative behavior result in economic institutions of any importance; only where allocative centers have been set up can individual acts of sharing produce a redistributive economy and only in the presence of a system of price-making markets will exchange acts of individuals result in fluctuating prices that integrate the economy. Otherwise such acts of barter will remain ineffective and therefore tend not to occur.*
> (1957:252)

This does not mean that institutional arrangements are static or inert; it simply means that they change slowly over time—that they evolve. The patterns of change are worthy of study.

One of the factors Polanyi uses to describe variation in forms of economic organization is time, here meant as duration or permanence of the unit (Polanyi 1957:254): "Redistribution, too, is apt to integrate groups at all levels and all degrees of permanence from the state itself to units of a transitory character." This last is not to be confused with the substitution of forms of integration for stages of evolution:

> *In any case, forms of integration do not represent*
> *"stages" of development. No sequence of time is*
> *implied. Several subordinate forms may be present*
> *alongside of the dominant one, which may itself*
> *recur after a temporary eclipse.*
> (POLANYI 1957:256)

The confusing thing here is that the above disclaimer has been interpreted to mean that Polanyi's framework fits into the static British structural-functional mold and that time itself is not an important aspect of Polanyi's work. Clearly, given the examples above, this statement is simply a rejection of unilineal evolution, not an eradication of time as a variable in forming economic processes and institutions.

Polanyi then proceeds to analyze forms of trade in terms of "the facts of anthropology and history" (1957:257). He starts from the proposition that all trade is not market trade because markets developed relatively late:

> *Trade, as well as some money uses, are as old as*
> *mankind; while markets, although meetings of an*
> *economic character may have existed as early as the*
> *Neolithic, did not gain importance until compara-*
> *tively late in history.*
> (1957:257)

Polanyi concludes the essay by talking about the development of price systems over time (1957:269). This follows an elaborate discussion of trade, its forms and components, and its development.

The Timing of Householding in Guatemala

> *How far, and in what ways, did this shift in time-*
> *sense affect labour discipline, and how far did it influ-*

> ence the inward apprehension of time of working
> people? If the transition to mature industrial society
> entailed a severe restructuring of working habits—
> new disciplines, new incentives, and a new human
> nature upon which these incentives could bite effec-
> tively—how far is this related to changes in the in-
> ward notation of time?
> (THOMPSON 1991:354)

As is evident from the above, E. P. Thompson's is one of the clearest discussions of capitalism's rhythms. These are very different from the rhythms of agrarian societies seen above. We need more investigations of the intricate timing and coordination processes required for rural people in nation-states to participate in industrial capitalist systems without becoming entirely dependent upon them for their livelihood and without giving up a strong degree of autonomy and cultural identity.[5] My discussion of householding as a form of integration in chapter 5 begins to address some of these issues. Here I want to highlight some points with respect to the specific issue of "Time and the Economy" by adding an additional case for comparative purposes—that recorded by Sheldon Annis for rural Guatemala (1987). I will suggest that what Annis describes for Guatemala as "*milpa* logic" can be understood as a form of householding that involves the coordination of time and timing in different economic arenas in a manner that is very similar to "the Kentucky way." The reader will recall from chapter 5 that householding in Kentucky involves three economic arenas each with separate and distinct, often conflicting, and sometimes overlapping schedules: (1) a pre-capitalist system of family farms and gardens, (2) a non-capitalist, informal rotating periodic marketplace system (flea markets), and (3) a capitalist system of factory-based wage labor.

The functional equivalents of these arenas in the Guatemalan case include: (1) *milpa* agriculture—a pre-capitalist traditional system very much like that of the family farms and gardens; (2) a series of family business enterprises that are very much like those that operate in the marketplace system in Kentucky; and (3) a system of wage labor that is not quite as rigid as that in the factories in Kentucky because it consists primarily of agricultural day labor. As we will see below, "*milpa* logic" has many features in common with "the Kentucky way." It is versatile and practical; it uses resources in ways that are quite foreign to capitalism; at the same time, however, it operates within an increasingly capitalistic context. In Polanyi's terms, this is a pattern of householding that is deeply embedded in a long-standing cultural system. In Annis' words: "production is both an idea and an expression of social circumstance . . . the *milpa* is not only an economically elegant way to produce corn and beans, it is an elegant expression of what is here called 'Indianness'" (1987:10).

The key characteristic of the system of "*milpa* logic" is that it is an internally driven (family and village) system that makes use of small quantities of resources that might otherwise be wasted. These resources include time as well as certain kinds of crops. Annis describes the *milpa* as "an agronomic system that operates by producing a very large number of very small quantities" (1987:36). The products of the *milpa* are quite varied; they can be consumed, sold, or fed to livestock: "Farmers often casually described plants by saying 'solo es monte' (just weeds) even though such 'weeds' can be sold as herbs, medicinal plants, dyestuffs, or can be fed to the turkey" (1987:36). Crops of very rapid maturation such as ornamental flowers and radishes can be sold and/or consumed. The choice of intercrops is very important, for these crops can be more important than the corn itself for the maintenance of the subsistence system and the cultural system. For example, the choice of intercrops depends on a variety of factors including the distance of the *milpa*, whether or not a man has other employment, and who is available to tend secondary crops:

> Is there a young son who can be sent daily to weed vegetables and watch for pests. Crops can be more or less processed (e.g., sorted, cleaned, cooked, bundled) before being sold at market. Is someone available who has the time and skills to do the processing—someone, moreover, who cannot earn a higher rate of return at some other occupation during that unit of time. (ANNIS 1987:36–37)

Here we see a kind of built-in flexibility and, as Annis says:

> What is most remarkable about the milpa *is its capacity to absorb inputs that might otherwise be wasted—microquantities of resources that the family may have in abundance but have no use for without the transformative superstructure. The* milpa *uses*

> *"resources" that may be abundant but are otherwise*
> *unusable, "down weeding" hours, after-school hours,*
> *knowledge of flower growing, a particular style of*
> *food preparation, waste water, human and animal*
> *feces, the fact of an upcoming fiesta . . .*
> (1987:37)

It is important to realize that the products grown in the *milpa* are, for the most part, consumed by the family or traded within the village. This is not an entrepreneurial strategy. Annis argues that "it works to assure nutritive security, even, ironically, if that means ensuring material poverty" (1987:37).

Another way to think about this is as a strategy that works against upward mobility and maintains the system of the status quo—a system that is traditionally entrenched.

> *It reinforces the family and household unit as the basis*
> *for social organization . . . (e.g., a grandmother's*
> *availability for weeding and her knowledge of herbs*
> *is a tangible resource within the context of a family-*
> *operated* milpa*) . . . because of its fundamentally*
> *anti-entrepreneurial character, it reinforces the egali-*
> *tarian character of the village.*
> (1987:38)

This last might sound a bit tautological (i.e., a cultural feature exists because it performs the function of "x"). However, given that we see very similar patterns all over the rural agrarian parts of the world, especially strong ideologies of equality, we can dismiss the tautology. One important point to emphasize is that these systems of householding designed to maintain the integrity of the group (whether the group is a family, a village, or a regionally based network) are predicated upon access to land (1987:40). Access to land allows people to maintain control over their time and thus to maintain "the stability of an egalitarian, internally self-sufficient, self-regulated culture" (1987:39).

As in the Kentucky case, the system of wage labor—here, agricultural day laborers (*mozos*)—is common, but relatively few people who practice "*milpa* logic" (San Antoneros) are full-time permanent *mozos*. Rather, *mozo* labor is used to stabilize the system of "*milpa*-centered livelihood" by generating supplemental income. It also provides flexibility in that it allows families with labor deficits to acquire labor (Annis 1987:51–53). People work outside in order to stabilize rather than abandon their primary occupation as *milperos*. Annis notes that in one case a man works as a caretaker while his elderly father, wife, and daughter take care of the *milpa* (1987:53). The importance of intergenerational ties is apparent here, as it is in Kentucky in maintaining the pattern of householding. Time flexibility is critical to the maintenance of multiple livelihood strategies; extended family members are essential. People also obtain work in cities; this work pays well, but is irregular. For example, the 1976 earthquake created a temporary construction boom in Antigua; as the reconstruction boom waned people returned to their *milpas* that were being maintained by family members (1987:56). These sorts of boom and bust cycles are legion, and livelihood strategies such as householding must be created to adapt to them.

As part of the householding strategy, enterprises crop up, but again these are subordinate to agriculture in the sense that they are organized as cash-generating strategies to support the family (1987:56). Selling is on a small scale (doorstep businesses) and when cash to maintain such enterprises in a village, for example, is short, or when the labor of family members is needed in the *milpa*, which operates through the pooling of household labor and resources, the business will cease temporarily. Clearly, then, work on the *milpa* takes priority, since agricultural products are essential to maintain both the nutritional base and the cultural system. If San Antoneros had to purchase their food with cash, they could not afford to maintain their current levels of nutrition and their cultural system, their "Indianness," would be in jeopardy, just as "the Kentucky way" is vulnerable to the same kinds of forces, albeit in different forms. The creative use of time is essential for these patterns to persist.[6]

Time and the Beginnings of Economic and Ecological Anthropology: Evans-Pritchard's "Oecological Time" vs. "Structural Time"

As Nancy Munn quite rightly points out, Evans-Pritchard analyzes time among the Nuer in two senses: ecological and (social) structural. As Evans-Pritchard defines these:

> *Ultimately most, perhaps all, concepts of time and space are determined by the physical ambient, but the*

values they embody are only one of many possible responses to it and depend also on structural principles, which belong to a different order of reality. . . .

In describing Nuer concepts of time we may distinguish between those that are mainly reflections of their relations to environment, which we call oecological time, and those that are reflections of their relations to one another in the social structure, which we call structural time. Both refer to successions of events which are of sufficient interest to the community for them to be noted and related to each other conceptually. The larger periods of time are almost entirely structural, because the events they relate are changes in the relationship of social groups.

(1944:94)

The parallels between ecological time, Marx's forces of production, and Polanyi's locational movements are striking; so too are the parallels between structural time, Marx's relations of production, and Polanyi's appropriational movements. Ecological time—while it has its rhythms and tempos, including cattle movements and the seasonal (transhumant) movements between dry season horticultural villages and wet season fishing and cattle camps—is limited to the yearly round and is cyclical in its repetition year after year (Evans-Pritchard 1944:95). Munn points out that time here "is understood as motion or process, not static units or concepts functioning to reckon time" (1992:96). By contrast, structural time is of longer duration; it is also more conceptual in that it deals with relationships between persons and between groups (kin groups and age grades, to name two important ones).

Reading Evans-Pritchard with the concepts of locational (forces of production) and appropriational (relations of production) movements in mind yields some interesting and important insights that can function as guideposts for economic anthropology. For example it is clear that Evans-Pritchard is careful to avoid ecological reductionism by saying that "the concept of seasons is derived from social activities rather than from the climatic changes which determine them" (1944:95). Thus seasonality is socially constructed with ecological referents.

Evans-Pritchard's discussion of the Nuer folk views of time is very illuminating and, in large measure, provides the beginnings of a model of time for fieldwork. His first point is that Nuer time is a relation between activities: "at the time of early camps, at the time of weeding, at the time of harvesting. . . . During the rains the stages in the growth of millet and the steps taken in its culture are often used as points of reference" (1944:100). Interestingly, he notes in passing that since pastoral activities are largely undifferentiated throughout the months and seasons, these do not provide suitable points for time reckoning. At the same time, Evans-Pritchard says that on a daily basis, "the daily timepiece is the cattle clock, the round of pastoral tasks" (1944:101).

Evans-Pritchard's attention to qualitative considerations, especially to the idea that the value of time varies throughout the year, is very important from the point of view of economic organization because it emphasizes the differential needs for coordination and cooperation in different seasons (the social, institutional, appropriational issues). He says:

> *Time has not the same value throughout the year.*
> *Thus in dry season camps, although daily pastoral*
> *tasks follow one another in the same order as in the*
> *rains, they do not take place at the same time, are*
> *more a precise routine owing to the severity of sea-*
> *sonal conditions, especially with regard to water and*
> *pasturage, and require greater co-ordination and co-*
> *operative action. On the other hand, life in the dry*
> *season is generally uneventful, outside routine tasks,*
> *and oecological and social relations are more monoto-*
> *nous from month to month than in the rains when*
> *there are frequent feasts, dances, and ceremonies.*
> *When time is considered as relations between activities*
> *it will be understood that it has a different connotation*
> *in rains and drought.*
> (1944:102–103)

Here Evans-Pritchard is moving towards a position that he finally states bluntly on the very next page. It is that the most important consideration, the highest analytic priority, if you will, must be given to the social relations of production (appropriational movements in Polanyi's terms). When Evans-Pritchard states that "all time is structural" he is establishing such priorities for the social over the ecological:

> *In a sense all time is structural since it is a conceptu-*
> *alization of collateral, co-ordinated, or co-operative*

activities: the movements of a group. Otherwise time
concepts of this kind could not exist, for they must
have a like meaning for everyone within a group. . . .
There is, however, a point at which we can say that
time concepts cease to be determined by oecological
factors and become more determined by structural in-
terrelations, being no longer a reflection of man's de-
pendence on nature, but a reflection of the interaction
of social groups.
(1944:104)

Notice the linkages here between locational and appropriational movements made by the use of words such as coordinated with "movements
of a group." Evans-Pritchard's analysis of the Nuer is a perfect model for
examining relationships between locational and appropriational movements in the context of time and the economy. Here also, methodological individualism is avoided:

Moreover, since time is to the Nuer an order of events
of outstanding significance to a group, each group has
its own points of reference and time is consequently
relative to structural space, locally considered. . . .
The structural system time-reckoning is partly the se-
lection of points of reference of significance to local
groups which give these groups a common and distinc-
tive history; partly the distance between specific sets
in the age-set system; and partly distances of a kin-
ship and lineage order.
(1944:105–106)

Evans-Pritchard clearly states, again through his discourse on time,
that while ecological time is limited to the yearly seasonal cycle, structural time is a conceptualization of the social structure. This includes,
again, an emphasis on relationships between individuals and between
groups, and a de-emphasis of individual action and events:

Beyond the annual cycle, time-reckoning is a concep-
tualization of the social structure, and the points of
reference are a projection into the past of actual rela-
tions between groups of persons. It is less a means of

coordinating events than of coordinating relationships,
and is therefore mainly a looking backwards, since re-
lationships must be explained in terms of the past.
(1944:108)

Chronotypes and the Timing of Work

In a recent edited volume, Bender and Wellbery
(1992) propose the concept of "chronotype" to capture the time patterns
in different cultural and historical contexts.

Chronotypes are models or patterns through which
time assumes practical or conceptual significance.
Time is not given but fabricated in an ongoing pro-
cess. Chronotypes are themselves temporal and plu-
ral, constantly being made and remade at multiple in-
dividual, social, and cultural levels . . . They change
over time and therefore have a history or histories . . .
(BENDER AND WELLBERY 1992:4)

It seems to me that the concept of chronotypes dovetails nicely with Polanyi's generic model of the economy, especially his concept of "the
economy as instituted process" because it accommodates changing processes and units of economic organization. The concept of chronotypes
also avoids many of the pitfalls of methodological individualism, precisely because its deals with patterns and relationships.

Jane Guyer's discussion of work rhythms and the timing of work in an
African "female farming system" and her critique of a "task-structure
approach" represents both an interesting application of the concept of
chronotype to the issue of time and the economy and a very powerful
critique of methodological individualism.

Guyer begins by reassessing the available methodologies for describing the gendered division of labor. Here Guyer's critique of researchers'
reliance on task specificity (or tasks) as the basic data for comparison is
worthy of close examination because it is essentially a sophisticated critique of methodological individualism. As Guyer points out, there are
legitimate reasons why task specificity has been used by researchers. The
first is that description of tasks is simple (straightforward) and less am-
biguous than any alternatives (1991:262). On the surface at least, a task
is a task and like tasks—for example, gardening, cooking, harvest-

ing—can be identified and compared. The large-scale comparative studies, such as one finds reported in the journal *Ethnology*, have used task lists and traits quite widely (Murdock and Provost 1973; see also Ember 1983; Burton and White 1984). Guyer's point, however, is that task lists are "too crude a mesh to capture the nuances of change in labor patterns as African agriculture has altered in this century." Her examples are very graphic and to the point:

> *If a male farmer uses hired labor and his wife cooks for them, is this "cooking" or something else? If women stretch the old rubric of harvesting crops for family provisioning to cover wage work on cash crops on local peasant farms or seasonal labor for agribusiness, is this still "harvesting" and in what sense? If women are doing the same tasks on the farm as at the beginning of the century, but doing them on larger areas and with greater control of the product, how does this figure as change? It is easy but deceptive to see any task over time as "the same thing" regardless of context. Cooking looks like cooking, whether done by a whole village collectively once a week in a clay oven or by an individual three times a day with a battery of implements and props for stage-managing the meal. But such a definition automatically generates static images, with major, even revolutionary, changes of technique and social relations automatically relegated to secondary and contingent importance.*
> (1991:262)

Here, using a very different vocabulary from that of Giddens, is an argument for seeing structure as primary over agency and action (task in this case). The argument is clearly derived from Marx whose famous statements about context determining everything from slavery to alienation are legion. With a slight shift of gears, Guyer proceeds to argue against a task-structure approach on the grounds (1991:263) that it "provides no way of addressing the comparative *value* of men's and women's work, nor any shifts in *labor time* or *claims* on resources and products."

She proceeds to analyze Beti agricultural history by focusing on the rhythmic structures of work in groundnut fields. Within the limitations of space, I will try to touch on the high points of her analysis while at the same time doing justice to the richness of Guyer's data. Basically the tasks involved in women producing groundnuts have not changed; neither have the features of groundnut fields or groundnuts themselves changed very much. What has changed is the context for production and the timing of productive tasks:

> *Women still carry out the same tasks they did in the*
> *precolonial period, with a similar repertoire of crops,*
> *tools, and field types. They are still responsible for*
> *the daily diet with some of the same valued compo-*
> *nents at its core, still work longer hours than men,*
> *still have little direct control over wealth and heritable*
> *resources.*
> (1991:264)

After acknowledging the centrality of groundnuts to women's production, their storability, and their flexible uses in the diet (including their transportability), the question Guyer proceeds to ask focuses on the groundnut field itself, specifically its internal organization and the nature of its external links to other productive activities and to the larger economy. From this point she describes the rhythms of work in the context of the whole productive system:

> *By focusing on this field, with its deep associations*
> *with female life and labor, one can ask, not what has*
> *happened to "female farming" but, how has this*
> field, *with all its symbolic gender load and pragmatic*
> *gender implications, changed in both its internal orga-*
> *nization and its external links to the entire field sys-*
> *tem, and to the wider productive economy? The*
> *changing rhythms of work and control of the produc-*
> *tion, taken as a whole, become the central subjects to*
> *describe. Subjects such as the "position of women" or*
> *"female farming" are then removed from the center of*
> *direct attention, to be replaced by a descriptive method*
> *that is intrinsically imbued with gender conceptions.*
> (1991:267)

It is extremely interesting that the above statement appears in a volume that is entitled *Gender at the Crossroads of Knowledge: Feminist Anthro-*

pology in the Postmodern Era. Were it not for Guyer's last sentence in the above quote, and were it not for the volume in which her statements appear, her methodology might be construed as un- or antifeminist. To my mind, as we will see below, she is not only practicing good feminism, but also good economic anthropology, by linking both to what is essentially a Marxist tenet that context (historical, political, ethnographic, cultural) is critical and should be taken into account at every stage of analysis.

Guyer proceeds then to delineate the changes in context that the women's groundnut fields have undergone since the late nineteenth century. At that point in history, the farming cycle as a whole, which consisted of various male and female periods of clearing followed by cultivation interspersed with periods of fallow, lasted over twenty years. The woman's groundnut field constituted one phase in this long cycle. Once cocoa production was introduced in the 1940s, however, the system of intercropping was interrupted by the fact that once cocoa trees grow beyond a certain height (after about seven years) there can be no intercrops and the land does not go through the full cycle back to fallow (1991:269). Guyer describes the consequences:

> *There are two results: the grand cycle and its dependent short cycles are severed from one another into two separate land-use cycles, and women lose— through their literal disappearance—the staple food crops from the male stages of the old cycle . . . the other predominantly male staple crop, yams, went into decline because of seasonal pressures on male labor.*
> (1991:269)

The entire timing of female groundnut production changed. Women began planting two groundnut fields a year instead of one large field that had been part of the longer cycle and had been grown only in the technically optimal of the two growing seasons (1991:270). More groundnuts were produced, however, along with greater quantities of cassava (female-produced) which compensated for the loss of yams (male-produced).

At about this same time (1940s) crop density was increased. Women also developed a whole series of subsidiary economic activities which claimed their time—liquor distilling, cooked-food selling, and trade in imported beer (1991:270). These activities, in effect, gave women access to men's cash. And in an economic world in which cash was becoming increasingly important, this was an important development. As Guyer points out, a series of interrelated cycles are involved in understanding the course of change for Beti men and women:

> One is then not working with dubiously measurable processes such as intensification, subordination, and increased work, but with changed elements, changed synchronies, and specific dissonances under particular historical conditions.
> (1991:273)

Having looked at these data, we can go one step beyond Guyer's analysis. That is, we can extrapolate specific chronotypes (patterns) that are important for future analysts to take into account. Cycles, for example, and the idea that there can be several cycles operating simultaneously, are important concepts. In all cultures, individual life cycles and seasonal cycles interdigitate with whatever cycles have been culturally constructed. These may be production cycles, wage labor cycles, or cycles of distribution such as those associated with periodic marketplace systems. The organization of production is the primary focus of the analysis, and we can see that it is possible to build gender into the analysis of production without making the position of women the central focus (Guyer 1991:274).

Using Time for Archaeoeconomic Analysis: The Case of Water Management

> Water management is the interruption and redirection of the natural movement or collection of water by society. With or without living consultants of extant texts, dams, reservoirs, canals, and wells reveal alterations to a landscape that permit an evaluation of a group's land-use practices. The scale and complexity of these features provide archaeologists, ethnographers, and geographers a powerful data base for examining economic behavior.
> (SCARBOROUGH 1993:1)

The slow accretive development of sophisticated water systems in the Maya area reflects the adaptability and longevity of this semitropical culture.
(SCARBOROUGH 1993 B:18)

By "slow" Scarborough is referring to centuries of labor inputs during which the landscape was carved and modified in response, partly, to a seasonally limited water supply. He contrasts this slow, accretive process with civilizations that occupied rapidly transformable landscapes associated with permanent, year-round rivers and streams, where intensive cultivation and flood recession management have allowed the rise and fall of many great civilizations.

The southern Maya Lowland system of water management is based, not on river and canal distributional systems, but on "human-modified watersheds and reservoir systems" (Scarborough 1993*b*:18). By A.D. 600, for example, the Maya of the urban center of Tikal, who lacked permanent water sources, had centralized a rainfall catchment area and associated reservoirs that permitted hydraulic control through water collection and storage (Scarborough and Gallopin 1991). Reservoirs were constructed at Tikal as adaptations to seasonally unavailable water. Scarborough argues that for the Classic period in the southern Maya Lowlands, Tikal manifests one of the most sophisticated water control systems in the New World.

Three types of reservoirs have been defined by Scarborough and Gallopin at Tikal, based on reservoir location and amount of water contained: (1) central precinct reservoirs, (2) residential reservoirs, and (3) *bajo*-margin reservoirs. The central precinct reservoirs are impressive with regard to their volume of water (10,000–25,000 cubic meters). They were formed behind clearly defined causeways, which connected various portions of the city's core, but also dammed water within the major catchment area. Residential reservoirs were located downhill from the central precinct within the most densely populated part of the city (Scarborough 1993*b*:47). The third type, *bajo*-margin reservoirs, are basins on the scalar order of the central precinct reservoirs, but located away from dense population aggregates associated with central Tikal (Scarborough and Gallopin 1991:660). All sizable catchment areas eventually terminated in *bajo*-margin reservoirs or natural *aguadas* (depressions near the edge of a *bajo*), ultimately leading into the flanking *bajos* (large,

PHOTO 5.   *Excavating a canal at Cerros, Belize. Courtesy Vernon Scarborough.*

PHOTO 6.   *A canal. Courtesy Vernon Scarborough.*

PHOTO 7.   *Looking up from a cenote (limestone sinkhole).*
Courtesy Vernon Scarborough.

PHOTO 8.   *A drainage ditch. Courtesy Vernon Scarborough.*

seasonally inundated, internally drained swamps) (Scarborough and Gallopin 1991:659).

Each of these types, one could argue, represents different amounts, organization, and timing of labor, and different locational and appropriational movements of water. Reservoirs in general require a great deal of maintenance work. They are organized differently from canals in which a ditch master's obligations dictate work at fixed points along narrowly defined canal lengths. Scarborough argues that source, or reservoir, systems emphasize community-wide activity, while allocation systems (canals) are more readily exploited by the special interests of an individual or a group (1993a:6). If we think about how these reservoir systems were constructed and maintained over hundreds of years, recognition of the amount of labor required is staggering. Scarborough delineates some of the labor requirements:

> *Although certain times of the year are more demand-*
> *ing in monitoring flows and generating water stores,*
> *focused maintenance of the catchment emphasizes*
> *seepage-proof surfaces and waste debris removal even*
> *during the dry season. Heavy rainfall is a period of*
> *community coordination to make sure that runoff is*
> *directed to reservoirs and the scouring action of mov-*
> *ing water is minimized.*
> (1993A:6)

These types, in turn, contrast with canal systems. There are implications for the organization of labor here that have not been explored. How is labor organized for the slow, accretive economies as opposed to the quick and explosive ones? Is a larger population required to sustain one or the other, or is it the arrangement of the population on the landscape that is critical?

Scarborough argues that both locational and appropriational movements are different in reservoir or catchment-area systems from those in canal-distributary systems. He posits, for example, that people did not relocate to plant, maintain, or harvest their agricultural plots in the still-water (humanly constructed reservoirs) systems. Rather, the adaptation was one to the immediate margins of the reservoir; the larger the capacity of the reservoirs in a system, the larger the population residing nearby (1993a:6). This means, of course, that travel time between fields and water source is reduced, in contrast to canal systems where field plots may be located large distances from the source. He suggests also that the appropriational movements associated with water systems that emphasize watershed construction and maintenance (reservoirs) have different ways of scheduling labor and different settlement patterns. The less-routinized scheduling of labor is based on the less-precise knowledge of when and how much rain actually will fall on a human-made watershed (1993a:7). The maintenance of the watershed also took high priority and it made sense for people to remain close by. One should keep in mind that these are systems that did not operate with private property; rather the polity (local, regional, or national) controlled all productive resources: land, labor, and water.

There are also questions to be addressed here concerning the longevity of certain kinds of states, and the forms of economic organization that support them. More simply, we can ask: How long does a form of economic organization last? In cases such as Moche, Peru, and Teotihuacan, the first indigenous states of the temporate world, there was a concentrated investment in landscape alteration, much of which was associated with water management technology. Scarborough argues that these primary states rose precipitously but did not last more than 800 years, approximately half the longevity of the Lowland Maya. There are implications here for the spatial arrangement of economies as well, for Scarborough notes that these other civilizations were limited by their needs for access to principal waterways—unlike the dispersed land use and occupation of the non-riverine Maya. Theirs was a gradual accretion, a modification of the environment in increments over a long and relatively stable 1,500-year period. Slowly developing water systems can lead to very complicated political and economic systems (Scarborough 1993:60) We can see that this case deals with time on two levels: (1) timing of water management systems themselves, especially as timing affects the organization of labor; and (2) the gradual evolutionary time in developing and maintaining the Maya state.

SUMMARY

In order to understand the organization and timing of economic processes, we need, to use Stephen J. Gould's terms, both arrows and cycles in different combinations. We also need arrows of different lengths and cycles of different durations and sizes. Seasonal and yearly cycles, for example, are relatively short; cycles of drought, on the other hand, can last many years. Qualitative considerations are very important with respect to the issue of time. For example, state-level economies have very different kinds of arrows and cycles than do pre-state economies. The difference between Evans-Pritchard's discussion of time for the Nuer and that of Scarborough's for the Maya is marked and certainly point to the fact that these two economies cannot be easily compared. We can see that, in order to understand time and the economy, economic anthropologists need to develop concepts and models that capture processes of gradual accretion as well as the seesaw-like movements of Nuer transhumance. We have not even begun to talk about the pace of culture change, but it is not difficult to understand that change deserves its own set of models, to accommodate gradual and sudden change, change that is rapid or slow, and also change that might be considered to be punctuated.

| Nine | LOOKING BACKWARD AND FORWARD ON CONCEPTS OF THE ECONOMY: THE DISCOURSE OF ECONOMIC ANTHROPOLOGY IN HISTORICAL AND COMPARATIVE PERSPECTIVE |

Anthropology has always been a case-based and place-oriented science that aims to produce ethnographic and archaeological data primarily, and comparative treatments only secondarily. For the most part, each individual anthropologist has the liberty of constructing concepts and descriptions that are unique, presumably, to his or her field situation. While it can certainly be argued that all case descriptions contain implicit models and suggest comparisons (if only in the decision that something is the case because it is or is not similar to or different from something else), historically anthropologists have made their careers studying one culture—in extreme cases, one site, ethnic group, or village. One of the reasons comparisons are so difficult in economic anthropology is that concepts and terms from capitalist economies have dominated the subfield—terms such as commodity, price, property. Alternative (non-market and mixed) models are scarce. Polanyi excepted, there are few writers who ask what, for example, a model of a non-market system of redistribution would look like in a positive sense. Pedro Carrasco (1978, 1982) is one of the very few to examine ancient state economies (Aztec and Inca) as they were embedded in political institutions (structures).[1]

This chapter uses Ruth Bunzel's comparative treatment of primitive

economies (1938), along with some other writers in the history of economic anthropology and culture theory (most notably those influenced
by Leslie White), as starting points for reviewing some of the discourse
of economic anthropology in its historical context and for examining
possibilities for alternative models of the economy. Bunzel's comparative treatment of the topic of economic organization is the first of its
kind, and it still stands as one of the few comprehensive attempts to deal
with a variety of economic processes—production, distribution, and exchange—in more than a single economy. The topics she treats and the
questions she asks are more important than the answers she provides. As
will be seen below, Bunzel was limited, to a great degree, by the terminology she had at hand, namely that of conventional economic theory.

Before Bunzel's lengthy piece, anthropologists had produced numerous weighty monographs describing single (pre-capitalist) economies
(Barton 1922; Firth 1929) or containing significant data on the economy.
Bunzel's chapter in Boas' *General Anthropology* textbook (1938), "The
Economic Organization of Primitive Peoples," was perhaps the first attempt to grapple with the problem of defining concepts for analyzing
pre-capitalist economies in a comparative framework. By drawing on a
rich ethnographic corpus, Bunzel provides a set of considerations—some
in the form of musings—about the components of economic organization. Her emphasis on economic organization, which is grounded ethnographically in her own detailed knowledge of Zuñi economy and theoretically in her very subtle, but sensitive, reading of Marx, allows her
to identify concepts, problems, and units of analysis that still remain in
need of comparative analysis in economic anthropology—concepts such
as property, ownership, the division of labor, and the nature of distribution and exchange. Her work anticipates issues that began to be addressed
much later in economic anthropology. What is especially noteworthy is
her focus on concepts and their relationships to data.

As we will see below, Bunzel is struggling with concepts and with
terminology. She is frustrated by the inappropriateness of existing
concepts and terms for the analysis of the economic organization of
primitive people but in places she does slip into the use of conventional
economic terminology and theoretical categories (Sahlins 1960).[2] The
implications of her discussion of terminology for the analysis of non-
market and mixed economies of various sorts remain to be spelled out.
It will become clear that some semblance of the institutional paradigm is
present in Bunzel's discussion. The paradigm is implicit, however, and
needs to be brought out. As we will see, her approach is consistent with

the analytic perspective of cultural economies taken in this book. Bunzel was opposed to methodological individualism.

Defining the Economy

Bunzel begins with a materialist definition that regards the economy as part of culture. The critical relationship is between culturally formed material needs (which are highly variable among economies) and the potential of the environment. For Bunzel "the uncovering of the basic assumptions underlying economic institutions of a people leads us to the very heart of culture" (1938:327). Tautologies aside, her point is that studying material provisioning is a way to get at culture.[3]

Bunzel discusses the economy in terms of three principles that roughly translate to Marx's: forces of production, relations of production, and ideology, or superstructure. In the first she talks about environment and technology, and conceptualizes these in terms of such problems as: "What does the environment offer? What is utilized? What techniques are employed to acquire and transform the materials at hand, and what forms are given to them?" (1938:327). Clearly, economy is neither ecology or technology, but rather a complex set of processes that involve not only ecological and technological input, but social organizational features as well. Again, this is consistent with the general institutional paradigm and with Polanyi's generic model of the economy. Her second principle refers to relations of production—or, in Bunzel's terms, social organizational features: "the structure of the group, the organization for production, the network of economic obligations between individuals, the position of each individual with reference to a group" (1938:327). In the third she covers a variety of issues related to ideology—for example, the question of value (1938:327). She summarizes by saying: "In these three aspects of economics we find answers to the three questions: What is done? Who does it? Why is it done?" (1938:328). Polanyi would refer to these as the physical, social, and cultural levels or aspects of economic organization (Pearson, personal communication).

Property

Bunzel's discussion of property emphasizes the inadequacy of existing terminology for analyses of the organization of resources such as land. She begins with a discussion of relationships between humans and things, and humans and their physical environments, and argues that the concept of property cannot be isolated from social structure (1938:340). Analyzing the principles underlying the relationships between humans, environments, and things is primary. She uses terms such as proprietorship and channels of ownership somewhat awkwardly, but is handicapped by a highly particularistic and ethnocentric existing lexicon.

While most of her discourse is descriptive, if one looks carefully at what it is that Bunzel chooses to describe, many components of economic organization begin to emerge. Even her seemingly offhand comments reveal features of economic and social structure. For example, her comment that people like the Eskimo "have absolutely no idea of permanent residence or exclusive rights" (1938:343) suggests a concept of *inclusive rights* that is foreign to economies based on private property. The implications of this statement for understanding how the Eskimo organize productive resources in terms of their access to and use of both land and sea has still not been systematically spelled out. What, for example, does inclusivity entail in terms of rights of access? What are its boundaries and domains? Drawing on Boas' work on the Central Eskimo, Bunzel discusses the organization of Eskimo resources. Again, the elements she describes have been carefully chosen. If initially they sound almost ethnocentric, the point of the description is to provide an interpretation of behavior that makes sense in a propertyless social context in which inclusivity, rather than exclusivity, prevails. Whether it is the only, or even the best, interpretation is not the issue:

> *These groups have no great permanence, no place of residence, no hunting grounds to which they claim many rights. The fact that a man is challenged when he comes to a strange camp is due to suspicion of personal aggression, and to a wish to test and rank the stranger's strength, it is not in any sense a defense of territorial claims against trespass.*
> (1938:343)

That Bunzel states all of these "facts" of Eskimo economic life in the negative only serves to indicate a dearth of concepts and terms for talking about relationships between humans and their resources (especially land) in the positive. The challenge: how to develop models and concepts for the analysis of cultural economies in which the notion of "private property no trespassing" is completely foreign.

For example, how do we create models of land systems that are not based on private property? Bunzel does attempt an alternative terminology by talking about "different property institutions," but the term property itself implies boundedness and exclusivity that, again, are not relevant to Eskimo processes of resource organization and material-means provisioning. Here Bunzel is really dealing with twelve problems of resource management, or, more simply, with how land resources are organized and used. Yet, for better or worse, she is stuck with the term property in what is really a statement about how land resources are used for survival:

> All kinds of property institutions exist among very simple people, and property institutions must be understood not with reference to a general economic level but with reference to specific problems of survival.
> (1938:343)

Here Bunzel is really dealing with the problem of how resources are organized in cultures where private property institutions are absent. She comes back to her original materialist definition of the economy. She still runs into terminological snags, though, when she tries to discuss how resources are used. For example, she points out that legal forms of property tell us very little about such substantive matters as

> whether all individuals have free access to the main sources of food supply; whether the control by certain groups of all or an important part of the food supply can be used as a means of class exploitation; whether there is any special form of wealth, the unequal distribution of which places certain individuals or groups in positions of control.
> (1938:344)

Here she is raising questions about the nature of inclusive rights to resources.

Common Property

The recent literature on common property (McCay and Acheson 1987; McCay 1987; Libecap 1989) evidences some of the same conceptual and terminological problems that are present in Bunzel's discussion of property. McCay and Acheson address three critical points: (1) the theoretical status of the thesis of the tragedy of the commons, (2) the nature of true common property situations, and (3) an ideal definition of common property as involving notions of exclusivity as well as inclusivity. Along the way they deal with the place of institutions and with the idea of restrictions. They say:

> The thesis of the tragedy of the commons fails to distinguish between common property as a theoretical condition in which there are no relevant institutions (open access) and common property as a social institution (the commons). The assumption that common property is the same thing as open access is historically inaccurate. . . . In true common property situations, rights of access or use are shared equally and are exclusive to a defined group of people. . . . Common property should refer to an exclusive as well as inclusive notion of the commonwealth involved. It should refer to specified sets of use-rights. . . . Designated common rights may be general and public or specific and contingent upon other rights, part of the "web of use rights" underlying the moral economy of human communities.
> (1987:8–9)

McCay and Acheson indicate their attention to the ecological and institutional contexts of common property as well as to its meaning:

> Common property—in the sense of communal use rights to extensive resources—is logical under certain conditions of production and environment. Just as important is the fact that common property can come about through the claims of a community to free and equal access to resources that could otherwise become the property of only a privileged few.
> (1987:19)

In a rather provocative article, "The Concept of Property among Shoshoneans" (1960), Stephen Cappannari argues that "property rights among the Shoshonean speaking groups differ *basically* from property rights among other, more advanced, societies" (1960:134). After objecting to the ethnocentric application of terms derived from capitalist economies to other kinds of economies, Cappannari suggests an alternative definition of the term "property." He says:

> *I shall use the term "property" as a thing or service which can satisfy a need, which quantitatively represents human labor and which functions in an economic context.*
> (1960:135)

He says that he agrees with Hobhouse (1922:7) that one would not speak of property if all the world alike could use something (Cappannari 1960:136). More importantly, the point for the Shoshonean group is that persons within the group have equal access to the resources of nature. Rights in land do not give rise to political power or control over the services of others (1960:136). In a summary statement Cappannari calls for new terminology:

> *The right of access to the resources of nature follows personal and kin ties among Shoshoneans. Shoshoneans have property rights or holdings in land but these differ profoundly from land ownership in modern societies. Among Shoshoneans private ownership of natural resources nowhere excludes people from access to the resources of nature. Nowhere among these Shoshoneans does "ownership" of any sort give rise to coercive power over other persons. If the term "primitive communism" must be abandoned because it has become ambiguous and emotionally laden, a new term should be devised to characterize a way of life, such as that enjoyed by the Shoshoneans and by similar societies.*
> (1960:141)

He concludes by arguing that the above distinctions are "necessary for the construction of a cross-culturally valid science of economics and for studies in the evolution of culture." This last statement indicates that this notion of a science of economics was not Polanyi's idea alone, but was prominent in the thinking of students of cultural evolution, particularly those influenced by Leslie White and Julian Steward.

The above questions about access to resources begin to get at organizational features of economies that are otherwise glossed over by descriptions of legal property rights. For example, the complexity of arrangements that organized Trobriand lands can be seen in the following, which is after a passage from the first volume of *Coral Gardens*. In Bunzel's words:

> *There are many kinds of restrictions upon ownership of real property. A commoner in the Trobriands owns his fields; they cannot be alienated from his lineage, but the chief claims an overlordship which entitles him to tribute in the form of first fruits. So does the garden magician who performs growth magic for all the gardens of the village. Since he makes it grow it is 'his' garden. The chief also owns the coconut trees on other men's lands.*
> (1938:347)

One should not lose sight of the fact that the term ownership is still problematical here. It should really be glossed as control, real or symbolic. The chief really administers land in such a way as to extract tribute, for example. Similarly, the garden magician symbolically controls the gardens. As Bunzel points out, it is rare among primitive people for owners to have free rights of disposal (1938:348), and, more positively, land is most often entailed with the kinship group and the rules of succession are set by custom (1938:348). In essence, this means that land is organized along kinship lines and according to kinship principles. Bunzel also notes that water is a resource that must be, and, in fact, is, organized differently in different cultural systems: "Among primitive peoples there are many special rules and guarantees regarding water rights, access to wells and springs, and access to special kinds of trees and shrubs" (1938:247). It should be pointed out that the organization of water has not received a great deal of attention in economic anthropology. Yet, beginning with Karl Wittfogel's classic work, *Oriental Despotism*, water management has been the source of debate for many topics in ethnology and archaeology: the origin of the state, the nature of stratification, the nature of the so-called Asiatic mode of production, to name just a few of the larger topics. As I have pointed out in chapter 8, water management is just now becoming a topic for economic anthropology.

Bunzel ends her discussion of property with two points that are critical to the understanding of primitive economies. The first is a statement about the Trobriand pre-capitalist economy. Although it is stated again in the negative, it nonetheless touches on some important aspects of trade, value, and the organization of labor:

> Still there is no capitalism in the Trobriands. Trade is conducted without profit, for profits have no reinvestment value. There is not much that one could do with capital—land cannot be alienated; "valuables" are not for sale; pigs belong to the chief. No man can exploit the labor of another, or make another dependent upon him for the necessities of life.
> (1938:350)

Translated into more positive terms, Bunzel is really raising questions about the raison d'être for trade, traffic in valuables, and the like. The fact that no man can exploit the labor of others does not tell us very much about the organization of labor, but it does call attention to the issue.

The second, and related, concluding point about property deals with the nature of value and valuables, especially the critical importance of prestige in pre-capitalist economies. Again, while there are parts that read to us in the 1990s as ethnocentric, the issues around value, the nature of exchange, the use of the resource base, and the symbolic elements of and relationships between people and material things remain important and are not by any means fully treated in contemporary economic anthropology. She says:

> The objects of wealth among primitive peoples are not always material instruments like land, animals and food, but articles whose value is culturally determined, and purely symbolic, like the blankets and coppers of the Kwakiutl, the valuables of the kula trade, the shell money (which is not really money in our sense at all) of other Melanesian Islands, the cowrie shells of West Africa. These objects frequently

do not even have an exchange value in terms of com-
modities, but their possession lends prestige. It is
about such objects, rather than land or houses or food,
that the competitive passions most frequently rage.
(1938:350)

Zuñi Economy as the Basis for Comparative Concepts

Bunzel's discussion of her own work on the Zuñi economy echoes some of the conceptual problems treated previously, but she is able to describe the Zuñi in more positive terms; these terms then take on comparative significance if we think of them in other contexts. For example, she points to such outstanding characteristics of the Zuñi economy as "the strong development of cooperative attitudes and techniques," and "the dominant role of women in economic affairs, the fluidity of wealth" (1938:352). Bunzel gives us a "thick description" of the organization of Zuñi production that deals with rights to resources, units of production, and a variety of other issues, including a definition of surplus land:

Men raise the crops and build the houses; women own
them. Men speak of "owning" fields. Actually the
title is entailed in the maternal lineage, passing from
mother to daughter, and exploited, according to expe-
diency, by brothers and husbands. This is the Zuñi
theory of land tenure, but its strictness is tempered by
the Zuñi insistence that property is for use, not for
power. Therefore surplus land is freely loaned, bar-
tered, or given away. Surplus land is that which the
household cannot cultivate . . . there is no such thing
as a "sale"; there are simply transfers of property
within the framework of personal relationships. In
"selling" a field, the size and location of the field are
less relevant than the kinship ties and relative ages of
the individuals concerned. "I bought this field (a good
cornfield) for a piece of calico because he was an old
man" (and presumably would not use the field). Al-
though good land is actually scarce, land has no scar-
city value because, according to native theory, it is la-

> bor to till the land that is scarce and expensive. . . .
> Agricultural work is done jointly on fields scattered
> in many places and "owned" individually by male
> members. The stores are pooled as the collective prop-
> erty of women. For any large task like planting, har-
> vest, or house-building the men invite a miscellaneous
> group of blood and affinal relatives, ceremonial associ-
> ates, and neighbors to assist.
> (1938:353)

Bunzel is one of the first, and still one of the few anthropologists to acknowledge heterogeneity in kin-based principles of economic organization. In contrast to land, which is organized matrilineally, herds are organized patrilineally, with age an additional consideration:

> The herding complex that has been superimposed
> upon the old agricultural base has a somewhat differ-
> ent ideology. Sheep are individually owned by men;
> they are inherited in the male line. But this rule, like
> that of land tenure, may always be set aside in the
> interests of expediency. A group of male relatives
> herd their sheep together at a distance from the vil-
> lage, and take turns in watching them, theoretically
> on a strictly reciprocal basis, each man going out for a
> month. But the whole system of reciprocities is unbal-
> anced by the feeling of social responsibility on the part
> of the old toward the young. If a boy goes to herd for
> his father, the whole cooperative group assumes re-
> sponsibility for him, giving him presents of animals;
> the leader, who is also richest in sheep, gives the
> most, so that the young man soon has a herd of his
> own. Direct reciprocity between individuals obviously
> is not a principle of Zuñi economic structure.
> (1938:354)

Among the important points here is that Bunzel demonstrates that the principles of Zuñi economic organization, specifically the organization of production, are not homogeneous. That is, land is organized one way (matrilineally), herds and herding, another (patrilineally). Also, the principle of reciprocity can be interrupted—indeed it can be cross-cut by the principles of age and generation.

Economic Mechanisms in Primitive Cultures: The Identification of Generic Economic Processes

In a section entitled "Economic Mechanisms in Primitive Cultures" Bunzel returns to her initial concept of the economy as the material provisioning process. Again, this is consistent with Polanyi's generic model. What she is really doing, however, is making a preliminary sketch of key economic processes that can be identified for analytical purposes in all economies. She selects four: the division of labor, distribution, gift-giving, and trade. In her first example, she is careful to point out that it is more difficult in pre-capitalist societies to identify empirically the boundaries between the four processes. Baking bread or gathering workers together can be analyzed variously as an aspect of production or as part of food distribution. Her concern for appropriate categories of analysis anticipates the formalist-substantivist debate:

> It is generally accepted as axiomatic that economic function can be divided into three separate processes: production, distribution, and consumption. We have organized our own economic life so as to differentiate these three aspects. The line between them is more fluid than is commonly assumed. The same act— baking bread, for instance—may be included in either the productive or consumptive structure, depending upon who does it. If we try to apply these categories to societies that are differently organized with reference to the economic problem, we see at once how inapplicable they are. It is not necessary to go to the simplest societies to see these processes merged . . . The Zuñi work party is a definite unit of social behavior that serves many purposes. It is not simply a matter of hiring workers at a certain wage to accomplish a certain end. It is just as fair to regard it as an invitation to participate in a food distribution. It is usual for women to emphasize the former aspect and men the latter. From the point of view of the host

(or employer) the social and ceremonial aspects are of
paramount importance.
(1938:367–368)

It is clear that anyone seriously interested in studying either production or distribution must take ethnographic facts, context, and interpretation into account.

The Division of Labor

The allotment of different tasks to different individuals occurs in all economies, albeit in many possible arrangements involving economic interdependencies of men and women, degrees of specialization, and relationships between highly differentiated skills and highly developed technologies. Writing eleven years before Margaret Mead's *Male and Female*, and almost forty years before anthropologists began to study gender systematically, Bunzel quickly eliminates biological explanations of the gendered division of labor in all cultures:

> *Among pastoral and agricultural people there is no*
> *obvious biological factor to account for the universal*
> *division of labor along sex lines. Men herd larger*
> *animals, as they hunt them, and perhaps for the same*
> *reasons; however, women herd cattle successfully in*
> *Europe, and Navajo women herd their own sheep.*
> *Throughout Melanesia women raise pigs. Nor does*
> *the division of labor always result in giving men the*
> *heavier share of work. Bogoras found that the Chuck-*
> *chee women work much harder than the men.*
> *(1938:369)*

Bunzel is not satisfied with simple descriptions of the division of labor; rather, she explores the conditions under which two groups with essentially the same "technological development" are either self-sufficient (producing all the skills they need internally) or specialized (in that they rely on other groups to provide certain needed skills). Here she is not satisfied with an argument that relies on technical efficiency; instead, she gives culture a major place in determining economic differentiation (1938:372). She points to ceremonial functions as one key basis of the division of labor in what was probably one of the first attempts at controlled comparison:

> *Zuñi and Quiche do not differ much in technological development. Among the Zuñi the economic ideal, now somewhat obscured by the intrusion of White traders, was the self-sufficient household within the self-sufficient tribe, with mechanisms to ensure cooperation and fluidity of wealth. Every man commanded all the major skills, every woman the major female skills. Organized trade and barter were negligible; only the feeble and the widowed were forced to exchange manufactures for food. . . . For all purposes of daily living each household was completely self-sufficient. This homogeneous economy is combined with the most minute differentiation in ceremonial function, which suggests that differentiation may have some other basis than simply technical efficiency.* (1938:372)

In contrast, the specialized economies of Mesoamerica look very different:

> *South of the Rio Grande no such ideal of self-sufficient units prevails. The Guatemalan or Mexican village swarms with specialists; a Quiche family head hires a mason to build his house and a carpenter to hang the doors; he buys the adobe from an adobe-maker and the tiles from a tile-maker, and orders the cloth for his suit from a professional weaver. These are all imported skills, as they are at Zuñi. He buys his pottery and baskets and mats and certain foodstuffs in the marketplace and hires laborers to till his fields while he himself earns his living as a witness and recorder of contracts, an ancient profession throughout Central America. The family does not constitute a closed economic unit. The same attitude prevails in the village economy also. The villages, although socially, politically, and often linguistically distinct,*

are industrially specialized and mutually dependent,
bound together by highly organized trade.
(1938:272)

The archaeological implications of these statements are enormous, especially given traditional concerns with trade and exchange, and the recent attention being paid to households. Archaeologically, it should not be difficult to determine the differences between what Bunzel calls homogeneous (self-sufficient) and what I will call heterogeneous (specialized) economies. The question remains: at what level are economies homogeneous or heterogeneous? At the household, the village, or the regional levels?

While Bunzel emphasizes that the Zuñi and the Quiche cultivate the same crops with the same technological equipment, she goes on to discuss variability, not only in degrees of specialization, but in units of production. Here she writes of several ways of organizing production. For example, "the extreme collectivism of the Maori, among whom all activities are carried out jointly," contrasts with patterns of "unformalized helpfulness," such as that found among the Arapesh of New Guinea. In the Maori case, the joint activities are organized and administered by the chief; this is a politically administered economy of a sort. Bunzel also points out, however, that collectivism in labor can exist without political organization as in the case of the Pueblos who conduct "all their major tasks in field and herd by a system of informal voluntary cooperation." They do this without concepts of rank or authority (1938:375).

Distribution

Bunzel's discussion of distribution is somewhat unusual in that it covers a rather wide set of cultural systems as well as a wide range of topics, including attention to time as a consideration in the organization of distribution processes and the implications of time management for the organization and technology of storage processes. Her analysis is also important because it links production and distribution processes. She says:

> *The problem of distribution is twofold: distribution in time, and distribution among the different members of the group . . .*
> *The problem of the distribution of produce over*

time arises wherever a people relies upon a seasonal
food supply. Its solution requires knowledge of tech-
niques for the preservation of food. Such knowledge is
basic not only to economic security but to the growth
of any complex organization. In most cases leisure is
not dependent upon the abundance of nature but upon
economic planning and, in particular, upon the ability
to utilize one day's surplus for the next day's hunger.
(1938:377)

Thus Bunzel, in a very subtle manner, makes an argument for rejecting ecological determinism in favor of examining how economies are organized by humans in cultural systems. Her reference to "economic planning" is contrasted with "abundance of nature." She also anticipates some of the arguments about "the original affluent society" (Sahlins 1972) that came thirty-five years later in arguing that:

Leisure and economic security are not the achieve-
ments of agricultural and pastoral peoples alone. The
Indians of Alaska, with only natural sources of food
supply, have greater economic security and certainly a
great deal more leisure than the Chukchee with their
huge herds of domesticated reindeer.
(1938:377)

Domestication of both plants and animals requires work. As Bunzel puts it, "the herds require constant attention." It is Bunzel's ability to link food storage to demography, settlement patterns, and the overall organization and rhythm of economic life that are particularly impressive and useful for archaeologists and ethnographers alike. Here we see, in her discussion of food source proximity, the anticipation of Binford's "forager"-"collector" models as well as attention to the problem of units of economic organization:

The existence of food stores not only offers some secu-
rity against calamity, but it profoundly affects the
whole rhythm and organization of economic life in
such fundamental aspects as distribution of popula-
tion and the permanence of settlements. Where daily
search for food is the rule, each unit must remain

*near a known source of food supply. This means that
either the units be small and widely dispersed, as
among the Northern Ojibwa, or they must be extremely mobile. . . .*
(1938:379)

Since the emphasis in Bunzel's writing is on economic organization,
she focuses on fundamental principles underlying the economy. Here her
detailed knowledge of the Zuñi is extremely useful because it enables her
to move analytically between abstract concepts and on-the-ground descriptions of economic activities. Thus, for example, she can begin with
the Zuñi principle of the fluidity of wealth and proceed to discuss feasting, food distributions, and distributions of products in general:

*the whole economy is based on the principle of the
fluidity of wealth, the preharvest season, which runs
imperceptibly into the season of harvest, is the season of maximum social activity, feasting, and open-
handed food distributions. Hospitality and generosity
are a social responsibility; so no household need go
hungry in the lean months. It is consistent with the
negative attitude toward hoarding that in a period of
panic following an earthquake, Zuñi housewives
gave away all their accumulated stores of food.*
(1938:380)

Some of the complexities of Bunzel's arguments about the mechanisms and objectives of distribution are illustrated by her recognition that
the relationships between production and distribution processes are not
always direct or positive. She argues below that what may really be distributed are not necessarily goods, but risks:

*Any joint enterprise requires some formal distribution
of the product among those who take part. But distribution does not always bear the obvious and direct
correlation to production that we might expect. There
may be some purely arbitrary division of the spoils of
the chase—an animal taken jointly by several men
may belong to the first man who saw it, or the man*

> who shot the first arrow, or the many who first
> touched it; or it may belong to nine of the hunters but
> may be given to someone who stands in a particular
> relationship to one of them. The theory upon which
> all such distributions work is that, assuming fairly
> uniform skill, it will all come out even in the end. It
> serves indeed to minimize the effects of striking in-
> equalities in skill, like insurance, it distributes risks.

For Bunzel, "economic forces are channeled by social forms" (1938: 380). The main social form is kinship, manifested by "compulsory payments between relatives by blood or marriage" (1938:381). These basic, kinship-driven distribution mechanisms include: bride price and dowry, affinal exchange, compulsory gifts, and the like. The important point is the link between economy and kinship—"the economic obligations of kinship" (1938:381). I should note here that this argument is very close to those of Cappannari (1960) and Sahlins (1960) exactly twenty-two years later.

From this point Bunzel moves to a rudimentary typology of kin-based exchanges, thereby anticipating the work of Lévi-Strauss, Dalton, and others. She says: "These exchanges may be individual or collective, direct or indirect, objects exchanged of similar or different kinds" (1938: 381). Dowry, or the distribution of marital property contributed by the man's or the woman's relatives takes many forms, as does bride price (1938:383). The African case is only one example:

> All of Africa must be regarded as a region in which
> both the father's line and the mother's line are recog-
> nized, different kinds of privileges being transmitted
> in each line. If we recognize this kind of organization
> as fundamental in Africa, then the bride price repre-
> sents the compensation which the patrilineal group
> pays for the rights which it acquires over a woman
> of another line; and over the children in whom her
> family also have an interest. In this connection it is
> notable that throughout Africa part of the bride price
> goes to the bride's maternal kinsmen, her mother and
> especially her mother's brother.
> (1938:384)

Institutionalized gift-giving is perhaps the most commonly known form of distribution. Bunzel points to variability in the principles and mechanisms of distribution. She points out that the importance of gift-giving in the overall economic organization is completely different for the Zuñi than it is for the Maori. In the Zuñi case, gift-giving and feasting are mechanisms for adjusting inequalities. In the Maori case, Bunzel argues that gift-giving drives the entire economy, but, importantly, is combined with redistribution. People give the products of their labor to the chief, who redistributes it while retaining a large portion for his own use. Gift-giving takes many forms, one of which is the intertribal feast. Food is both consumed on the spot and given away to guests to take home (Firth 1929).

Gift-Giving and Trade

The relationships between gift-giving and trade are extremely important, but as Bunzel points out, not always easy to distinguish (1938:393). When a Maori chief exchanges gifts with a visitor, he can be considered to be engaging in trade. How to distinguish, analytically, between ordinary exchange and trade is difficult, especially because the terms are often used interchangeably. Bunzel suggests the following distinctions between trade and exchange. She does so in a rather groping and ethnocentric-sounding way, but the distinction she is making between processes internal to the group and those external to it is important. For Bunzel, trade is "intertribal economics."

> In preceding paragraphs we have discussed various forms of internal exchange which result in the redistribution of products—often products of different kinds—but which cannot be called trade. These exchanges are obligatory, or at least demanded by prestige; they follow prescribed channels, without regard for such economic factors as the needs or resources of the individuals concerned. But trade is primarily an economic mechanism. It may have a secondary social function as in the markets of Africa or Central America. Or else the prestige and ceremonial aspects may completely overshadow the economic, as in the kula trade already described. However the manner of conducting trade may differ from one group to an-

other, however much the interest in trade may vary,
the main economic motivations are clear and every-
where the same.
(1938:397)

SUMMARY

Despite Sahlins' arguments to the contrary, Bun-
zel's discussion represents an approach that is very close to his in its focus, however awkward, on the institutional arrangements that organize
economic processes. Bunzel, for example, talks about "institutions called
by the same name" such as the Chukchee or Zuñi or Kwakiutl feasts and
how different these are. While her details may not be accurate by today's
ethnographic standards, her descriptions of the institution of the trade
friendship in Melanesia, and of trade functioning within certain institutions for neither accumulation nor profit, indicate her sharp awareness of
the variety of institutional arrangements that organize kin-based economies. She is also aware of some of the complex relationships between
trade and marketplaces, especially those in Central America. Indeed, the
range of topics and problems covered in her piece is quite remarkable.
She drew on virtually every economic ethnography of her time, from
those of Boas and Malinowski on the Kwakiutl and the Trobrianders,
respectively, to more specialized writers on money (Armstrong 1924).

More importantly to us, Bunzel has touched on virtually all of the
major concepts discussed in this book. While she did not have the vocabulary that we have today, and she certainly did not have the ethnographic or archaeological data at her disposal, the fact that all of the key
concepts appear in one form or other is a testimony to her farsightedness
as well as to the generic quality and cross-cultural importance of the perspective I have called "cultural economies."

In 1982 Robert Dunnell (1982:3) took the new archaeology to task for
its lack of introspection and for using disembedded concepts as "articles
of faith." He laments the absence of bases for evaluating the "application,
relevance, and meaning" of concepts. "Theory defines unit: theory supplies the substantive meaning, the unit of observation, the means of asking and answering questions, and the means to bring the entire process
under the control of the investigator so that it can be examined, chal-
lenged, and evaluated. . . . Observation requires units and the means of
linking observations within those units" (1982:6). One of the main con-

cepts addressed by Dunnell is time (1982:13). Here he says that cultural history has had to conceptualize time "because common sense does not embody a usable notion of time" (1982:13).

The same can be said for all of the concepts in this book. Common sense does not tell us how to observe and analyze the economy. Ultimately common sense is ethnocentric and not useful for comparing like processes within like cultural systems. I have taken the opposite of a common sense approach to concepts of the economy. All of the concepts presented here, from the economy itself to equivalencies, storage, householding, and the informal economy—to name a few—must be understood as processes in cultural systems. These processes are explainable only in cultural and institutional terms. These are, as Leslie White would have it, culturally determined. This is the meaning of cultural economies past and present.

Notes

INTRODUCTION

1. Ellanna takes on the task of comparing four "Eskimo" groups, with the idea of shattering the common stereotype of Eskimo hunter-gatherers as "residing in relatively small, highly mobile social units that are flexibly organized and that undergo seasonal fission and fusion to facilitate survival in an environment where resources are both sparse and inconstant in their availability and abundance" (1988:74). Here she cites some of the standard materials on a range of Arctic groups (Balikci 1970; Damas 1969; Guemple 1972; Mauss and Beuchat 1979; Moran 1982; Spencer 1959). Among other things, she documents populations in excess of 200 for all four groups, depending upon historic period, and she argues further that "the relevance of overall population size to the successful exploitation of large marine mammals is central to an understanding of the economic systems of these populations" (1988:77–78). She also notes named patrilineal descent groups with a core of related males, and a high degree of community endogamy (1988:80–81). She argues then that "the adaptive strategies of the study populations are dependent upon reduced mobility, a relatively large population base, and a relatively conservative and rigid social organization." Production systems depend on these factors that "are typically considered to be maladaptive in generalized Inupiat and hunter-gatherer models" (1988:85).

Arguing in a similar vein, but with a different set of social organizational factors, Mark Cassell emphasizes organizational features of Inupiat economy and says that: "What is important is not whether people hunt caribou, drive rabbits, plant rice, or harvest millet, but rather how people organize themselves to hunt, drive, plant, and harvest. . . . I propose that the social organization of the traditional Inupiat whale hunt is best viewed in terms of models of relations of production derived from studies of agricultural peoples" (Cassell 1988:90). His theoretical backing comes primarily from Claude Meillassoux, whose framework is consistent with what I have called "the institutional paradigm" (Meillassoux 1973, 1978a, 1978b, 1980, 1981; see also Woodburn 1980, 1982) and with the distinction between "immediate-return" and "delayed-return" production systems for foragers.

2. Some archaeologists, especially classical archaeologists, have adopted an ethnocentric market-oriented stance (Knapp and Stech 1985; Runnels 1985).

1. METHODOLOGICAL INDIVIDUALISM: STRUCTURE AND AGENCY IN ECONOMIC ANTHROPOLOGY

1. Perhaps the best example of this naive brand of methodological individualism can be found in the anthropological literature on the roles and status of women. As Jane Guyer (1991) points out, and as I later discuss in chapter 8, mere descriptions of tasks, whatever these may be, without attention to the larger organizational and historical contexts within which a particular task is carried out, result in a kind of naive methodological individualism.

2. Polanyi's term for divorcing individuals from their societal context is the "disembedded economy." Samir Amin's concept of economistic alienation is similar. Kari Polanyi-Levitt points out that both Polanyi and Amin derive these concepts from Marx (Polanyi-Levitt 1990:116). See also F. Block 1991; Granovetter 1985; Schroyer 1991.

3. The influence of Marshall and the marginal-utility school of neo-classical economics is clear throughout Herskovits' work.

4. For an excellent critique of optimal foraging models see Wimsatt, who described "model-building activity . . . performed against a background of presumed mechanisms operating in the interaction of presumed units" (1982: 190–193).

2. MARX'S INSTITUTIONAL PARADIGM AND POLANYI'S GENERIC MODEL OF THE ECONOMY

1. While the whole corpus of Marx's work is certainly relevant to the discussion of the institutional paradigm, I am drawing primarily on his *Early Writings* and on *The Grundrisse*.

2. It is important to recognize that the history of anthropological theory plays

a critical role in the elaboration of the institutional paradigm in that it determines the methods and concepts by which anthropologists organize their research. As we will see in the penultimate chapter, Leslie White and his students probably practiced better institutional economic anthropology than any other group of anthropologists (Sahlins, Cappannari, and others). White himself was adamant about the separation of psychology from anthropology and strongly criticized methodological individualism. The reader edited by Dole and Carneiro (1960) is important to consult for an elaboration of these points.

3. One of the first and most articulate advocates of this position was the historian of ancient Greece, Moses Finley (1954, 1973).

4. The numerous discussions on the issue of structure and agency all harken back to the relationships between individuals and larger structures as units of analysis for formulating models, etc. See Ortner 1984, Bourdieu 1977. It is true that some economic anthropologists do not seem to recognize the issues involved in discussions of structure and agency (Plattner 1989). Plattner's collection focuses on economic behavior. See more recently Granovetter 1985.

5. There is a huge literature here. I have reviewed much of it in chapter 5 of *Economies Across Cultures* (Halperin 1988). See also Winterhalder 1986, Webster 1986, Thomas 1986, Speth and Spielmann 1983, Belovsky 1987.

6. Notes of a Week's Study on THE EARLY WRITINGS OF KARL MARX and summary of discussions on BRITISH WORKING CLASS CONSCIOUS-NESS. January 1, 1938. Prepared by a Christian Left Group. Bulletin 2.

4. EQUIVALENCIES IN ECONOMIC ANTHROPOLOGY

1. In *Barter, Exchange and Value: An Anthropological Approach*, Humphrey and Hugh-Jones delineate the features of barter as follows: "(a) The focus is on demand for particular things which are different in kind; in other cases it may be for services exchanged for goods or other services. (b) The protagonists are essentially free and equal, either can pull out of the deal and at the end of it they are quits. (c) There is no criterion by which, from the outside, it can be judged that the oxen are equal in value to the carving. Some kind of bargaining is taking place, but not with reference to some abstract measure of value; each simply wants the object held by the other. (d) In the case above, the two parts of the transaction occur simultaneously; sometimes the two may be separated in time. (e) Finally the act is transformative; it moves objects between the 'regimes of value' (Appadurai 1986) sustained by the two actors" (Humphrey and Hugh-Jones 1992:1). There are some major confusions, however, especially in their failure to define "barter."

2. See Berdan 1978, 1983; Blom 1932; Carrasco 1978; Casson 1984; Chapman

1957; Curtin 1984; Grierson 1977; Lamberg-Karlovsky 1975; Silver 1938; Simkin 1968; Wright and Johnson 1975; and Zeitlin 1991.

3. See Mitchell 1991a, 1991b.

5. HOUSEHOLDING: RESISTANCE AND LIVELIHOOD IN RURAL ECONOMIES

1. The market system is hierarchically organized and resembles many marketplaces described elsewhere in the world. In fact, it is quite reminiscent of the dendritic marketplaces described by Carol Smith (1985) for Guatemala and by Cook and Diskin (1976) for Oaxaca, Mexico. In Kentucky, however, the marketplace system is a major component of the informal economy. See also Orlove 1986; Skinner 1964, 1985; Carol Smith 1974, 1976, 1977; R. H. T. Smith 1971; Granovetter 1985; Katzin 1960; Mintz 1961, 1964; and Trager 1981.

2. It should be clear that householding encompasses all sorts of locational and appropriational movements in various combinations, depending upon season, provisioning needs, people available to perform work tasks, etc. It would be a revealing exercise to take each exchange and analyze it in terms of locational and appropriational movements.

6. STORAGE AS AN ECONOMIC PROCESS

1. Croes (1992:345) also takes a seasonal, ecological approach to storage by modeling storage practices for the Northwest coast Hoko archaeological site: "When we model for storage by increasingly making resources available in off-seasons through the storage practices we initially see a heavy reliance on off-shore fisheries in the spring/summer, and especially for flatfish, which can be sun-dried for winter uses . . ." Matson, in the same volume (1992), says that the large-scale harvesting, processing, and storage of salmon must be recognized as the economic underpinning of the Northwest coast, and that storage practices play a major role in subsistence change. He notes also that these coastal cultures have many features usually associated with agriculturally based societies: ascribed status, elaborate art, permanent dwelling, large villages, property ownership. Yet they lack any significant use of domesticated plants or animals.

2. See Baksh 1985; Carneiro 1960; Johnson 1983; Johnson and Baksh 1987; Maybury-Lewis 1974; Murphy and Murphy 1985; Rappaport 1967; and Weiner 1976, 1983.

3. Scarborough adds to the evidence for intensification of storage activities in his discussion of jar-to-bowl (serving bowl) ratios. In contrast to the Meyer Pit-

house Village, where storage jars were barely in the majority—with the jar-to-bowl ratios nearly 1:1 (1.08)—was the Hot Wells Pueblo site, where the ratio was 3:1.

4. T. Gross (1992:248) examines eleven independent variables: (1) the degree of dependence on stored materials, (2) the form of the stored materials, (3) the diversity of the stored materials, (4) the availability of building materials, (5) the need to buffer fluctuations in food availability, (6) the size of the population dependent on the facility, (7) the permanence of the settlement containing the facility, (8) the density of the human population, (9) the accumulation of surpluses for use in hosting gatherings, (10) the accumulation of individual surpluses for attracting followers, and (11) the need to build contiguous facilities. The implications for economic organization, for example labor use and intensity, are not explored by Gross. It would be possible, by using certain ethnoarchaeological techniques, to make some projections about the different labor requirements of corn storage in various forms. This is an important article.

5. A *milpa* is translated literally as "cornfield." In reality, though, *milpas* are large gardens with a mixture of crops, depending upon the environment.

8. TIME AND THE ECONOMY: A SUBSTANTIVE PERSPECTIVE

1. By narrowly I really mean in a manner that relies strongly on methodological individualism (e.g., studies of how much time people spend doing this or that). Time allocation studies are cases in point (Hames 1979, 1989; Hames and Vickers 1982; Johnson and Baksh 1975; Minge-Kalman 1980; Werner et al. 1979; Winterhalder 1983; O'Connell and Hawkes 1983; Hawkes et al. 1982). These studies focus on a variety of topics, including what determines how much hunting versus how much fishing a given Amazon Basin group will engage in. From an evolutionary-ecological perspective, all humans are resource maximizers and time is one resource. Hames (1989:57–58), for example, writes: "In optimal foraging theory a resource maximization strategy is chosen if and only if an increase in time spent foraging will lead to an increase in fitness. This strategy is opposed to a time minimization strategy, which is followed whenever a decrease in foraging time will lead to an increase in fitness. Both strategies are optimized when the net rate of return while foraging is maximized. This is true for energy maximizers because it leads to the maximum possible rate of resource consumption, and it is true for time minimizers because it allows them to satisfy energy needs in the shortest time possible."

2. Exceptions include the Yucatecan village of Chan Kom, which has been studied at three different points in time (Redfield and Villa Rojas 1934; Redfield 1950; Goldkind 1965); the Guatemalan village of Panajachel; and a Yugoslav case

(Halpern and Wagner 1984; Halpern 1967, 1981; Halpern and Kerewsky-Halpern 1972).

3. Bourdieu 1964, 1977, 1979, 1990; Giddens 1979, 1981, 1984; Weiner 1976, 1983. Even Bourdieu and Giddens treat time and the economy in the abstract.

4. We should note that Munn seems to have overlooked a much earlier piece by Bourdieu entitled: "The attitude of the Algerian peasant toward time" (1963). It is not inconsistent, however, with methodological individualism. As E. P. Thompson (1991:356) points out: "Pierre Bourdieu has explored more closely the attitudes towards time of the Kaabyle peasant (in Algeria) in recent years: 'An attitude of submission and of nonchalant indifference to the passage of time which no one dreams of mastering, using up, or saving. . . . Haste is seen as a lack of decorum combined with diabolical ambition.' The clock is sometimes known as 'the devel's mill'; there are no precise meal-times; 'the notion of an exact appointment is unknown; they agree only to meet "at the next market".'"

5. I am grateful to Joel Halpern for emphasizing to me the point that peasant workers exist within multiple time frames. See Holmes 1989; Holmes and Quataert 1986; R. Johnson 1979; and Lockwood 1973.

6. Swetnam's discussion of time and timing in the context of Guatemalan markets would be another case for analysis here (1993).

9. LOOKING BACKWARD AND FORWARD ON CONCEPTS OF THE ECONOMY: THE DISCOURSE OF ECONOMIC ANTHROPOLOGY IN HISTORICAL AND COMPARATIVE PERSPECTIVE

1. See also Stanish 1992. It is noteworthy that Kahn and Llobera refer to Polanyi to elaborate Marx on the anthropology of pre-capitalist economies (1981). Among other points, in their concluding chapter entitled "Towards a New Marxism or a New Anthropology," Kahn and Llobera point to the limitations of Marxist economic anthropology and of Marx himself. They begin with Althusser's realization that Marx was creating a new science of history: "For Althusser this means that at that moment in time (1845–1846 as recorded in *The German Ideology*), Marx broke radically with every approach which based history in the essence of man. Marx proposed a new conception based on the notion of social totality and associated concepts like mode of production, relations of production, forces of production, ideology, etc. Althusser is aware that Marx never succeeded in giving a systematic exposition to this science. On the other hand, the novelty of this conception of history lies in the fact that it puts forward a new criterion for periodization, that is, the succession of social totalities (modes of production). . . . Althusser remarks that for Marx each unit of periodization has

laws of its own that cease to be effective once that stage has passed. This means that although there are a number of general concepts of historical materialism, each mode of production has laws of its own and, consequently, requires specific concepts.

According to Althusser, the two basic and most general concepts of historical materialism, namely mode of production and social formation, are both social totalities, or to be more precise, structures in dominance. The former is a theoretical and abstract object, the latter a real, concrete one, and historical materialism constructs the former in order to understand, that is, to produce the scientific knowledge of, the latter. Failure to distinguish one concept from the other—a deep-rooted empiricist practice—makes it impossible to produce the desired knowledge effect . . .

In Althusser's view Marx only formulated the general and specific concepts of historical materialism in a rather sketchy, incomplete and uneven way; thus, the economic instance was elaborated more than the other. On the other hand, and with respect to specific concepts, although Marx considered a number of modes of production he studied only the capitalist mode of production in detail" (1981:274–277).

Kahn and Llobera go on to point out that those writers who followed in the Marxist tradition (Meillassoux and Godelier at first, Terray, Rey, and others later) "who saw as their task as an intervention in anthropology either by the critical appropriation of anthropological discourse by historical materialism or the use of a Marxist approach in anthropology, or a combination of the two" also had their limitations. Rey became interested in the work of Meillassoux and Polanyi when he realized that mathematical economics could not explain problems of economic development (Kahn and Llobera 1981:283). I should note that this is an excellent review of French Marxist economic anthropology.

2. Sahlins (1960:391) states categorically that primitive economic behavior is largely an aspect of kinship behavior, and must be understood to be organized by means completely different from capitalist production and market transactions (cf. White 1949:379). For Sahlins, following Polanyi, modern (conventional) economic theory fails to apply to primitive economies.

3. The definition of the economy has been a topic of great debate in economic anthropology, and in fact was at the heart of the formalist-substantivist debate. As Sahlins (1960:391) states the issue: "Anthropologists were wont to identify the economic subsystem of a culture, an economy, with 'economizing'—applying scarce means against alternate ends—which is the typical transactional feature in our society." Where there is economizing, it is argued, there is an economy (Firth 1954:15; Herskovits 1952, Ch. 1). In a general sense it is true that primitives economize and make allocative choices. To live is to economize, but this indicates the worthlessness of so defining an economy. The question is whether economic choices are specifically determined by the relative value of the goods involved. If so, as can be true only in a price-setting market system, then

the entire economy is organized by the process of maximization of economic value. If not, as in primitive societies where price-fixing markets are absent and social relations channel the movement of goods, then the economy is organized by these relations. To say that primitives economize tells us nothing about their economy; it is simply misleading. We are indebted to Karl Polanyi for pointing out the logical weakness of the identification of economy with economizing (Polanyi 1957).

Sahlins notes another disadvantage to adopting conventional economic theory: economics uses the individual, rather than the society, as the unit of analysis (1960:391). This is an important point because some of the newer models, such as optimal foraging models, do the same thing. That is, they use the individual, rather than culture or society, as the unit of analysis. I deal with some of these issues in chapter 5 of *Economies Across Cultures* (1988).

Bibliography

Adams, R. M.

1966   *The Evolution of Urban Society: Early Mesopotamia and Pre-Hispanic Mexico.* Chicago: Aldine.

1974   "Anthropological Perspectives on Ancient Trade." *Current Anthropology* 15:239–258.

Aguirre Beltrán, Gonzalo

1967   *Regiones de Refugio.* Mexico City: Instituto Indigenista.

Alland, A., Jr.

1967   *Evolution and Human Behavior.* Garden City, N.Y.: Natural History Press.

Althusser, Louis

1970   "From Capital to Marx's Philosophy." In *Reading Capital*, edited by L. Althusser and E. Balibar, 11–70. London: Lowe and Brydonne.

Amir, Samir

1974   "In Praise of Socialism." *Monthly Review.*

Anderson, James N.

1973   "Ecological Anthropology and Anthropological Ecology." In *Handbook of Social and Cultural Anthropology*, edited by J. Honigmann, 179-239. Chicago: Rand McNally.

Annis, Sheldon

1987   *God and Production in a Guatemalan Town.* Austin: University of Texas Press.

Appadurai, Arjun, ed.

1986   *The Social Life of Things.* Cambridge: Cambridge University Press.

Arizpe, Lourdes
    1977   "Women in the Informal Sector: The Case of Mexico City."
                Signs: Journal of Women in Culture and Society Fall: 45–59.
Armstrong, W. E.
    1924   "Shell Money from Rossell Island, Papua." *Man* 24:119.
Babb, Florence E.
    1985   "Middlemen and 'Marginal' Women: Marketers and Dependency
                in Peru's Informal Sector." In *Markets and Marketing*, edited by
                Stuart Plattner, 287–308. Lanham, Md.: University Press of
                America.
Baksh, M.
    1985   "Faunal Food as a 'Limiting Factor' on Amazonia Cultural Be-
                havior: A Machiguenga Example." In *Research in Economic An-
                thropology*, vol. 7, edited by B. L. Isaac, 145–176. Greenwich,
                Conn.: JAI Press.
Balikci, Asen
    1970   *The Netsilik Eskimo*. Garden City, N.Y.: Natural History Press.
Barlett, Peggy F.
    1980   *Agricultural Decision Making: Anthropological Contributions to Rural
                Development*. New York: Academic Press.
    1989   "Industrial Agriculture." In *Economic Anthropology*, edited by
                Stuart Plattner, 253–291. Stanford: Stanford University Press.
Barth, F.
    1956   "Ecological Relationships of Ethnic Groups in Swat, North Pak-
                istan." *American Anthropologist* 58:1079–1089.
Bates, M.
    1961   *Man in Nature*. Englewood Cliffs, N.J.: Prentice-Hall.
Batteau, Alan, ed.
    1983   *Appalachia and America: Autonomy and Regional Dependence*. Lex-
                ington: University Press of Kentucky.
Beaman, Anne W.
    1983   "Women's Participation in Pastoral Economy: Income Maximi-
                zation among the Rendille." *Nordic Peoples* 12:20–25.
Beaver, Patricia D.
    1986   *Rural Community in the Appalachian South*. Lexington: University
                Press of Kentucky.
Belshaw, C. S.
    1965   *Traditional Exchange and Modern Markets*. Englewood Cliffs, N.J.:
                Prentice-Hall.
Bender, John, and David E. Wellbery, eds.
    1991   *Chronotypes: The Construction of Time*. Stanford: Stanford Univer-
                sity Press.

Bennett, J. W.

1969   *Northern Plainsmen: Adaptive Strategy and Agrarian Life.* Chicago: Aldine.

Berdan, Frances F.

1978   "Ports of Trade in Mesoamerica: A Reappraisal." In *Cultural Continuity in Mesoamerica*, edited by D. Browman. World Anthropology Series. The Hague: Mouton Publishers.

1983   "The Reconstruction of Ancient Economies: Perspectives from Archaeology and Ethnohistory." In *Economic Anthropology: Topics and Theories*, edited by Sutti Ortiz, 83–95. SEA vol. 1. Lanham, Md.: University Press of America.

Bernstein, Gail

1983   *Haruko's World.* Palo Alto: Stanford University Press.

Bettinger, R. L.

1980   "Explanatory/Predictive Models of Hunter-Gatherer Adaptation." In *Advances in Archaeological Method and Theory, vol. 3*, edited by M. B. Schiffer. New York: Academic Press.

Billings, Dwight, Kathleen Blee, and Louis Swanson

1986   "Culture, Family, and Community in Preindustrial Appalachia." *Appalachian Journal* 13:154–170.

Binford, Lewis

1980   "Willow Smoke and Dogs' Tails: Hunter-Gatherer Settlement Systems and Archaeological Site Formation." *American Antiquity* 45:4–20.

1989   "The 'New Archaeology,' then and now." In *Archaeological Thought in America*, edited by C. C. Lamberg-Karlovsky, 50–62. Cambridge: Cambridge University Press.

Bloch, Andrzej

1985–86   "The Private Sector in Poland." *Telos* 66:129–131.

Bloch, M.

1989   "The Symbolism of Money in Imerina." In *Money and the Morality of Exchange*, edited by M. Bloch and J. Parry, 165–190. Cambridge: Cambridge University Press.

Bloch, M., and J. Parry, eds.

1989   *Money and the Morality of Exchange.* Cambridge: Cambridge University Press.

Block, F.

1990   *Postindustrial Possibilities: A Critique of Economic Discourse.* Berkeley: University of California Press.

1991   "Contradictions in Self-Regulating Markets." In *The Legacy of Karl Polanyi*, edited by Marguerite Mendell and Daniel Salee, 86–106. New York: St. Martin's Press.

Blom, Franz
    1932   "Commerce, Trade, and Monetary Units of the Maya." *Middle American Research Series Publication* 4:531–552.

Boas, Franz, ed.
    1938   *General Anthropology*. Washington, D.C.: Heath and Company.

Boeke, J. H.
    1953   *Economics and Economic Policy of Dual Societies as Exemplified by Indonesia*. New York: Institute of Pacific Relations.

Bohannan, Paul
    1955   "Some Principles of Exchange and Investment Among the Tiv." *American Anthropologist* 57:60–70.

    1959   "The Impact of Money on an African Subsistence Economy." *The Journal of Economic History* 19:491–503. (Reprinted in *Tribal and Peasant Economies*, edited by George Dalton.)

Bohannan, Paul, and Laura Bohannan
    1968   *Tiv Economy*. London: Longmans.

Bohannan, Paul, and George Dalton, eds.
    1962   *Markets in Africa*. Evanston, Ill.: Northwestern University Press.

Bourdieu, Pierre
    1964   "The attitude of the Algerian peasant towards time." In *Mediterranean Countrymen*, edited by J. Pitt-Rivers, 55–72. The Hague: Mouton.

    1977   *Outline of a Theory of Practice*. Cambridge: Cambridge University Press.

    1979   "The disenchantment of the world." In *Algeria 1960*, 1–94. Cambridge: Cambridge University Press.

    1990   *The Logic of Practice*. Stanford: Stanford University Press.

Braudel, F.
    1982   *The Wheels of Commerce*. London: Collins.

Bromley, Ray
    1978a   "Introduction: The Urban Informal Sector: Why is it Worth Discussing?" *World Development* 6:1033–1039.

    1978b   "Organization, Regulation, and Exploitation in the So-Called 'Urban Informal Sector': The Street Traders of Cali, Columbia." *World Development* 6:1161–1171.

Bromley, Ray, ed.
    1985   *Planning for Small Enterprises in Third World Cities*. Oxford: Pergamon Press.

Bronitsky, Gordon
    1984   "'Banking' at Arroyo Hondo, New Mexico, A.D. 1300–1424." In *Research in Economic Anthropology*, *vol. 6*, edited by B. L. Isaac, 171–190. Greenwich, Conn.: JAI Press.

Brown, James S.

    1952   *The Family Group in a Kentucky Mountain Farming Community.* Lexington: University Press of Kentucky, Agricultural Experiment Station Bulletin 588.

Brumfiel, Elizabeth M., and Timothy K. Earle

    1987   "Specialization, Exchange, and Complex Societies." In *Production, Exchange, and Complex Societies,* edited by Elizabeth M. Brumfiel and Timothy K. Earle. Cambridge: Cambridge University Press.

Bryant, Carlene

    1981   *We're All Kin: A Cultural Study of an East Tennessee Mountain Neighborhood.* Knoxville: University of Tennessee Press.

    1983   "Family Group Organization in a Cumberland Mountain Neighborhood." In *Appalachia and America: Autonomy and Regional Dependence,* edited by Alan Batteau. Lexington: University Press of Kentucky.

Bunzel, Ruth

    1938   "The Economic Organization of Primitive Peoples." In *General Anthropology,* edited by Franz Boas. Washington, D.C.: Heath.

Burling, Robbins

    1962   "Maximization Theories and the Study of Anthropology." *American Anthropologist* 66:20–28.

Burton, Michael L., and Douglas R. White

    1984   "Sexual Division of Labor in Agriculture." *American Anthropologist* 86:568–583.

Cancian, Frank

    1965   *Economics and Prestige in a Maya Community: The Religious Cargo System in Zinacantan.* Stanford: Stanford University Press.

    1966   "Maximization as Norm, Strategy, and Theory: A Comment on Programmatic Statements in Economic Anthropology." *American Anthropologist* 68:465–470.

Cappannari, Stephen C.

    1960   "The Concept of Property Among Shoshoneans." In *Essays in the Science of Culture in Honor of Leslie White,* edited by Gertrude Dole and Robert Carneiro, 133–144. New York: Thomas Crowell Co.

Carneiro, Robert L.

    1960   "Slash-and-Burn Agriculture: A Closer Look at Implications for Settlement Patterns." In *Men and Culture,* edited by A. Wallace. Philadelphia: University of Pennsylvania Press.

    1961   "Slash-and-Burn Cultivation Among the Kuikuru and Its Implications for Cultural Development in the Amazon Basin." In *The Evolution of Horticultural Systems in Native South America: Causes* and *Consequences*, edited by J. Wibert. Caracas: Sociedad de Ciencias Naturales LaSalle.

1981*a*   "Leslie A. White." In *Totems and Teachers: Perspectives on the History of Anthropology*, edited by Sydel Silverman, 209–251. New York: Columbia University Press.

1981*b*   "The Chiefdom: Precursor of the State." In *The Transition to Statehood in the New World*, edited by Grant D. Jones and Robert R. Krautz. New York and London: Cambridge University Press.

Carrasco, Pedro

1978   "La Economía del Mexico Prehispánico." In *Economía Politica e Ideología en el Mexico Prehispánico*, edited by Pedro Carrasco and Johanna Broda, 15–76. Mexico: Instituto Nacional de Antropología e Historia.

1982   "The Political Economy of the Aztec and Inca States." In *The Inca and Aztec States 1400–1600: Anthropology and History*, edited by G. A. Collier, R. I. Rosaldo, and J. D. Wirth, 24–39. New York: Academic Press.

Cashdan, Elizabeth

1983   "Territoriality among Human Foragers: Ecological Models and Application to Four Bushman Groups." *Current Anthropology* 24: 47–66.

1989   "Hunters and Gatherers: Economic Behavior in Bands." In *Economic Anthropology*, edited by Stuart Plattner, 21–48. Stanford: Stanford University Press.

Cassell, Mark S.

1988   "Farmers of the Northern Ice: Relations of Production in the Traditional North Alaskan Inupiat Whale Hunt." In *Research in Economic Anthropology*, *vol. 10*, edited by B. L. Isaac. Greenwich, Conn.: JAI Press.

Casson, Lionel

1984   *Ancient Trade and Society*. Detroit: Wayne State University Press.

Chang, K. C.

1975   "Ancient Trade as Economics or as Ecology." In *Ancient Civilization and Trade*, edited by J. A. Sabloff and C. C. Lamberg-Karlovsky, 211–224. Albuquerque: University of New Mexico Press.

Chapman, Anne

1957   "Port of Trade Enclaves in Aztec and Maya Civilization." In *Trade and Market in the Early Empires*, edited by Karl Polanyi et al., 114–153. New York: The Free Press.

1980   "Barter as a Universal Model of Exchange." *L'Homme* 20:33–88.

Chayanov, A. V.

1966   "On the Theory of Non-capitalist Economic Systems." In *On the*

Theory of Peasant Economy, edited by D. Thorner, 1–13. Homewood: Richard D. Irvin.

Chevalier, Jacques M.

1982   *Civilization and the Stolen Gift: Capital, Kin and Cult in Eastern Peru*. Toronto: University of Toronto Press.

Clammer, John

1978a   (Ed.) *The New Economic Anthropology*. New York: St. Martin's Press.

1978b   "Concepts and Objects in Economic Anthropology." In *The New Economic Anthropology*, edited by John Clammer, 1–20. New York: St. Martin's Press.

Codere, Helen

1950   *Fighting with Poverty*. Seattle: University of Washington Press.

1968   "Exchange and Display." In *International Encyclopedia of the Social Sciences*, edited by D. Sills, 239–245. New York: The Free Press.

Cohen, Mark N.

1989   "Paleopathology and the interpretation of economic change in prehistory." In *Archaeological Thought in America*, edited by C. C. Lamberg-Karlovsky, 117–132. Cambridge: Cambridge University Press.

Cohen, Yehudi A.

1968   "Culture as Adaptation." In *Man in Adaptation: The Cultural Present*, edited by Y. Cohen, 40–60. Chicago: Aldine.

Comaroff, Jean

1985   *Body of Power, Spirit of Resistance: The Culture and History of a South African People*. Chicago: University of Chicago Press.

Cook, Scott

1966a   "The Obsolete 'Anti-Market' Mentality: A Critique of the Substantive Approach to Economic Anthropology." *American Anthropologist* 68:323–345.

1966b   "Maximization, Economic Theory, and Anthropology: A Reply to Cancian." *American Anthropologist* 68:1494–1498.

1969   "The 'Anti-Market' Mentality Re-Examined: A Further Critique of the Substantive Approach to Economic Anthropology." *Southwestern Journal of Anthropology* 25:378–406.

1973   "Production, Ecology, and Economic Anthropology: Notes Toward an Integrated Frame of Reference." *Social Science Information* 12:25–52.

Cook, Scott, and Martin Diskin, eds.

1976   *Markets in Oaxaca*. Austin: University of Texas Press.

Cordell, Linda S.

1984   *Prehistory of the Southwest*. New York: Academic Press.

Cowgill, George L.

    1989   "Formal approaches in archaeology." In *Archaeological Thought in America*, edited by C. C. Lamberg-Karlovsky, 74–88. Cambridge: Cambridge University Press.

Croes, Dale

    1992   "Exploring Prehistoric Subsistence Change on the Northwest Coast." In *Long-Term Subsistence Change in Prehistoric North America*, edited by Dale Croes, R. Hawkins, and B. L. Isaac. Research in Economic Anthropology Supplement 6, 337–366. Greenwich, Conn.: JAI Press.

Cross, John R.

    1993   "Craft Specialization in Nonstratified Societies." In *Research in Economic Anthropology, vol. 14*, edited by B. L. Isaac, 61–84. Greenwich, Conn.: JAI Press.

Curtin, Philip D.

    1984   *Cross-Cultural Trade in World History*. Cambridge: Cambridge University Press.

Dalton, George

    1961   "Economic Theory and Primitive Society." *American Anthropologist* 63:1–25.

    1974   "How Exactly are Peasants 'Exploited'?" *American Anthropologist* 76:553–561.

    1980   "Introduction." In *Research in Economic Anthropology: A Research Annual 3*, edited by George Dalton, pp. vii–xiii. Greenwich, Conn.: JAI Press.

    1981   "Comment on 'Symposium: Economic Anthropology and History: The Work of Karl Polanyi.'" In *Research in Economic Anthropology: A Research Annual 4*, edited by George Dalton. Greenwich, Conn.: JAI Press.

D'Altroy, Terence N., and Christine A. Hastorf

    1984   "The Distribution and Content of Inca State Storehouses in the Xauxa Region of Peru." *American Antiquity* 49(2):334–349.

Damas, David

    1969*a*   *Contributions to Anthropology: Ecological Essays*, edited by Ottawa: National Museums of Canada Bulletin No. 230, Anthropological Series No. 86.

    1969*b*   "Environment, History, and Central Eskimo Society." In *Contributions to Anthropology: Ecological Essays*, edited by David Damas. Ottawa: National Museums of Canada Bulletin No. 230, Anthropological Series No. 86.

    1969*c*   "Characteristics of Central Eskimo Band Structure." In *Contributions to Anthropology: Band Societies*, edited by David Damas.

Ottawa: National Museums of Canada Bulletin No. 230, Anthropological Series No. 86.

Damon, Frederick

1993   "Representation and Experience in Kula and Western Exchange Spheres." *Research in Economic Anthropology, vol. 14*, edited by B. L. Isaac, 235–254. Greenwich, Conn.: CAI Press.

Davies, R.

1979   "Informal Sector or Subordinate Mode of Production? A Model." In *Casual Work and Poverty in Third World Cities*, edited by R. Bromely and C. Gerry. New York: John Wiley and Sons.

DeWalt, Billie

1975   "Changes in the Cargo Systems of Mesoamerica." *Anthropological Quarterly* 45:87–105.

Dilley, Roy, ed.

1992   *Contesting Markets: Analysis of Ideology, Discourse and Practice*. Edinburgh: Edinburgh University Press.

Dole, Gertrude E.

1960   "Techniques of Preparing Manioc Flour as a Key to Culture History in Tropical America." In *Men and Cultures*, edited by Anthony F. C. Wallace. Philadelphia: University of Pennsylvania Press.

Douglas, Mary

1967   "Raffia Cloth Distribution in the Lele Economy." In *Tribal and Peasant Economies: Readings in Economic Anthropology*, edited by George Dalton. New York: Natural History Press (originally published 1958 in *Africa* 28:109–122).

Douglas, M., and B. Isherwood

1979   *The World of Goods: Towards an Anthropology of Consumption*. London: Allen Lane.

Dow, Leslie M., Jr.

1977   "High Weeds in Detroit: The Irregular Economy Among a Network of Appalachian Migrants." *Urban Anthropology* 6:111–128.

Dowling, John

1968   "Individual Ownership and the Sharing of Game in Hunting Societies." *American Anthropologist* 70:502–507.

Drucker, Philip

1955   *Indians of the Northwest Coast*. New York: McGraw-Hill.

Dufour, Darna L.

1980   "Manioc as a Dietary Staple: Implications for the Budgeting of Time and Energy." Paper prepared for the 1980 Annual Meeting of the American Anthropological Association.

Dumont, L.

1986   *Essays on Individualism: Modern Ideology in Anthropological Perspectives*. Chicago and London: University of Chicago Press.

Dunnell, Robert C.

1982   "Science, Social Science, and Common Sense: The Agonizing Dilemma of Modern Archaeology." *Journal of Anthropological Research* 38:1–25.

1989   "Aspects of the application of evolutionary theory in archaeology." In *Archaeological Thought in America*, edited by C. C. Lamberg-Karlovsky, 35–49. Cambridge: Cambridge University Press.

Earle, T. K., and A. L. Christenson, eds.

1980   *Modeling Change in Prehistoric Subsistence Economies*. New York: Academic Press.

Earle, Timothy, and Terrence D'Altroy

1989   "The political economy of the Inka empire: the archaeology of power and finance." In *Archaeological Thought in America*, edited by C. C. Lamberg-Karlovsky, 183–204. Cambridge: Cambridge University Press.

Earle, Timothy, and Terrence D'Altroy

1982   "Storage Facilities and State Finance in the Upper Mantaro Valley, Peru." In *Contexts for Exchange*, edited by Timothy Earle and Terrence D'Altroy. New York: Academic Press.

Ellanna, Linda J.

1988   "Demography and Social Organization as Factors in Subsistence Production in Four Eskimo Communities." In *Research in Economic Anthropology, vol. 10*, edited by B. L. Isaac, 73–88. Greenwich, Conn.: JAI Press.

Ellen, Roy

1982   *Environment, Subsistence, and System: The Ecology of Small-Scale Social Formations*. Cambridge: Cambridge University Press.

Eller, Ronald

1982   *Miners, Millhands, and Mountaineers: Industrialization of the Appalachian South 1880–1930*. Knoxville: University of Tennessee Press.

Ember, Carol R.

1983   "The Relative Decline in Women's Contribution to Agriculture with Intensification." *American Anthropologist* 85:285–304.

Epstein, T. S.

1968   *Capitalism, Primitive and Modern*. East Lansing: Michigan State University Press.

Ericson, J., and Earle, T., eds.

1982   *Contexts for Prehistoric Exchange*. New York: Academic Press.

Evans-Pritchard, E. E.
   1944   *The Nuer.* Oxford: Clarendon Press.

Fabian, Johannes
   1983   *Time and the Other: How Anthropology Makes its Object.* New York: Columbia University Press.

Ferguson, J.
   1988   "Cultural Exchange: New Developments in the Anthropology of Commodities." *Current Anthropology* 3:488–513.

Ferman, Louis A., S. Henry, and M. Hoyman
   1987a   (Eds.) *The Informal Economy. The Annals of the American Academy of Political and Social Science.* Newbury Park, Calif.: Sage Publications.
   1987b   "Preface." In *The Informal Economy. The Annals of the American Academy of Political and Social Science.* Newbury Park, Calif.: Sage Publications.

Finley, M. I.
   1954   *The World of Odysseus.* New York: The Viking Press.
   1973   *The Ancient Economy.* Berkeley and Los Angeles: University of California Press.

Firth, Raymond
   1929   *Primitive Economics of the New Zealand Maori.* New York: Dalton.
   1939   *Primitive Polynesian Economy.* London: Routledge.
   1954   "Orientations in Economic Life." In *The Institutions of Primitive Society*, edited by E. E. Evans-Pritchard, Raymond Firth, et al. Glencoe: The Free Press.
   1964   "Capital, Savings, and Credit in Peasant Societies: A Viewpoint from Economic Anthropology." In *Capital, Savings, and Credit in Peasant Societies*, edited by Raymond Firth and B. S. Yamey. Chicago: Aldine.
   1967   *Themes in Economic Anthropology.* A. S. A. Monograph No. 6. London: Tavistock.

Flannery, Kent V.
   1969   "The Ecology of Early Food Production in Mesopotamia." In *Environment and Cultural Behavior*, edited by A. P. Vayda. Garden City, N.Y.: Natural History Press.

Forde, C. D.
   1934   *Habitat, Economy, and Society: A Geographical Introduction to Ethnology.* New York: Dutton.

Foster, Robert
   1990   "Value without Equivalence: Exchange and Replacement in a Melanesian Society." *Man* 25:54–69.

Foster, Stephen William
    1988   *The Past is Another Country*. Berkeley and Los Angeles: University of California Press.

Foster-Carter, A.
    1978   "The Mode of Production Controversy." *New Left Review* 107: 47–78.

Fratkin, Elliot
    1987   "Age-Sets, Household, and the Organization of Pastoral Production: The Ariaal, Samburu, and Rendille of Northern Kenya." In *Research in Economic Anthropology, vol. 9*, edited by B. L. Isaac, 295–314. Greenwich, Conn.: JAI Press.

Fried, Morton
    1967   *The Evolution of Political Society*. New York: Random House.

Friedman, Jonathan
    1974   "Marxism, Structuralism, and Vulgar Materialism." *Man* 9: 444–469.

Fry, R. E., ed.
    1980   *Models and Methods in Regional Exchange*. Washington, D.C.: Society for American Archaeology, Papers, 1.

Gaertner, Wulf, and Alois Wenig, eds.
    1985   *Economics of the Shadow Economy*. New York: Springer-Verlag.

Galaty, John
    1980   "The Maasai Group-Ranch: Politics and Development in an African Pastoral Society." In *When Nomads Settle: Processes of Sedentarization as Adaptation and Response*, edited by P. C. Salzman. New York: J. F. Bergin.

Galaty, John, Dan Aronson, Philip C. Salzman, and Amy Chouinard, eds.
    1981   *The Future of Pastoral Peoples*. Ottawa: International Development Research Center.

Gaughan, Joseph P., and Louis A. Ferman
    1987   "Toward an Understanding of the Informal Economy." In *The Informal Economy. The Annals of the American Academy of Political and Social Science,* edited by L. A. Ferman, S. Henry, and M. Hoyman. Newbury Park, Calif.: Sage Publications.

Geertz, C.
    1963   *Agricultural Involution: The Process of Ecological Change in Indonesia*. Berkeley: University of California Press.

Gerry, Chris
    1987   "Developing Economies and the Informal Sector in Historical Perspective." In *The Informal Economy. The Annals of the American Academy of Political and Social Science*, edited by L. A. Ferman, S. Henry, and M. Hoyman. Newbury Park, Calif.: Sage Publications.

Giddens, Anthony

1971   *Capitalism and Modern Social Theory: An Analysis of the Writings of Marx, Durkheim, and Weber.* Cambridge: Cambridge University Press.

1979   *Central Problems in Social Theory.* London: MacMillan.

1981   *A Contemporary Critique of Historical Materialism.* Berkeley: University of California Press.

1982   *Profiles and Critiques in Social Theory.* Berkeley: University of California Press.

1984   *The Constitution of Society: Outline of the Theory of Structuration.* Berkeley: University of California Press.

Gillin, John

1936   "The Barama River Caribs of British Guiana." *Papers of the Peabody Museum of American Archaeology and Ethnology Vol. 14, No. 2.* Cambridge, Massachusetts.

Gilman, Antonio

1989   "Marxism in American anthropology." In *Archaeological Thought in America*, edited by C. C. Lamberg-Karlovsky, 63–73. Cambridge: Cambridge University Press.

Gilman, Patricia

1983   "Changing Architectural Forms in the Prehistoric Southwest." Ph.D. diss., University of New Mexico, Albuquerque.

1987   "Architecture as Artifact: Pit Structures and Pueblos in the American Southwest." *American Antiquity* 52:538–564.

Gladwin, Christina H.

1975   "A Model of the Supply of Smoked Fish from Cape Coast to Kumasi." In *Formal Methods in Economic Anthropology*, edited by Stuart Plattner, 77–127. Washington: American Anthropological Association.

1982   "Off-Farm Work and Its Effect on Florida Farm Wives' Contribution to the Family Farm." In *World Development and Women*, vol. 2., edited by M. Rojas. Blacksburg, Va.: Virginia Tech Title XII Women in International Development Office.

1989   "On the Division of Labor between Economics and Economic Anthropology." In *Economic Anthropology*, edited by Stuart Plattner, 397–425. Stanford: Stanford University Press.

Gledhill, John, and Mogens Larsen

1982   "The Polanyi Paradigm and a Dynamic Analysis of Archaic States." In *Theory and Explanation in Archaeology: The Southampton Conference*, edited by Colin Renfrew, Michael Rowlands, and Barbara Abbott Segraves, 197–229. New York: Academic Press.

Godelier, Maurice

1966   *Rationality and Irrationality in Economics*. New York and London: Monthly Review Press.

1976   *Perspectives in Marxist Anthropology*. Cambridge: Cambridge University Press.

1978*a*   "The Object and Method in Economic Anthropology." In *Relations of Production*, edited by David Seddon. London: Frank Cass.

1978*b*   "Infrastructures, Societies, and History." *Current Anthropology* 19:763–771.

Goldkind, Victor

1965   "Social Stratification in the Peasant Community: Redfield's Chan Kom Reinterpreted." *American Anthropologist* 67:863–884.

1966   "Class Conflict and Cacique in Chan Kom." *Southwestern Journal of Anthropology* 22:325–345.

Granovetter, Mark

1985   "Economic Action and Social Structure: The Problem of Embeddedness." *American Journal of Sociology* 91:481–510.

Greenberg, James

1981   *Santiago's Sword*. Berkeley: University of California Press.

Gregory, C.

1982   *Gifts and Commodities*. London: Academic Press.

Gregory, S.

1980   "Gifts to Men and Gifts to God: Gift Exchange and Capital Accumulation in Contemporary Melanesia." *Man* 15:625–652.

1982   *Gifts and Commodities*. London: Academic Press.

Grierson, Philip

1977   *The Origins of Money*. The Creighton Lecture in History, 1970. London: The Athlone Press.

Gross, Daniel

1975   "Protein Capture and Cultural Development in the Amazon Basin." *American Anthropologist* 77:536–549.

1983   "The Ecological Perspective in Economic Anthropology." In *Economic Anthropology: Topics and Theories*, edited by Sutti Ortiz. Latham, Md.: University Press of America, Society for Economic Anthropology, Monograph 1.

Gross, Timothy

1992   "Subsistence Change and Architecture: Anasazi Storerooms in the Dolores Region, Colorado." In *Long-Term Subsistence Change in Prehistoric North America*, edited by Dale Croes, R. Hawkins, and B. L. Isaac. Research in Economic Anthropology Supplement 6, 241–266. Greenwich, Conn.: JAI Press.

Grossman, Gregory, ed.

1988   *Studies in the Second Economy of Communist Countries*. Berkeley: University of California Press.

Gudeman, S.

1986   *Economics as Culture: Models and Metaphors of Livelihood*. London: Routledge and Kegan Paul.

Gudeman, S., and M. Penn

1982   "Models, Meaning, and Reflexivity." In *Semantic Anthropology*, edited by D. Parkin. London: Academic Press.

Guemple, Lee, ed.

1972   *Alliance in Eskimo Society*. Seattle: American Ethnological Society.

Guyer, Jane I.

1991   "Female Farming in Anthropology and African History." In *Gender at the Crossroads of Knowledge: Feminist Anthropology in the Postmodern Era*, edited by Micaela di Leonardo, 257–277. Berkeley: University of California Press.

Halperin, Rhoda

1975   *Administración Agraria y Trabajo: Un caso de la economía política mexicana*. Mexico: Instituto Nacional Indigenista, No. 36.

1984   "Polanyi, Marx, and the Institutional Paradigm in Economic Anthropology." In *Research in Economic Anthropology, vol. 6*, edited by B. L. Isaac., 245–272. Greenwich, Conn.: JAI Press.

1985   "The Concept of the Formal in Economic Anthropology." In *Research in Economic Anthropology*, vol. 7, edited by B. L. Isaac, 339–368. Greenwich, Conn.: JAI Press.

1988   *Economies Across Cultures*. London: MacMillan.

1989   "Ecological vs. Economic Anthropology." In *Research in Economic Anthropology*, vol. 11, edited by B. L. Isaac, 13–41. Greenwich, Conn.: JAI Press.

1990   *The Livelihood of Kin: Making Ends Meet "The Kentucky Way."* Austin: The University of Texas Press.

1991   "Karl Polanyi's Concept of Householding: Resistance and Livelihood in an Appalachian Region." In *Research in Economic Anthropology*, vol. 13, edited by B. L. Isaac, 93–116. Greenwich, Conn.: JAI Press.

Halpern, Joel M.

1967   *A Serbian Village*. New York: Harper and Row.

1981   "Demographic and Social Change in the Village of Orasac: A Perspective over Two Centuries." *Serbian Studies* 1 : 51–70.

Halpern, Joel M., and T. Laird Christie

1992   "Time: A Tripartite Sociotemporal Model." Prepared for presentation at the International Society for the Study of Time, July 1992. In press.

Halpern, Joel M., and B. Krewsky-Halpern
   1972   *A Serbian Village in Historical Perspective*. New York: Holt, Rinehart, and Winston.
Halpern, Joel M., and Richard A. Wagner
   1984   "Time and Social Structure: A Yugoslav Case Study." *Journal of Family History* 9: 229–244.
Hames, R.
   1979   "A Comparison of the Efficiencies of the Shotgun and the Bow in Neotropical Forest Hunting." *Human Ecology* 7:219–252.
   1989   "Time, Efficiency, and Fitness in the Amazon Protein Quest." In *Research in Economic Anthropology, vol. 11*, edited by B. L Isaac, 43–85. Greenwich, Conn.: JAI Press.
Hames, R., and W. Vickers
   1982   "Optimal Foraging Theory as a Model to Explain Variability in Amazonia Hunting." *American Ethnologist* 9:358–378.
Hardesty, Donald L.
   1977   *Ecological Anthropology*. New York: John Wiley and Sons.
Harding, Thomas
   1967   *Voyagers of the Vitiaz Strait*. Seattle: University of Washington Press.
Harner, Michael
   1973   *The Jivaro*. New York: Anchor Books.
Harris, Marvin
   1966   "The Cultural Ecology of India's Sacred Cattle." *Current Anthropology* 7:51–66.
   1968   *The Rise of Anthropological Theory*. New York: Crowell Company.
   1979   *Cultural Materialism*. New York: Random House.
Hart, Keith
   1973   "Informal Income Opportunities and Urban Employment in Ghana." *Journal of Modern African Studies* 11:61–89.
   1992   "Market and State after the Cold War: The Informal Economy Reconsidered." In *Contesting Markets*, edited by Roy Dilley, 214–227. Edinburgh: Edinburgh University Press.
Hatch, E.
   1973   "The Growth of Economic, Subsistence, and Ecological Studies in American Anthropology." *Journal of Anthropological Research* 29:221–243.
Hawkes, Kristen, Kim Hill, and James F. O'Connell
   1982   "Why Hunters Gather: Optimal Foraging and the Ache of Eastern Paraguay." *American Ethnologist* 9:379–398.

Hawley, A.

1950   *Human Ecology: A Theory of Community Structure.* New York: Ronald Press.

Heidegger, M.

1982   *The Basic Problems of Phenomenology.* Bloomington: Indiana University Press.

Helm, J.

1962   "The Ecological Approach in Anthropology." *American Journal of Sociology* 17:630–639.

Henn, Jeanne K.

1984   "Women in the Rural Economy: Past, Present, and Future." In *African Women South of the Sahara,* edited by J. Hay and S. Stichter. London: Longman.

Henry, Stuart

1987   "The Political Economy of Informal Economies." In *The Informal Economy. The Annals of the American Academy of Political and Social Science,* edited by L. A. Ferman, S. Henry, and M. Hoyman. Newbury Park, Calif.: Sage Publications.

Herskovits, M. J.

1952   *Economic Anthropology: A Study of Comparative Economics.* New York: Knopf.

Hesiod

1973   *Works and Days.* New York: Penguin.

Hicks, George L.

1973   *Appalachian Valley.* New York: Holt, Rinehart and Winston.

Hindess, B.

1986   *Freedom, Equality, and the Market.* London: Tavistock.

1988   *Choice, Rationality, and Social Theory.* London: Unwin Hyman.

Hirth, Kenneth, ed.

1984   *Trade and Exchange in Early Mesoamerica.* Albuquerque: University of New Mexico Press.

Hobhouse, L. T.

1922   "The Historical Evolution of Property, in Fact and in Idea." In *Property, Its Duties and Rights,* new edition. New York: MacMillan.

Hodder, Ian

1980   "Trade and Exchange: Definitions, Identification, and Function." In *Models and Methods in Regional Exchange,* edited by R. Fry, 151–156. Washington, D.C.: Society for American Archaeology, Papers, 1.

Holmes, Douglas

1989   *Cultural Disenchantments.* Princeton: Princeton University Press.

Holmes, Douglas, and Jean Quataert

1986   "An Approach to Modern Labor: Worker Peasantries in Historic Saxony and the Friuli Region over Three Centuries." *Comparative Studies in Society and History* 28:191–216.

Hoyman, Michelle

1987   "Female Participation in the Informal Economy: A Neglected Issue." In *The Informal Economy. The Annals of the American Academy of Political and Social Science*, edited by L. A. Ferman, S. Henry, and M. Hoyman. Newbury Park, Calif.: Sage Publications.

Hugh-Jones, Christine

1979   *From the Milk River: Spatial and Temporal Processes in Northwest Amazonia*. Cambridge: Cambridge University Press.

Humphrey, Caroline, and Stephen Hugh-Jones

1992   *Barter, Exchange, and Value: An Anthropological Approach*. Cambridge: Cambridge University Press.

Illich, Ivan

1981   *Shadow Work*. London: Marion Boyars.

Ingold, T.

1979   "The Social and Ecological Relations of Culture-bearing Organisms: An Essay in Evolutionary Dynamics." In *Social and Ecological Systems*, edited by P. Bernham and R. Ellen. London: Academic Press.

1980   *Hunters, Pastorialists, and Ranchers*. Cambridge: Cambridge University Press.

1983   "The Significance of Storage in Hunting Societies." *Man* 18: 553–571.

Isaac, Barry L.

1979   "The Economic, Ethic, and Sexual Parameters of Petty Trading in Pendembu, Sierra Leone." In *Essays on the Economic Anthropology of Liberia and Sierra Leone*, edited by V. R. Dorjahn and B. L. Isaac. Philadelphia: Institute for Liberian Studies, Monograph 6.

1984   "Introduction." In *Research in Economic Anthropology, vol. 6*, edited by B. L. Isaac, 1–25. Greenwich, Conn.: JAI Press.

1993   "Retrospective on the Formalist-Substantivist Debate." In *Research in Economic Anthropology, vol. 14*, edited by B. L. Isaac, 213–233. Greenwich, Conn.: JAI Press.

Jameson, F.

1990–91   *Postmodernism, or, The Cultural Logic of Late Capitalism*. London and New York: Verso.

Jochim, Michael

1981   *Strategies for Survival*. New York: Academic Press.

Johnson, A.

1983   "Machiguenga Gardens." In *Adaptive Responses of Native Amazo-*

nians, edited by R. Hames and W. Vickers. New York: Academic Press.

Johnson, A., and M. Baksh

1975 "Time Allocation in a Machiguenga Community." *Ethnology* 14: 301–310.

1987 "Ecological and Structural Influences on the Proportions of Wild Foods in the Diets of Two Machiguenga Communities." In *Food and Evolution*, edited by M. Harris and E. Ross. Philadelphia: Temple University Press.

Johnson, Allen

1989 "Horticulturalists: Economic Behavior in Tribes." In *Economic Anthropology*, edited by Stuart Plattner, 49–77.

Johnson, Robert

1979 *Peasant and Proletarian: The Working Class of Moscow in the Late Nineteenth Century*. New Brunswick: Rutgers University Press.

Kahn, J.

1990 "Towards a History of the Critique of Economism: The 19th Century German Origins of the Ethnographer's Dilemma." *Man* 25:230–249.

Kahn, Joel S., and Josep R. Llobera

1981 *The Anthropology of Pre-Capitalist Societies*. London: MacMillan.

Kaplan, David

1968 "The Formalist-Substantivist Controversy in Economic Anthropology: Some Reflections on its Wider Implications." *Southwest Journal of Anthropology* 24:228–247.

Katzin, Margaret

1960 "The Business of Higglering in Jamaica." *Social and Economic Studies* 9:297–331.

Keegan, William F.

1986 "The Optimal Foraging Analysis of Horticultural Production." *American Anthropologist* 88:92–107.

Keene, A. S.

1979 "Economic Organization Models and the Study of Hunter-Gatherer Subsistence-Settlement Systems." In *Transformation: Mathematical Approaches to Culture Change*, edited by C. Renfrew and K. L. Cook, 369–404. New York: Academic Press.

Kehoe, Alice B.

1993 "How the Ancient Peigans Lived." In *Research in Economic Anthropology*, vol. 14, edited by B. L. Isaac, 87–105. Greenwich, Conn.: JAI Press.

Knapp, A. Bernard, and Tamara Stech, eds.

1985 *Prehistoric Production and Exchange: The Aegean and Eastern Medi-*

terranean. Los Angeles: University of California, Institute of Archaeology Monograph 25.

Knight, Frank H.
1941   "Anthropology and Economics." *Journal of Political Economy* 49: 247–268.

Kohl, Philip L.
1989   "The use and abuse of world systems theory: the case of the 'pristine' West Asian state." In *Archaeological Thought in America*, edited by C. C. Lamberg-Karlovsky, 218–240. Cambridge: Cambridge University Press.

Kopytoff, Igor
1986   "The Cultural Biography of Things." In *The Social Life of Things*, edited by Arjun Appadurai. Cambridge: Cambridge University Press.

Kroeber, A. L.
1917   "The Superorganic." *American Anthropologist* 19:163–213.

Kuhn, Thomas
1962   *The Structure of Scientific Revolutions*. Chicago: University of Chicago Press.

La Lone, Darrell E.
1982   "The Inca as a Nonmarket Economy: Supply on Command Versus Supply and Demand." In *Contexts for Prehistoric Exchange*, edited by Jonathan Ericson and Timothy Earle. New York: Academic Press.

Lambek, M.
1990   "Exchange, Time and Person in Mayotte." *American Anthropologist* 92(3):647–671.

Lamberg-Karlovsky, C. C.
1975   "Third Millennium Modes of Exchange and Modes of Production." In *Ancient Civilization and Trade*, edited by Jeremy A. Sabloff and C. C. Lamberg-Karlovsky, 341–368. Albuquerque: University of New Mexico Press.
1989   "Introduction." In *Archaeological Thought in America*, edited by C. C. Lamberg-Karlovsky, 1–16. Cambridge: Cambridge University Press.

Langebaek, Carl Henrik
1991   "Highland Center and Foothill Periphery in 16th Century Eastern Colombia." In *Research in Economic Anthropology, vol. 13*, edited by B. L. Isaac, 325–339. Greenwich, Conn.: JAI Press.

Lave, Charles A., and James V. Mueller
1975   "The Economic Success of Tribal Migrants in Liberia." In *Formal Methods in Economic Anthropology*, edited by Stuart Plattner, 38–76. Washington: American Anthropological Association.

Leacock, E. B.

1972   "Introduction." In *The Origin of the Family, Private Property and the State*, edited by Frederick Engels, 7–67. New York: International Publishers.

LeClair, E., and H. Schneider, eds.

1968   *Economic Anthropology: Readings in Theory and Analysis*. New York: Holt, Rinehart and Winston.

Lee, Richard B.

1965   "Subsistence Ecology of !Kung Bushmen." Ph.D. diss., University of California-Berkeley.

1969   "!Kung Bushman Subsistence: An Input-Output Analysis." In *Environment and Cultural Behavior*, edited by A. P. Vayda. Garden City, N.Y.: Natural History Press.

1979   *The !Kung San: Men, Women, and Work in a Foraging Society*. New York: Cambridge University Press.

1984   *The Dobe !Kung*. New York: Holt, Rinehart and Winston.

Lee, Richard B., and Irven DeVore

1968   *Man the Hunter*. Chicago: Aldine.

Leeds, A., and A. P. Vayda, eds.

1965   *Man, Culture, and Animals: The Role of Animals in Human Ecological Adjustments*. Washington, D.C.: American Association for the Advancement of Science.

Lévi-Strauss, Claude

1969   *The Elementary Structures of Kinship*. Boston: Beacon Press.

Libecock, G. D.

1989   *Contracting for Property Rights*. Cambridge: Cambridge University Press.

Llobera, Josep R.

1979   "Techno-Economic Determinism and the Work of Marx on Pre-Capitalist Societies." *Man* 14:249–270.

Lockwood, William

1973   "The Peasant-Worker in Yugoslavia." *Studies in European Society* 1:91–110.

Lomnitz, Larissa A.

1988   "Informal Exchange Networks in Formal Systems." *American Anthropologist* 90:42–55.

Long, Norman, and Paul Richardson

1978   "Informal Sector, Petty Commodity Production, and the Social Relations of Small-Scale Enterprise." In *The New Economic Anthropology*, edited by John Clammer. New York: St. Martin's Press.

Maclachlan, Morgan D.

1987   *Household Economies and Their Transformations*. Lanham, Md.:

University Press of America, Monographs in Economic Anthropology No. 3.

Malinowski, Bronislaw

1915   "The Mailu." *Transactions of the Royal Society of South Australia* 4:612–629.

1921   "The Primitive Economics of the Trobriand Islanders." *The Economic Journal* 31:1–16.

1922   *Argonauts of the Western Pacific*. London: Routledge and Kegan Paul.

1926   *Crime and Custom in Savage Society*. London: Routledge.

1935   *Coral Gardens and Their Magic*. Vol. 1: *Soil-Tilling and Agricultural Rights in the Trobriand Islands*. Bloomington: Indiana University Press.

Malinowski, B., and J. de la Fuente

1982   *The Economics of a Mexican Market System*. London: Routledge and Kegan Paul (originally published in 1957).

Marshall, John

1980   *N!ai: The Story of a !Kung Woman* [ethnographic film]. Odyssey Television Series.

Martin, John F.

1983   "Optimal Foraging Theory: A Review of Some Models and Their Applications." *American Anthropologist* 85:612–629.

Marx, Karl

1904   *Capital*, vol. 1. London: Sonnenschein.

1964   *Pre-Capitalist Economic Formations*. Edited by E. J. Hobsbawm. Trans. Jack Cohen. London: Lawrence and Eishart.

1973   *The Grundrisse*. Trans. Martin Nicolaus. New York: Vintage.

Matson, R. G.

1992   "The Evolution of Northwest Coast Subsistence." In *Long-Term Subsistence Change in Prehistoric North America*, edited by Dale Croes, R. Hawkins, and B. L. Isaac. Research in Economic Anthropology Supplement 6, 367–428. Greenwich, Conn.: JAI Press.

Mattera, Philip

1985   *Off the Books: The Rise of the Underground Economy*. New York: St. Martin's Press.

Mauss, Marcel

1925   "Essai sur le Don: Forme et raison de l'exchange dans les societes archaiques." *L'Année Sociologique* 1:30–186 (for 1923–24). [Republished in 1954 as "The Gift: Form and Functions of Exchange in Archaic Society." Trans. Ian Cunnison. London: Cohen and West.]

1969   *The Gift: Forms and Functions of Exchange in Archaic Societies.* London: Cohen and West.
Mauss, M., and H. Beuchat
    1968   "Variations saisonnieres des societes Eskimos: etude de morphologie sociale." Paris: *L'Année Sociologique* (ser. I).
Maybury-Lewis. D.
    1974   *Akwe-Shavante Society.* New York: Oxford University Press.
McCay, B. J.
    1987   "The Culture of the Commoners." In *The Question of the Commons: The Culture and Ecology of Human Resources*, edited by B. J. McCay and J. M. Acheson. Tucson: University of Arizona Press.
McCay, B. J., and J. M. Acheson
    1987   "Human Ecology of the Commons." In *The Question of the Commons: The Culture and Ecology of Human Resources*, edited by B. J. McCay and J. M. Acheson. Tucson: University of Arizona Press.
Meggers, B.
    1954   "Environmental Limitations on the Development of Culture." *American Anthropologist* 56:301–324.
    1957   "Environment and Culture in the Amazon Basin: An Appraisal of the Theory of Environmental Determinism." In *Studies in Human Ecology*, edited by L. Krader and A. Palerm. Washington, D.C.: The Anthropological Society of Washington.
Meillassoux, C.
    1973   "On the Mode of Production of the Hunting Band." In *French Perspective in African Studies*, edited by P. Alexandre. London: Oxford University Press.
    1978a   "'The Economy' in Agricultural Self-Sustaining Societies: A Preliminary Analysis." In *Relations of Production*, edited by D. Seddon. London: Frank Cass.
    1978b   "The Social Organization of the Peasantry: The Economic Basis of Kinship." In *Relations of Production*, edited by D. Seddon. London: Frank Cass.
    1980   "From Reproduction to Production: A Marxist Approach to Economic Anthropology." In *Articulation of Modes of Production*, edited by H. Wolpe. London: Routledge and Kegan Paul.
    1981   *Maidens, Meal, and Money.* Cambridge: Cambridge University Press.
Miller, S. M.
    1987   "The Pursuit of Informal Economies." In *The Informal Economy. The Annals of the American Academy of Political and Social Science*, edited by L. A. Ferman, S. Henry, and M. Hoyman. Newbury Park, Calif.: Sage Publications.

Minge-Kalman, W.
1980   "Does Labor Time Decrease with Industrialization? A Survey of Time-Allocation Studies." *Current Anthropology* 21:279–298.

Mintz, Sidney
1961   "Pratik: Haitian Personal Economic Relationships." *Proceedings of the 1961 Annual Spring Meeting of the American Ethnological Society.*
1964   "The Employment of Capital by Market Women in Haiti." In *Capital, Savings, and Credit*, edited by R. Firth and B. Yamey. Chicago: Aldine.

Mitchell, William P.
1991a   "Some are More Equal than Others: Labor Supply, Reciprocity, and Redistribution in the Andes." In *Research in Economic Anthropology, vol. 13*, edited by B. L. Isaac, 191–219. Greenwich, Conn.: JAI Press.
1991b   *Peasants on the Edge: Crop, Cult, and Crisis in the Andes.* Austin: University of Texas Press.

Monaghan, John
1990   "Reciprocity, Redistribution, and the Transaction of Value in the Mesoamerican Fiesta." *American Ethnologist* 17:758–774.

Moran, Emilio
1979   *Human Adaptability: An Introduction to Ecological Anthropology.* North Scituate, Mass.: Duxbury Press.
1982   *Human Adaptability.* Boulder, Colo.: Westview Press.

Morris, Craig
1967   "Storage in Tawantinsuyu." Ph.D. diss., University of Chicago.
1972   "Reconstructing patterns of non-agricultural production in the Inca economy." In *Reconstructing Complex Societies*, edited by C. B. Moore. Chicago: American School of Oriental Research.

Munn, Nancy D.
1992   "The Cultural Anthropology of Time: A Critical Essay." *Annual Review of Anthropology* 21:93–123.

Murdock, George P., and Cateria Provost
1973a   "Factors in the Division of Labor by Sex: A Cross-Cultural Analysis." *Ethnology* 12:203–226.
1973b   "Measurement of Cultural Complexity." *Ethnology* 12:379–392.

Murphy, Robert F.
1981   "Julian Steward." In *Totems and Teachers: Perspectives on the History of Anthropology*, edited by Sydel Silverman, 171–206. New York: Columbia University Press.

Murphy, Yolanda, and Robert F. Murphy
1985   *Women of the Forest.* New York: Columbia University Press.

Murra, J. V.

1956   "The Economic Organization of the Inca State." Ph.D. diss., University of Chicago.

1972   "El 'Control Vertical' de un máximo de pisos ecológicos en la economía de las sociedades andinas." In *Visita de la provincia de Leon de Huanuco en 1562, Tomo 2*, edited by J. V. Murra. Huanuco: Universidad Nacional Hermilio Valdizán.

1980   *The Economic Organization of the Inca State*. Greenwich, Conn.: JAI Press.

Netting, Robert M.

1965   "A Trial Model of Cultural Ecology." *Anthropological Quarterly* 38:81–96.

1968   *Hill Farmers of Nigeria: Cultural Ecology of the Kofyar of the Jos Plateau*. Seattle: University of Washington Press.

1977   *Cultural Ecology*. Menlo Park, Calif.: Cummings Publishing Company.

Netting, Robert M., Richard W. Wilk, and Eric J. Arnould, eds.

1984   *Households: Comparative and Historical Studies of the Domestic Group*. Berkeley and Los Angeles: University of California Press.

Nietschmann, B.

1973   *Between Land and Water*. New York: Seminar Press.

Nugent, David

1993   "Property Relations, Production Relations, and Inequality: Anthropology, Political Economy, and the Blackfeet." *American Ethnologist* 20:336–362.

Obregon, Anibal Quijano

1980   "The Marginal Role of the Economy and the Marginalized Labor Force." In *The Articulation of Modes of Production: Essays from Economy and Society*, edited by H. Wolpe. Boston: Routledge and Kegan Paul.

O'Connell, James F., and Kristen Hawkes

1984   "Food Choice and Foraging Sites among the Alyawara." *Journal of Anthropological Research* 40:504–535.

O'Laughlin, Bridget

1975   "Marxist Approaches in Anthropology." In *Annual Review of Anthropology*, edited by B. Siegel et al. Palo Alto: Annual Reviews, Inc.

Orlove, Benjamin

1980   "Ecological Anthropology." In *Annual Review of Anthropology*, edited by B. Siegel et al. Palo Alto: Annual Reviews, Inc.

1986   "Barter and Cash Sale on Lake Titicaca: A Test of Competing Approaches." *Current Anthropology* 27:85–106.

Ortner, Sherry B.
    1984   "Theory in Anthropology Since the Sixties." *Comparative Studies in Society and History* 22:126–166.

Parry, J.
    1986   "The Gift, the Indian Gift, and the 'Indian Gift.'" *Man* 21: 453–473.
    1989   "On the Moral Perils of Exchange." In *Money and the Morality of Exchange*, edited by J. Parry and M. Bloch, 64–93. Cambridge: Cambridge University Press.

Parry, J., and M. Bloch
    1989   "Introduction: Money and the Morality of Exchange." In *Money and the Morality of Exchange*, edited by J. Parry and M. Bloch, 1–32. Cambridge: Cambridge University Press.

Pasternak, Burton
    1972   "The Sociology of Irrigation: Two Taiwanese Villages." In *Economic Organization in Chinese Society*, edited by W. Willmott. Stanford: Stanford University Press.

Peace, William J.
    1993   "Leslie White and Evolutionary Theory." *Dialectical Anthropology* 18:123–151.

Pearsall, Marion
    1959   *Little Smoky Ridge*. Tuscaloosa: University of Alabama Press.

Peattie, Lisa R.
    1980   "Anthropological Perspectives on the Concepts of Dualism: The Informal Sector, and Marginality in Developing Urban Economies." *International Regional Science Review* 5:1–31.
    1982   "What is to be Done with the 'Informal Sector'? A Case Study of Shoe Manufacturers in Columbia." In *Towards Political Economy of Urbanization in Third World Countries*, edited by Helen I. Safa. Oxford: Oxford University Press.

Perlman, S. M.
    1980   "An Optimum Diet Model, Coastal Variability, and Hunter-Gatherer Behavior." In *Advances in Archaeological Method and Theory, vol. 3*, edited by M. B. Schiffer. New York: Academic Press.

Peterson, Jean Treloggen
    1984   "Cash, Consumerism, and Savings: Economic Change Among the Agta Foragers of Luzon, Philippines." In *Research in Economic Anthropology, vol. 6*, edited by B. L. Isaac, 53–73. Greenwich, Conn.: JAI Press.

Piddock, S.
    1965   "The Potlatch System of the Southern Kwakiutl: A New Perspective." *Southwestern Journal of Anthropology* 21:244–264.

Piot, Charles

1991   "Of Persons and Things: Some Reflections on African Spheres of Exchange." *Man* 26:405–424.

Plattner, S.

1975a   (Ed.) *Formal Methods in Economic Anthropology*. Washington, D.C.: American Anthropological Association, Special Publication No. 4.

1975b   "The Economics of Peddling." In *Formal Methods in Economic Anthropology*. Washington, D.C.: American Anthropological Association, Special Publication No. 4.

1985   (Ed.) *Markets and Marketing*, Monographs in Economic Anthropology, No. 4. Lanham: University Press of America.

1989   (Ed.) *Economic Anthropology*. Palo Alto: Stanford University Press.

Plattner, Stuart

1989   "Economic Behavior in Markets." In *Economic Anthropology*, edited by Stuart Plattner, 209–221. Stanford: Stanford University Press.

Polanyi, Karl

1944   *The Great Transformation*. New York: Holt, Rinehart and Winston.

1957a   "The Economy as Instituted Process." In *Trade and Market in the Early Empires*, edited by K. Polanyi, C. Arensberg, and H. W. Pearson, 243–270. New York: The Free Press.

1957b   "Aristotle Discovers the Economy." In *Trade and Market in the Early Empires*, edited by K. Polanyi, C. Arensberg, and H. W. Pearson, 64–94. New York: The Free Press.

1968   *Primitive, Archaic, and Modern Economies*, edited by George Dalton. Garden City, N.Y.: Anchor Books.

1977   *The Livelihood of Man*, edited by Harry Pearson. New York: Academic Press.

n.d.a.   "Early Economies." Manuscript. Box 10, Archive of the Karl Polanyi Institute of Political Economy. Montreal, Quebec, Canada. Written 1960.

n.d.b.   "Money and Related Institutions in Early Societies." Manuscript. Archive of the Karl Polanyi Institute of Political Economy. Montreal, Quebec, Canada. Written 1958.

n.d.c.   Unpublished Manuscripts. Karl Polanyi Institute of Political Economy. Montreal, Quebec, Canada.

Polanyi, Karl, C. Arensberg, and H. W. Pearson, eds.

1957   *Trade and Market in the Early Empires*. New York: The Free Press.

Polanyi-Levitt, Kari

1990   "The Origin and Significance of *The Great Transformation*." In

The Life and Work of Karl Polanyi, edited by Kari Polanyi-Levitt, 111–124. Montreal: Black Rose Books.

Popov, A. A.
1966   *The Nganasan: The Material Culture of the Tavgi Samoyeds.* Bloomington: Indiana University Uralic and Altaic Series 56.

Pospisil, Leopold
1963   *Kapauka Papuan Economy.* New Haven: Yale University Press.

Precourt, Walter
1983   "The Image of Appalachian Poverty." In *Appalachia and America: Autonomy and Regional Dependence,* edited by Alan Batteau. Lexington: University Press of Kentucky.

Rappaport, R. A.
1968*a*   "Ritual Regulation of Environmental Relations Among a New Guinea People." *Ethnology* 6:17–30.

1968*b*   *Pigs of the Ancestors.* 2nd ed. New Haven: Yale University Press.

Redfield, Robert, and Alfonso Villa Rojas
1934   *Chan Kom, A Maya Village.* Washington: Carnegie Institute. Reprinted by the University of Chicago Press.

1950   *A Village that Chose Progress: Chan Kom Revisited.* Chicago: University of Chicago Press.

Rey, P.-P.
1983   "The Lineage Mode of Production." *Critique of Anthropology* 3: 27–79.

Rice, Prudence M.
1980   "Peten Postclassic Pottery Production and Exchange: A View from Macanche." In *Models and Methods in Regional Exchange,* edited by R. Fry. Washington, D.C.: Society for American Archaeology, Papers, 1.

Robbins, Lionel
1962   *An Essay On the Nature and Significance of Economic Science.* London: MacMillan.

Runnels, Curtis N.
1985   "Trade and the Demand for Millstones in Southern Greece in the Neolithic and the Early Bronze Age." In *Prehistoric Production and Exchange: The Aegean and Eastern Mediterranean,* edited by A. Bernard Knapp and Tamara Stech. Los Angeles: University of California, Institute of Archaeology Monograph 25.

Sabloff, J. A., and D. A. Freidel
1975   "A Model of a Pre-Columbian Trading Center." In *Ancient Trade and Civilization,* edited by J. Sabloff and C. C. Lamberg-Karlovsky, pp. 369–408. Albuquerque: University of New Mexico Press.

Sabloff, J., and C. C. Lamberg-Karlovsky, eds.

1975   *Ancient Civilization and Trade*. Albuquerque: University of New Mexico Press.

Sahlins, Marshall

1960   "Political Power and the Economy in Primitive Society." In *Essays in the Science of Culture in Honor of Leslie White*, edited by G. Dole and Robert Carneiro, 390–415. New York: Thomas Crowell Co.

1964   "Culture and Environment: The Study of Cultural Ecology." In *Horizons of Anthropology*, edited by S. Tax. Chicago: Aldine.

1965   "On the Sociology of Primitive Exchange." In *The Relevance of Models for Social Anthropology*, edited by M. Banton, A. S. A. Monograph No. 1. London: Tavistock.

1972   *Stone Age Economics*. Chicago: Aldine.

Sampson, Steven

1985–86   "The Informal Sector in Eastern Europe." *Telos* 66:44–66.

1987   "The Second Economy of the Soviet Union and Eastern Europe." In *The Informal Economy. The Annals of the American Academy of Political and Social Science*, edited by L. A. Ferman, S. Henry, and M. Hoyman. Newbury Park, Calif.: Sage Publications.

Samuelson, Paul

1967   *Economics: An Introductory Analysis*. 7th ed. New York: McGraw-Hill.

Sanders, W. T.

1962   "Cultural Ecology of Nuclear Meso-America." *American Anthropologist* 64:34–44.

1965   *The Cultural Ecology of the Teotihuacan Valley*. University Park, Pa.: Pennsylvania State University.

Sanders, W. T., and B. J. Price

1968   *Mesoamerica: The Evolution of a Civilization*. New York: Random House.

Scarborough, Vernon

1992   "Ceramics, Sedentism, and Agricultural Dependency at a Late Pithouse/Early Pueblo Period Village." In *Long-Term Subsistence Change in Prehistoric North America*, edited by Dale Croes, R. Hawkins, and B. L. Isaac. Research in Economic Anthropology Supplement 6, 307–333. Greenwich, Conn.: JAI Press.

1993*a*   "Introduction." In *Research in Economic Anthropology: Economic Aspects of Water Management in the Prehispanic New World*, edited by Vernon Scarborough and B. L. Isaac, 1–14. Greenwich, Conn.: JAI Press.

1993*b*   "Water Management in the Southern Maya Lowlands: An Accretive Model for the Engineered Landscape." In *Research in Eco-*

nomic Anthropology: Economic Aspects of Water Management in the Prehispanic New World*, edited by Vernon Scarborough and B. L. Isaac, 17–67. Greenwich, Conn.: JAI Press.

Scarborough, Vernon, and G. G. Gallopin
1991   "A water storage adaptation system in the Maya Lowlands." *Science* (February 8):658–662.

Schneider, Harold K.
1964   "Economics in East African Aboriginal Society." In *Economic Transition in Africa*, edited by Melville J. Herskovits and Mitchell Harwitz. Evanston, Ill.: Northwestern University Press.

1974   *Economic Man*. New York: The Free Press.

Schrire, Carmel
1984   *Past and Present in Hunter-Gatherer Studies*. New York: Academic Press.

Schroyer, Trent
1991   "Karl Polanyi's Post-Marxist Critical Theory." In *The Legacy of Karl Polanyi*, edited by Marguerite Mendell and Daniel Salee, 66–85. New York: St. Martin's Press.

Schwarzweller, Harry K., James G. Brown, and J. J. Mangalam, eds.
1971   *Mountain Families in Transition*. University Park: Pennsylvania State University Press.

Schwerin, Karl H.
1971   "The Bitter and the Sweet: Some Implications of Techniques for Preparing Manioc." Paper presented at the 1971 Annual Meeting of the American Anthropological Association. New York.

Scott, James
1976   *The Moral Economy of the Peasant: Rebellion and Subsistence in Southeast Asia*. New Haven, Conn.: Yale University Press.

1985   *Weapons of the Weak: Everyday Forms of Peasant Resistance*. New Haven, Conn.: Yale University Press.

Seddon, David, ed.
1978   *Relations of Production*. London: Frank Cass.

Service, E. R.
1962   *Primitive Social Organization*. New York: Random House.

1969   "Models for the Methodology of Mouthtalk." *Southwestern Journal of Anthropology* 25:68–80.

Shipton, Parker
1989   *Bitter Money*. Washington D.C.: American Ethnological Society Monograph Series, Number 1. James L. Watson, series editor.

Silver, Morris
1983   "Karl Polanyi and Markets in the Ancient Near East: The Challenge of the Evidence." *Journal of Economic History* 43:795–829.

Silverbauer, George

 1981   *Hunter and Habitat in the Central Kalahari Desert.* Cambridge: Cam-
             bridge University Press.

Simkin, C. G. F.

 1968   *The Traditional Trade of Asia.* London: Oxford University Press.

Simon, Carl P., and Ann D. White

 1982   *Beating the System: The Underground Economy.* Boston: Auburn
             House.

Skinner, William G.

 1964   "Marketing and Social Structure in Rural China." *Journal of Asian
             Studies* 24:3–43.

 1985   "Rural Marketing in China: A Revival and Reappraisal." In
             Markets and Marketing, edited by Stuart Plattner. Lanham, Md.:
             University Press of America for the Society for Economic
             Anthropology.

Smith, A.

 1904   *An Inquiry into the Nature and Causes of the Wealth of Nations, Vols.
             1 and 2.* London: Methuen (originally published in 1776).

 1976   *The Theory of Moral Sentiments.* Oxford: Clarendon (originally
             published in 1759).

Smith, Carol A.

 1974   "Economics of Marketing Systems: Models from Economic Ge-
             ography." *Annual Review of Anthropology* 3:167–201.

 1976   *Regional Analysis, Vols. 1 and 2.* New York: Academic Press.

 1977   "How Marketing Systems Affect Economic Opportunity in
             Agrarian Societies." In *Peasant Livelihood*, edited by R. Halperin
             and J. Dow, 117–146. New York: St. Martin's Press.

 1985   "Methods for Analyzing Periodic Marketplaces as Elements in
             Regional Trading Systems." In *Research in Economic Anthropology*,
             vol. 7, edited by B. L. Isaac, 291–337. Greenwich, Conn.: JAI
             Press.

Smith, E. A., and B. Winterhalder

 1981   "New Perspectives on Hunter-Gatherer Socioecology." In
             *Hunter-Gatherer Foraging Strategies: Ethnographic and Archaeologi-
             cal Analyses*, edited by Bruce Winterhalder and Eric Alden Smith.
             Chicago: University of Chicago Press.

Smith, M. Estellie

 1989   "The Informal Economy." In *Economic Anthropology*, edited by
             Stuart Plattner. Stanford: Stanford University Press.

Smith, R. H. T.

 1971   "West African Marketplaces: Temporal Periodicity and Loca-
             tional Spacing." In *The Development of Indigenous Trade and Mar-*

kets in West Africa, edited by Claude Meillassoux. London: Oxford University Press.

Smith, Waldemar
    1977   *The Fiesta System and Economic Change*. New York: Columbia University Press.

Smyth, Michael P.
    1988   "Storage Behavior in the Puuc Region of Yucatan, Mexico: An Ethnoarchaeological Investigation." Ph.D. diss., University of New Mexico, Albuquerque.

    1991   *Modern Maya Storage Behavior: Ethnoarchaeological Case Examples from the Puuc Region of Yucatan*. Pittsburgh: University of Pittsburgh Memoirs in Latin American Archaeology No. 3.

Spencer, R. F.
    1959   "The North Alaskan Eskimo: A Study in Ecology and Society." *Smithsonian Institution Bureau of American Ethnology, Bulletin 171.* Washington, D.C.: U.S. Government Printing Office.

Speth, John D., and Katherine A. Spielmann
    1983   "Energy Source, Protein Metabolism, and Hunter-Gatherer Subsistence Strategies." *Journal of Anthropological Archaeology* 2:1–31.

Spriggs, Matthew
    1984   *Marxist Perspectives in Archaeology*. Cambridge: Cambridge University Press.

Stack, Carol
    1972   *All Our Kin*. New York: Harper and Row.

Stanish, Charles
    1992   *Ancient Andean Political Economy*. Austin: University of Texas Press.

Stephenson, John B.
    1968   *Shiloh: A Mountain Community*. Lexington: University Press of Kentucky.

Steward, J. H.
    1955   *Theory of Culture Change: The Methodology of Multilinear Evolution*. Urbana: University of Illinois Press.

Strathern, M.
    1984   "The Social Meanings of Localism." In *Locality and Rurality: Economy and Society in Rural Regions*, edited by T. Bradley and P. Lowe. Norwich: Geo Books.

    1985   "Kinship and Economy: Constitutive Orders of a Provisional Kind." *American Ethnologist* 12:191–209.

Susser, Ida
    1982   *Norman Street: Poverty and Politics in an Urban Neighborhood*. New York: Oxford University Press.

Suttles, W.

1960   "Affinal Ties, Subsistence, and Prestige Among the Coastal Sa-
         lish." *American Anthropologist* 62:296–305.

Sweet, L. E.

1965   "Camel Raiding of North Arabian Bedouin: A Mechanism of
         Ecological Adaptation." *American Anthropologist* 67:1132–1150.

Swetnam, John

1993   "The Annual Market Cycle at Antigua Guatemala." In *Research
         in Economic Anthropology, vol. 14*, edited by B. L. Isaac, 141–151.
         Greenwich, Conn.: JAI Press.

Tadesse, Zenebeworke

1982   "The Impact of Land Reform on Women: The Case of Ethiopia."
         In *Women and Development: The Sexual Division of Labor in Rural
         Societies*, edited by Lourdes Beneria. New York: Praeger.

Taussig, Michael

1980   *The Devil and Commodity Fetishism in Latin America*. Chapel Hill:
         The University of North Carolina Press.

Tax, Sol

1953   *Penny Capitalism: A Guatemalan Indian Economy*. Washington,
         D.C.: Smithsonian Institute for Social Anthropology, Publica-
         tion No. 16.

Teilhet-Waldorf, Saral, and William H. Waldorf

1983   "Earnings of the Self-Employed in an Informal Sector: A Case
         Study of Bangkok." *Economic Development and Cultural Change*
         31:587–607.

Terray, Emmanual

1972   *Marxism and "Primitive" Societies*. New York and London:
         Monthly Review Press.

1975   "Classes and Class Consciousness in the Abron Kingdom of
         Gyaman." In *Marxist Analyses and Social Anthropology*, edited by
         M. Bloch. London: Malaby Press.

Testart, Alain

1982   "The Significance of Food Storage among Hunter-Gatherers:
         Residence Patterns, Population Densities, and Social Inequali-
         ties." *Current Anthropology* 23:523–537.

Thomas, David Hurst

1979   "Complexity among Great Basin Shoshoneans: The World's
         Least Affluent Hunter-Gatherers?" In *Affluent Foragers: Pacific
         Coasts East and West*, edited by S. Koyama and D. Thomas.
         Osaka: National Museum of Ethnology, Senri Ethnological Se-
         ries, 9.

1986   "Contemporary Hunter-Gatherer Archaeology in America." In
         American Archaeology, Past and Future: A Celebration of the Soci-

ety for American Archaeology 1935–1985, edited by D. J. Meltzer,
D. D. Fowler, and J. A. Sabloff. Washington, D.C.: Smithsonian
Institution Press.

Thompson, E. P.

1971   "The Moral Economy of the 18th Century English Crowd." Past
        and Present 50:76–136.

1991   "Time, Work-Discipline, and Industrial Capitalism." In Customs
        in Common, edited by E. P. Thompson, 352–403. New York: The
        New Press.

Thurnwald, Richard C.

1932   Economics in Primitive Communities. London: Oxford University
        Press.

Trager, Lillian

1981   "Customers and Creditors: Variations in Economic Personalism
        in a Nigerian Marketing System." Ethnology 20:133–146.

1985   "From Yams to Beer in a Nigerian City: Expansion and Change
        in Informal Sector Trade Activity." In Markets and Marketing, ed-
        ited by Stuart Plattner . New York: University Press of America.

1987   "The Urban Informal Sector in West Africa." Canadian Journal of
        African Studies 21:238–255.

Trigger, Bruce G.

1989   "History and contemporary American archaeology: a critical
        analysis." In Archaeological Thought in America, edited by C. C.
        Lamberg-Karlovsky, 19–34. Cambridge: Cambridge University
        Press.

Tuden, Arthur

1979   "An Exploration of a Pre-Capitalist Mode of Production." In
        New Directions in Political Economy, edited by Madelaine B. Leons
        and R. Rothstein. Westport, Conn.: Greenwood Press.

Vayda, A. P.

1967   "Pomo Trade Feasts." In Tribal and Peasant Economies, edited by
        A. P. Vayda. Garden City, N.Y.: Natural History Press.

1969   Environment and Cultural Behavior. Garden City, N.Y.: Natural
        History Press.

Vayda, A. P., and B. McCay

1975   "New Directions in Ecology and Ecological Anthropology." An-
        nual Review of Anthropology 4:293–306.

Vayda, A. P., and R. A. Rappaport

1968   "Ecology: Cultural and Non-Cultural." In Introduction to Cultural
        Anthropology, edited by J. A. Clifton. Boston: Houghton Mifflin.

Villamarin, Juan A., and Judith E. Villamarin

1975   Indian Labor in Mainland Colonial Spanish America. Newark, Del.:

University of Delaware, Latin American Studies Program, Occasional Papers and Monographs, 1.

Wachtel, Nathan

1982   "The Mitimas of the Cochabamba Valley: The Colonization of Huayna Capac." In *The Inca and Aztec States 1400–1800*, edited by G. A. Collier et al., 199–235. New York: Academic Press.

Ward, H. Trawick

1985   "Social Implications of Storage and Disposal Patterns." In *Structure and Process in Southeastern Archaeology*, edited by R. S. Dickens and H. T. Ward. Tuscaloosa: University of Alabama Press.

Webster, Gary S.

1986   "Optimization Theory and Pre-Columbian Hunting in the Tehuacan Valley." *Human Ecology* 14:415–435.

Wedel, Janine

1986   *The Private Poland*. New York: Facts on File.

Weinberg, Daniela

1975   *Peasant Wisdom: Cultural Adaptation in a Swiss Village*. Berkeley and Los Angeles: University of California Press.

Weiner, A.

1976   *Women of Value, Men of Renown*. Austin: University of Texas Press.

1983   "A World of Made Is Not a World of Born: Doing Kula in Kiriwina." In *The Kula: New Perspectives on Massim Exchange*, edited by J. Leach and E. Leach. Cambridge: Cambridge University Press.

Weissner, Polly

1982   "Beyond Willow Smoke and Dogs' Tails: A Comment on Binford's Analysis of Hunter-Gatherer Settlement Systems." *American Antiquity* 47:171–177.

Werner, D., N. Flowers, M. Ritter, and D. Gross

1979   "Subsistence Productivity and Hunting Effort in Native South America." *Human Ecology* 7:303–315.

White, Leslie

1949   *The Science of Culture*. New York: Grove Press, Inc.

1959   *The Evolution of Culture*. New York: McGraw-Hill Book Company, Inc.

1975   *The Concept of Cultural Systems*. New York: Columbia University Press.

Wienpahl, Jan

1984   "Women's Roles in Livestock Production among the Turkana of Kenya." In *Research in Economic Anthropology*, vol. 6, edited by B. L. Isaac, 193–215. Greenwich, Conn.: JAI Press.

Wilk, Richard R., and Wendy Ashmore, eds.
 1987   *Household and Community in the Mesoamerican Past*. Albuquerque: University of New Mexico Press.

Winter, Marcus Cole
 1972   "Tierras Largas: A Formative Community in the Valley of Oaxaca, Mexico." Ph.D. diss., University of Arizona.

Winterhalder, Bruce
 1983   "Opportunity Cost Foraging Models for Stationary and Mobile Predators." *American Naturalist* 122:73–84.
 1986   "Diet Choice, Risk, and Food Sharing in a Stochastic Environment." *Journal of Anthropological Archaeology* 5:369–392.

Winterhalder, Bruce, and Eric Alden Smith, eds.
 1981   *Hunter-Gatherer Foraging Strategies: Ethnographic and Archaeological Analysis*. Chicago: University of Chicago Press.

Wittfogel, Karl A.
 1957   *Oriental Despotism*. New Haven: Yale University Press.

Woodburn, J.
 1980   "Hunter-Gatherers Today and Reconstruction of the Past." In *Soviet and Western Anthropology*, edited by E. Gellner. New York: Columbia University Press.
 1982   "Egalitarian Societies." *Man* 17:431–451.

Wright, Henry T., and Gregory A. Johnson
 1975   "Population, Exchange, and Early State Formation in Southwestern Iran." *American Anthropologist* 77:267–289.

Yang, Martin
 1945   *A Chinese Village*. New York: Columbia University Press.
 1967   "The Family as a Primary Economic Group [China]." In *Tribal and Peasant Economies*, edited by George Dalton. New York: Natural History Press.

Yellen, John E.
 1989   "The present and the future of hunter-gatherer studies." In *Archaeological Thought in America*, edited by C. C. Lamberg-Karlovsky, 103–116. Cambridge: Cambridge University Press.

Yesner, David R.
 1981   "Archaeological Implication of Optimal Foraging Theory: Harvest Strategies of Aleut Hunter-Gatherers." In *Hunter-Gatherer Foraging Strategies: Ethnographic and Archaeological Analysis*, edited by Bruce Winterhalder and E. A. Smith. Chicago: University of Chicago Press.

Index

Acheson, J. M., 237
adaptation, 66, 68
administered trade, 125, 132
administrative exchange, 136–137
Africa, 123–131, 197–199, 207, 220–224, 249. *See also specific countries*
agency and structure, 13–15, 18–20, 26–32, 75, 207, 221
agriculture: African female farming system, 220–224; in Mesopotamia, 64; *milpa* agriculture, 27, 30, 184, 213–216, 257n.5; and storage, 177–181; of Tiv, 197–199. *See also* family; horticulture
Algeria, 258n.4
Althusser, Louis, 19, 258–259n.1
Amazon Basin, 56, 175–177, 196–197, 257n.1
Amin, Samir, 254n.2
ancient Near East, 134, 136
Anderson, James, 63–64
animal ecology, 68
Annis, Sheldon, 213–216
anthropology. *See* ecological anthropology; economic anthropology; and *specific concepts, groups, and countries*

anti-economy, 194–195, 203. *See also* informal economy
Appadurai, Arjun, 86, 89, 114–118, 120
Appalachia, 31–32, 149–162, 165–166, 201–202
Appalachian Valley (Hicks), 201–202
appropriation, 70–72, 77
appropriational movements. *See* locational and appropriational movements
Arapesh, 246
archaeology, 11, 96, 97, 246, 251
Arensberg, Conrad, 52, 123–126, 129, 131
Argonauts of the Western Pacific (Malinowski), 56, 58
Arnold, Rosemary, 123–131, 132, 141
atomistic models, formal, 22–23
Australian Aborigines, 169
Aztec culture, 52, 232

Bajo-margin reservoirs, 225, 229
banana plantations, 27, 30
banking trade, 189
bartering, 122–123, 255n.1

Cordell, Linda S., 178
corvée system, 99–100
counter-gifting, 85
Cozumel, 181, 187
Croes, Dale, 256n.1
cultural ecology, 63–66
cultural economies, definition of, 1.
    See also ecological anthropology;
    economic anthropology; equiva-
    lencies; householding; Polanyi,
    Karl; time
Cultural Materialism (Harris), 56
culture: Kroeber's superorganic con-
    cept of, 19; Marx on, 18; subcate-
    gories of, 17–18; White on, 16–18
culture core, 64
culturology, 17
currency, 121–122

Dalton, George, 2, 56, 67, 249
D'Altroy, Terrence, 96–99, 107, 133,
    185–186
Darwinian theory, 68
decision-making models, 22
delayed exchange, 73
dialectic, 50
Dickens, Charles, 208
diet choice, optimal, 24–25
disembedded economy, 254n.2
Diskin, Martin, 256n.1
distribution: Bunzel on, 246–250;
    food distribution, 91; Marx on,
    40–41; Polanyi on, 50, 51, 62–63;
    in pre-1980 period, 67–68; and
    production, 246–247. *See also*
    redistribution
division of labor. *See* labor divisions
Dorfman, Robert, 123, 125, 129, 130,
    131
Douglas, Mary, 101–102
dowry, 249

Dufour, Darna L., 176
Dunnell, Robert, 251–252
Durkheim, Emile, 17, 42

Earle, Timothy, 96–99, 107, 133,
    185–187
East Africa, 66
Eastern Europe, 199–200
ecological anthropology: compared
    with economic anthropology, 56–
    58; early period (pre-1980), 63–66;
    Ellen on environment, subsistence,
    and system, 69–72, 82; Jochim's
    survival strategies, 72–74; and lo-
    cational movements, 76; material-
    ism of, 76; patterns of thinking in,
    62–63; post-1980 period of, 68–74
ecological time versus structural time,
    216–220
ecological zoning maps, 72
ecology: animal ecology, 68; cultural
    ecology, 63–66; definition of, 56–
    57; economy/ecology separation,
    56–57; origin of term, 56
economic anthropology: and appro-
    priational movements, 76; begin-
    nings of, 58; Bunzel on, 232–236,
    239–251; compared with ecologi-
    cal anthropology, 56–58; concepts
    and terms in, 8–11; early period
    (pre-1980), 66–68; formalist school
    of, 20; forms of methodological in-
    dividualism in, 20–21; historical
    and comparative perspectives on,
    232–252; new formalism in, 21–
    26; new Marxist economic anthro-
    pology, 68–69, 74–76; patterns of
    thinking in, 62–63; post-1980 pe-
    riod of, 68–69, 74–76; structures
    and agents in fieldwork in, 26–32.
    See also equivalencies

Economic Anthropology (Herskovits), 20
economic integration: dominant mode
of, 193; and equivalency-formation
processes, 94–100, 141–142; forms
of, 51–52, 94–100, 211; and householding, 144, 147–148
Economic Man (Schneider), 21
economics: conventional economics,
20, 21; origin of term, 56
Economies Across Cultures (Halperin):
vii, 2, 9, 260n.3
economism, Marx on, 39–40
economistic alienation, 254n.2
economy: anti-economy, 194–195;
Bunzel on, 234; cross-cultural treatment of informal economy, 191–
204; definition of, 8, 83, 234, 259–
260n.3; definition of cultural
economies, 1; definition of empirical economy, 60; disembedded
economy, 254n.2; economy/
ecology separation, 56–57; formal
economy, 193, 209; generic model
of, 34–35, 43–54, 83–84, 92–94,
120; informal economy, 191–204;
as instituted process, 210; materialist and humanistic approaches to,
8–11; origin of term, 56; Polanyi's
definition of, 60; state versus community economy, 99; substantive
economy, 47–48, 49, 60, 144–149,
209–216; and time, 205–231
Ecuador, 196–197
ejido, 99–100, 120, 184
elites, 127
Ellana, Linda J., 253n.1
Ellen, Roy, 69–72, 77, 82, 83
Eller, Ronald, 149–150
energy, 65, 66, 69, 70, 76
equivalencies: Appadurai on, 114–
118; Arnold on, 126; in Chinese

farm family in 1920s, 110–112; in
Chinese peasants in 19th century,
113–114; in Colombian chiefdom,
106–107; at Columbia University
seminars, 123–131; and context,
91–92; definition of, 86; and economic integration, 94–100, 141–
142; ethnographic examples of,
100–114; exchange equivalencies,
135, 137–138; external equivalencies, 91, 97–98; and forms of economic integration, 94–100; as generic problem, 89–100; historical
views on, 87–89; internal equivalencies, 91, 98–100; in Japan, 112–
113; Kopytoff on, 118–119; and
Kula, 85, 118; and locational and
appropriational movements, 93–
94; in peasant societies, 110–114;
Polanyi on, 86–89, 92–94, 120,
121–142; and Polanyi's generic
model of the economy, 92–94,
120; in Polanyi's *Great Transformation*, 121–123; in Polanyi's *Livelihood of Man*, 135–139; in Polanyi's
*Trade and Market in the Early Em-
pires*, 132–135; political nature of,
132; in post-industrial economies,
90; in primitive societies, 138–139;
problems of, 87–100; quantitative and qualitative dimensions of,
100–114; raffia cloths as kin-based
equivalencies, 101–102; and reciprocity, 94, 95–96; and redistribution, 94, 96–97, 98–100, 133;
sociology of, 138–139, 141; state
and, 136; substitutive equivalencies, 135–137, 138; Tiv spheres
of exchange, 102–104; trade and
equivalency-formation processes,
106–110; types of, 135–139; versus
equivalents, 104–106

equivalency-formation processes, 86, 91–104, 106–110, 112–113, 115–116, 140

equivalents, versus equivalencies, 104–106

Eskimo, 70, 101, 235–236, 253n.1

ethnicity, 66

Evans-Pritchard, E. E., 56, 206, 207, 216–220, 231

Evolution of Political Society, The (Fried), 65

evolutionary biology, 68

exchange: administrative exchange, 136–137; Binford on, 82; delayed exchange, 73; Jochim on, 73–74; kin-based exchanges, 249; Kopytoff on, 119; as model, 145; Polanyi on, 35, 47, 50, 51–53, 67, 145; spheres of exchange, 102–104; value of exchange objects, 105–106; without prices, 91

exchange equivalencies, 135, 137–138

exchange value. *See* equivalencies

extended family. *See* family

external equivalencies, 91, 97–98

Fabian, Johannes, 7, 18, 206–207, 208

family: Chinese farm family in 19th century, 113–114; Chinese farm family in 1920s, 110–112; in Deep Rural area of Kentucky, 150, 151–154; Japanese farm family, 112; in Kentucky, 149–162, 165–166; and resistance to dependency on capitalism, 161–162; in Shallow Rural area of Kentucky, 150–151, 154–155; Smith family network in Kentucky, 155–161; urban extended-family in U.S., 31–32; and wage labor, 120. *See also* householding; kinship

farinha, 177

farm family. *See* family

farming. *See* agriculture

feasting, 52, 73, 93, 107–110, 171–172, 188, 251

Finley, Moses, 87–88, 89, 255n.3

Firth, Raymond, 20–21, 35, 56, 60, 122, 168–169, 195

fishing: seine fishing in Grenada, 27–31

Flannery, Kent V., 64

food procurement, 65, 69, 76. *See also* Hunter-gatherers

food production. *See* agriculture; horticulture

food sharing, 22

foragers, 10, 78–79, 82, 247

foraging models, optimal, 22, 24–26, 68, 254n.4

forces of production, 42–43, 217

formal atomistic models, 22–23

formal economy, 193, 209

formalism: assumptions of, 20; definition of, 48; formal atomistic models, 22–23; formal processual models, 23–24, 53; new formalism in economic anthropology, 21–26; old version of, 20, 23; and optimal foraging analyses, 24–26; of Polanyi, 44–48, 51, 53–54, 61

formalist-substantivist debate, 61, 66–67, 259n.3

Formal Methods in Economic Anthropology (Plattner), 23

formal processual models, 23–24, 53, 165–166

forms of economic integration, 51–52, 94–100, 211

Foster, Robert J., 89, 104–106

France, 62

Freidel, D. A., 181–182

Fried, Morton, 65, 66, 195

Gallopin, G. G., 225
gardening in Grenada, 27, 30
Geertz, C., 3, 64
Gender at the Crossroads of Knowledge, 222–223
gender divisions. *See* labor divisions
General Anthropology (Boas), 233
generic model of the economy: advantages of, 83–84; diagram of, 45; economic processes in, 50, 51; and equivalencies, 92–94, 120; locational and appropriational movements in, 47–50, 53, 57–62, 145, 217; Polanyi on, 34–35, 43–54, 83, 120; structure of, 45, 46, 92–93; summary of, 50–54
Giddens, Anthony, 13–15, 18–20, 49, 75, 207, 221, 258n.3
gift-giving, 85, 250–251
Gillin, John, 176
Gilman, Patricia, 178, 179–180
gold standard, 122
Gould, Stephen J., 205, 230
Great Transformation, The (Polanyi), 43, 48, 60, 86, 121–123, 144, 147, 208
Greece, 87, 88–89, 134
Grenada, 27–31
Gross, Daniel, 56
Gross, T., 257n.4
groundnut production, 222–224
Guatemala, 62, 66, 207, 212–216, 245–246, 256n.1, 257n.2, 258n.6
Guinea Coast, 123–131
Guyer, Jane, 11, 18, 207, 220–224, 254n.1
Gwi San, 78

habitus, 19
Haeckel, Ernst, 56–57
Hames, R., 257n.1
Harner, Michael, 196–197
Harris, Marvin, 56, 64

Hart, Keith, 191
Hastorf, Christine A., 186–187
Hatch, E., 55
Helm, J., 64
Herskovits, Melville, 20–21, 56, 60, 168, 254n.3
Hesiod, 87, 89
Hganasan, 171
Hicks, George, 201–202
Hobhouse, L. T., 238
Hoko, 256n.1
Homer, 88
horticulture: in Africa, 207; tropical horticulturists, 175–177. *See also* agriculture
Hot Wells Pueblo site, 257n.3
householding: community-based householding in Deep Rural area, 151–154; definition of, 147; and economic integration, 144; as formal processual model, 165–166; in Guatemala, 212–216; and institutional arrangements, 147–148; in Kentucky, 149–162, 165–166, 213; and locational and appropriational movements, 166, 256n.2; as model, 145–147; as peasant resistance, 162–165; Polanyi's model of, 35, 47, 51–53, 67, 143, 144, 147–149, 214; problematical relationship between actual households and, 143–144, 148–149; regional basis of, in Shallow Rural area, 154–155; and resistance to dependency on capitalism, 161–162; and self-sufficiency, 149–150; and Smith family network, 155–161; and substantive economy, 144–149; and time, 207, 212–216
households, versus householding, 143–144, 148–149
Hugh-Jones, Stephen, 255n.1
Humphrey, Caroline, 255n.1

hunter-gatherers: Binford on, 77–81; food sharing among, 22; optimal foraging analyses of, 24–26; organizational types of, 10; reciprocal sharing processes among, 23; seasonal variation among, 26; storage among, 168, 169–175; Weissner on, 81–82

Inca state, 97–99, 107, 168, 184–187, 232
individualism. *See* methodological individualism
informal economy: as anti-economy, 194–195, 203; in Appalachia, 201–202; and centrally planned economies, 199–200; cross-cultural treatment of, 191–204; definitions of, and assumptions on, 193–195, 203; of Jivaro, 196–197; of !Kung, 196; as model, 192–193; periodic marketplace system in eastern Kentucky, 202–203; in prestate societies, 196–199; of state systems, 199–203; of Tiv, 197–199
Ingold, T., 70, 170–175
institutedness, 210–211
institutional arrangements, 75, 147–148
institutional history, 134
institutional paradigm: and appropriational movements, 75–76; diagram of, 37; of Marx, 13, 34–43, 46, 75; and Polanyi, 13, 34–35, 75
institutions: definition of, 19, 75; and householding, 147–148
internal equivalencies, 91, 98–100
Inupiat, 253–254n.1
Isaac, Barry L., 21

Japan, 112
Jivaro, 196–197

Jochim, Michael, 72–74, 76, 187, 188
just price, 139

Kaabyle peasants, 258n.4
Kahn, Joel S., 258–259n.1
Kalahari Desert, 101
Kapauku, Papuans, 21
Karinya, 176–177
Kentucky: Deep Rural part of, 150–154; farm size in, 150, 152, 154; householding in, 62, 149–162, 165–166, 213; informal economy in, 202–203, 256n.1; periodic marketplace system in, 202–203; resistance to dependency on capitalism in, 161–162; self-sufficiency of family units in, 149–150; Shallow Rural part of, 150–151, 154–161; Smith family network in, 155–161; timing of householding in, 207
kinship: and informal economy in Appalachia, 201–202; as institution, 75; raffia cloths as kin-based equivalencies, 101–102; and reciprocity, 67; Smith family network in Kentucky, 155–161; and Tiv spheres of exchange, 103; in U.S. urban areas, 31–32. *See also* family; householding
kitchen gardening, 27, 30
Knight, Frank, 53–54
Kofyar, 56, 64
Kopytoff, Igor, 86, 118–119, 120
Kroeber, A. L., 19
kula trade, 42, 56, 85, 95, 118, 240
!Kung, 101, 169, 196
Kwakiutl, 251

labor: chronotypes and timing of work, 220–224; and equivalencies, 120; *mozo* labor, 215–216; recruitment for work, 59–60; resistance to dependency on wage labor, 161–165

labor divisions: African female farming system, 220–224; Bunzel on, 244–246; in Grenada, 27–31; in Kentucky family network, 155–161; Mead on, 244; in storage facilities building, 183; of Tiv, 197–199; among women in U.S. urban areas, 32; of Zuñi, 241–243

labor organization, 59, 76

La Lone, Darrell E., 184–185

land transfers, 59

Langebaek, Carl Henrik, 106–107

LeClaire, E., 21

Lele, 101–102

Levesque, Andre, 2

Lévi-Strauss, Claude, 249

life-course, 32

Little Laurel, 201–202

Livelihood of Man, The (Polanyi), 43, 135–139

Llobera, Josep R., 258–259n.1

locational and appropriational movements: and Binford, 77–81; and comparison of economic and ecological anthropology, 57–58, 75–76; definitions of, 58–62; as dichotomy, 63, 77; ecological and economic anthropology associated with, 63, 68; Ellen on locational movements, 70; and equivalencies, 93–94; examples of, 59–60; and householding, 166, 256n.2; and hunter-gatherers, 77–82; Jochim on, 73–74; and Marxist economic anthropology, 74–76; in Polanyi's generic model of the economy, 47–50, 53, 57–62, 83, 145, 187–188, 217; production and distribution asssociated with, 62–63; and storage, 173–174, 187–188; synthesis of, while keeping analytically separate, 76, 83; and time, 217, 219; and Weissner, 77, 81–82

locations, versus sites, 79, 80

Logic of Practice, The (Bourdieu), 207–208

long-distance trade, 75, 97–98

Lowie, Robert, 60

maintenance strategies, 72–73

maize storage, 182–184

Male and Female (Mead), 244

Malinowski, Bronislaw, 35, 42, 56, 58, 60, 85, 194–195, 251

manioc processing, 176–177

Mantaro Valley, 185–187

Maori, 246, 250

maps of ecological zoning, 72

market exchange. *See* Exchange

marketplaces, versus market systems, 67, 88, 90–91, 202–203, 256n.1

market systems, versus marketplaces, 67, 88, 256n.1

Markets in Africa (Bohannan and Dalton), 67

Martin, John F., 25

Marx, Karl: on agency and structure, 18; Althusser on, 258–259n.1; and anthropology, 47; associations with Polanyi, 2, 43, 45, 46–47, 254n.2; on capitalism, 39, 41, 45; on commodities, 114, 116; on context, 221; on culture, 18; on the dialectic, 50; on distribution, 40–41, 63; on economism, 39–40; influence of, on White, 16–17; and institutional paradigm, 13, 34–43, 46; on production, 15, 37–43, 63, 81, 114, 217; on social totality, 74; on society, 75; on time, 210

Marxism: hidden aspects of, in American anthropology, 65; institutional

patch-use model, 24

Peace, William J., 18

Pearson, Harry, 123, 127

peasant economies: in China in 19th century, 113–114; Chinese farm family in 1920s, 110–112; equivalencies in, 110–114; and exchange equivalencies, 137–138; formal processual models of, 23, 24; in Japan in 20th century, 112; peasant resistance, 162–165; relationship with landlords, 113–114

peasant resistance, 162–165

penny capitalists, 66

periodic marketplace systems, 202–203

Peru, 133, 185–186, 196–197

Plattner, Stuart, 15, 22, 23, 255n.4

pluralism, 199–203

Polanyi, Karl: associations with Marx, 2, 43, 45, 46–47, 63, 254n.2; and Bunzel, 234; on capitalism, 44, 47; codes of, 43–44, 63, 210; and Columbia University seminars, 86–87, 121, 123–131, 132, 141; on currency, 121–122; definition of economy, 60; on disembedded economy, 254n.2; on distribution, 50, 51, 62–63; on equivalencies, 86–89, 92–94, 101, 120, 121–142; formalism of, 44–48, 51, 53–54, 61; on forms of economic integration, 51–52, 94–100, 193, 211; and generic model of the economy, 34–35, 43–54, 83, 92–94, 120; on gold standard, 122; on householding, 35, 47, 51–53, 67, 143, 144, 147–149, 214; humanistic approach of, 43–44; on institutedness, 210–211; and institutional paradigm, 13, 34–35, 75; on locational and appropriational movements, 47–50, 53, 57–62, 83, 93, 145, 187–188,

217; major elements of thought of, 47; models used by, 35, 44–48, 53, 67, 92; on process, 60; on production, 41–42, 62–63; on staple finance, 97; on submonetary device, 185; on substantive economy, 47–48, 49, 60, 144–145, 209–212; on time, 206, 208, 212

—works: *The Great Transformation*, 43, 48, 60, 86, 121–123, 144, 147, 208; *The Livelihood of Man*, 43, 135–139; *Trade and Market in the Early Empires*, 43, 47, 48, 60, 67, 121, 132–135, 144

Polanyi group, 2, 89

Polanyi Institute, 2

Polanyi-Levitt, Kari, 2, 254n.2

political economics, 36

political society, evolution of, 65

Pomo trade feasts, 73, 93, 107–110, 188

population pressure, 76

Pospisil, Leopold, 21, 56, 66

pre-capitalist economies: Polanyi on, 43; and redistribution, 91

prestige systems, 67, 103–104, 109–110

prices: and Columbia University seminars, 123, 124, 127, 128, 131; as equivalency, 88, 132–135, 139, 142; Polanyi on, 88, 132–135, 139, 141, 142

primitive cultures. *See* specific cultures

Primitive Polynesian Economy (Firth), 56

private property, 75

process, definition of, 60

processual concept of time, 206

processual models, formal, 23–24, 53, 165–166

production: and distribution, 246–247; forces of production, 42–43, 217; Marx on, 15, 37–43, 81, 114,

storage: and agriculture, 177–181; definition of, 167–168; facilities for, 179–184; Firth on, 168–169; Gross's variables of, 257n.4; among hunter-gatherers, 169–175; Inca storage, 184–187; Jochim on, 72–73, 187, 188; and locational and appropriational movements, 172–174, 187–188; Maya storage, 181–184, 187; as part of production, 175–177, 189–190; Polanyi on, 50, 51; and reciprocity, 171–172; and redistribution, 171–172; and sharing, 170, 175; significance of food containers, 174–175, 256–257n.3; social storage, 173, 175; and states, 181–187; and time, 170–171; and trade, 181–182; and transportation factors, 173; and tropical horticulturalists, 175–177; Weissner on, 81

Strategies for Survival (Jochim), 72

structural Marxism, 74–75

structural time versus oecological time, 216–220

structuration, theory of, 19

structure and agency, 13–15, 18–20, 26–32, 75, 207

submonetary device, 185

subsistence patterns: Ellen on, 69–72; kin-organized subsistence, 98–99; in new Marxist economic anthropology, 68; optimal foraging analyses of hunter-gatherers, 24–26; and Tiv spheres of exchange, 102–103; variability within types of, 10

substantive economy, 47–48, 49, 60, 144–149, 209–212

substitutive equivalencies, 135–137, 138

survival strategies, 72–74

Swetnam, John, 258n.6

symbolic capital, 75

Tannenbaum, Frank, 123, 124, 127, 131

Tax, Sol, 66

taxation, 136

temporality. *See* time

Testart, Alain, 169–170, 180

Thompson, E. P., 212–213, 258n.4

Thurnwald, Richard C., 138

Tikal, 225

Tikopia, 122–123

time: and African female farming system, 220–224; and capitalism, 209; chronotypes and timing of work, 206, 220–224; Dunnell on, 252; and economy, 205–231; and equivalency-formation processes, 112–113; in Guatemala case, 207, 212–216; and householding, 207, 212–216; in Kentucky case, 207; and Nuer case, 216–220; oecological time versus structural time, 216–220; Polanyi on, 206, 208, 212; processual concept of, 206; and storage, 170–171; and substantive economy, 209–212; and water management, 224–230

Time and the Other (Fabian), 7, 206–207, 208

Tiv, 102–104, 197–199

total caloric input and output, 76

trade: administered trade versus reciprocity, 125, 132; banking trade, 189; Bunzel on, 250–251; in Colombian chiefdom, 106–107; definition of, 125; and equivalency-formation processes, 106–110; Guinea Coast trade in 18th century, 123–131; historical links between rulers and traders, 117–118; *kula* trade, 42, 56, 85, 95, 118, 240; long-distance trade, 75, 97–98;

Pomo trade feasts, 73, 93, 107–110, 188; silent trade, 115–116; and storage, 181–182

Trade and Market in the Early Empires (Polanyi), 43, 47, 48, 60, 67, 121, 132–135, 144

trade beads, 107–110, 188

trade feasts, 73, 93, 107–110, 188

Traditional Exchange and Modern Markets (Belshaw), 67

transportation: and storage, 173

tribute systems, 75

Trobriand Islands, 95, 118, 239–240, 251

tropical horticulturalists, 175–177

urban areas, extended family in, 31–32

value: Bunzel on, 240–241; of exchange objects, 105–106; regimes of, 115

Vayda, A. P., 64, 107–110

Vickery, William, 123

wage labor, resistance to dependency on, 161–165

water management, 224–230, 239–240

Weber, Max, 135

Weissner, Polly, 77, 81–82, 188

Wellbury, David E., 220

West Indies, 27–31

White, Leslie, 16–18, 66, 70, 233, 252, 255n.2

Winterhalder, Bruce, 24

Wittfogel, Karl, 239–240

women's labor. *See* labor divisions

work and workers. *See* labor; labor divisions

Yang, Martin, 110–112

Yesner, David R., 24

Yokaia village chiefs, 107–110

Yucatan, 182

Yucatecan, 257n.2

Yugoslavia, 257n.2

Zuñi, 233, 241–246, 248, 250, 251